Red Room Rendezvous

Red Room

Rendezvous

For my dear friends Julie - with love,

Paulette Crain

Paulette Crain

Oak Tree Press   Springfield, IL

Oak Tree Press

Oak Tree Books may be purchased for educational, business, or sales promotional use. Contact Publisher for quantity discounts.

Although the publisher has exhaustively researched and verified so far as possible the accuracy of statements in this book, we assume no responsibility for errors, inaccuracies, omissions, or any inconsistencies herein. Any slights of people or organizations are unintentional, and we advise readers to keep in mind that much of the information included in this book is anecdotal, as presented to the author.

First Edition, October 2002

Cover Design by Dazzling Dew

10 9 8 7 6 5 4 3 2

Limited Edition Hardcover, April 2002
ISBN 1892343-33-9

Library of Congress Cataloging-in-Publication Data
Crain, Paulette, 1942-
Red Room Rendezvous/Paulette Crain
P. cm.
ISBN 1892343-24-X
1.   Paulette Crain, 1942——Anecdotes. I. Title

CT275.C86498 A3 2000

973.9'092—dc21   00-040664

Dedication

In memory of my dear friend, Shirley Angelle, who first asked if I would host a charity event at my home. Many events followed as well as my introduction to Maryflynn Thomas.

Maryflynn has made it a priority to introduce me to every living soul in every prestigious organization in New Orleans.

Shirley Angelle will always be in my thoughts.
Maryflynn is still introducing.

Prologue

"I never could find out exactly where New Orleans is. I have looked for it on the map without much enlightenment. It is dropped down there somewhere in the marshes of the Mississippi and the bayous and lakes. It is below the one and tangled up among the others, or it might some day float out to the Gulf and disappear. How the Mississippi gets out I never could discover. When it first comes in sight of the town, it is running east: at Carrollton, it abruptly turns its rapid, broad, yellow flood and runs south, turns presently eastward, circles a great portion of the city, then makes a bold push for the north in order to avoid Algiers and reach the foot of Canal Street, and encountering then the heart of the town, it sheers off again along the old French Quarter and Jackson Square due east, and goes no one knows where."

Harper's New Monthly Magazine
(New York: Harper and Brothers)
"Sui Generis," by
Charles Dudley Warner (1887)

Chapter 1

He was quite decorous, noticeably fastidious, and was capable of intimidating even the most courtly of blue bloods. He was medium height with thick silver hair and beard. He would give one pause at the sight of him. Had Ernest Hemingway miraculously risen from the dead? It was no wonder that confusion had set in when hearing the words "food stamps" pass his lips. And he was not referring to someone else's. These were *his* food stamps.

So it was on that day in October of 1999 that I met William Lafayette Holcomb. I was helping out my friend, Les Wisinger, at his interior design shop on Magazine Street in New Orleans. I had lived in New Orleans for a little over three years. The exotic city had captivated my husband and me, body and soul. Since his business kept him in another exotic city, San Francisco, we decided to live bicoastal. My first novel had yet to land me in the company of the rich and famous. Succumbing to credit card debt for a third go around, I often helped out at Harper's Interiors to pay off items I simply could not live without.

That was my excuse for being there.

I could not imagine why this erudite man was wasting his time trimming cord, answering phones and helping customers search for European antiquities. Surely he was a scholar or at the very least, a writer of extreme literary proportion.

Having been cursed with a hefty dose of curiosity for most of my life, I found it difficult to trim miles of cording with this man and not plunge into matters that were absolutely none of my business. I suspected a book somewhere inside his life, and though I had never attempted nonfiction, I had not ruled it out. So, as the day progressed, I listened intently, roaring with laughter at Bill's Southern wit and British humor, which he acquired while living in London. Within a short six hours or so, I found myself in blissful adoration of this man. To me, he was a cross between my dearest friend, the aristocratic Joseph Piazza, and my wild and crazy first cousin, professor and scholar William Banks Taylor III, who had also lived in London. Since Will Taylor now resided somewhere in a remote area of Mississippi and Joseph Piazza in Los Angeles, I was ecstatic to have run across Bill Holcomb.

The next day or so, after copious conversations accompanied by blinding laughter, I still had no clue about the food stamps. However, I did learn a snippet more about my newfound friend. To my amazement, this elegant man was savvy about every thrift store in New Orleans from St. Vincent-DePaul to Bloomingdeals. He had clothes with the original tags still intact—and he had paid next to absolutely nothing for them. Could it be, I pondered, that his brilliance had simply twisted into eccentric penuriousness and he took delight in beating the hell out of the system? If so, I knew my equally thrifty husband would be thrilled at the prospect of meeting my new friend.

Bill Holcomb continued to keep me perpetually amused with outrageous stories of New Orleans' aristocracy. He seemed to have known every living soul of aristocratic importance in the Garden District and Uptown area—and he had been married to two such women. The house on St. Charles Avenue where his family—which dated back to the late 1800s—had lived, was nothing less than a palatial estate. Though my curiosity roiled, I uncharacteristically kept the questions at bay—an enormous burden and unfamiliar one. Probing and outspoken pretty well sums up my character. So why the reticent behavior? Other than fate's ruling hand, there was no explanation. However, I did invite him to dinner, hoping to stumble across a clue to his curious situation.

After a non-eventful but enjoyable dinner, I suggested that we take Max, my Scottish terrier, for a walk. The summer nights had succumbed to autumn's chill, a perfect evening for a stroll through the Garden District. Or as Bill so eloquently put it, The Garbage District—a self-deprecating term used by the locals to label the decay and decline of the once-fashionable area bounded by Louisiana, Jackson, Magazine and St. Charles. However, a renaissance was in progress, and the Garden District was emerging from its doldrums and back to its former grandeur.

Bill and I left my house on Washington with Max in tow, and

headed down Chestnut toward First. The night was crisp and we seemed to enjoy the walk in silence while Max placed his mark at every bush and shrub surrounded by crumbling bricks. As we approached the corner of Philip and Chestnut, Bill turned, lifted his hand and pointed to—as he put it—a wonderful kind of a slightly butt-sprung house once owned by a Mrs. Baker who played bridge eighteen hours a day, six days a week. On the seventh day she played gin without benefit of cards.

"It was 1957," he said. "I was seventeen, living on my own for the first time, and I needed a place that was nice and cheap. Considering that my take-home salary was thirty-five dollars per week, cheap was imperative. So after meeting Mrs. Baker, and passing muster, she introduced me to the boy whose apartment I would be taking. His name was Gary Bergeron and he was from New Roads, Louisiana."

I had never heard of New Roads, Louisiana, but I had a vivid picture of a remote area that had boredom written all over it. Bill quickly informed me that New Roads was where *The Long Hot Summer* had been filmed, the movie where Paul Newman and Joanne Woodward first met and fell in love.

I thought about that for a minute and said, "No it wasn't, *The Long Hot Summer* was filmed in Clinton, LA, not New Roads. I know, because my good friend Sandy Robert was there. She and several other teenagers went to the Bellemont Hotel where Paul Newman and Joanne Woodward were staying. In fact, she said that Lee Remick was also there, but no one knew who she was then. And guess what? Paul Newman invited them into their room. She said everyone was so friendly and not the least bit effected by their fame."

Bill seemed to mull this over, then continued as though I had never spoken.

"After talking with Gary for a bit," Bill reminisced, "I came to realize he was directly related to all of the Morrison, Boggs, Bounachaud, Blackshear, Buffington families, from whom had evolved Mayor Chep Morrison of New Orleans and Congressman Hale Boggs. Gary took me around the corner to meet his aunt, Rowena Buffington, who had a lovely home on First Street, right off the corner of Chestnut."

Bill turned to me with a gleam in his eye. He lifted his hand, pivoted, and continued walking. "This was my *entrée*," he said. "The beginning of a long association with the treasures of all these families."

We turned onto First Street, and while pulling Max from another unfortunate shrub, I prodded Bill for more.

"Rowena," and he pointed to a Greek Revival house. With a roll of his eyes, he explained that even the slums in New Orleans were Greek Revival. "Rowena lived in that house with her mother, Rhettie, who was in her late nineties.

"Now Miss Rhettie," he sighed, "went and complicated the entire family tree by marrying her deceased sister's husband." Bill paused introspectively. "And then Miss Rhettie up and gave birth to six children, therefore, giving her six nieces and nephews six stepbrothers and sisters." Bill looked at me in a state of bewilderment, as if musing over this genealogical feat. "Were they stepbrothers and sisters?' he asked. "Half brothers and sisters or were they merely nieces and nephews?"

We finally came to the conclusion that, at the very least, they all had the same father, which was a heap more than could be attributed to some of their neighbors.

Bill seemed to have pacified his quandary and had no problem picking up exactly where he had left off.

"Rowena and her mother," he said, "also had as perennial house guests, Rowena's sisters, Eustacia, the widow of the Lieutenant Governor of Louisiana, and dear Coco Jacobs, Lindy Boggs' mother, and although less frequently, Frosty Blackshear. At this time," he informed authoritatively, "when Hale and Lindy weren't occupying their congressional digs in Washington, they stayed in the house next to Rowena's which she also owned."

Bill walked up next to the wrought-iron gate and cupped his hand around one of the spikes. "This place was a 24-hour a day open house. I found myself being invited over to dinner night after night, never knowing whether or not fellow guests would number six or twenty." Bill turned on his heel and, with hands in rapid animation, continued. Max tugged at his leash, so I released more line and leaned against a nearby fence. Bill walked in circles, head down, his arms moving in all directions. There was no doubt that the past was rumbling inside his head and was determined to get out. I could not have been more attentive. At last a history lesson which did not bore me. I wanted more. The words spilled from Bill's mouth, painting a visual masterpiece.

"Coco was absolutely delightful," he said with sincere adoration. "She was a recovering alcoholic and had not touched a drop in years. It was her birthday, and we were all looking forward to the cook, Naomi's, fried chicken feast. A gastronomical *fait accompli*. When I arrived, I could sense hostility in the air, and the circumstances were strained, totally unlike any past visits. It seems that just moments before I arrived, the Prytania Liquor Store attempted to deliver four cases of bourbon to Rowena's house, and since no one there had ordered it, all eyes were cast upon poor Coco. Unbeknownst to any of the *madames* in the house, cousin Al, an on-again-off-again favorite drunk, had arrived earlier that afternoon from New Roads. After taking the liberty to call and order two cases of bourbon for himself, albeit to be charged to the Buffington account, he squirreled himself away in an upstairs bedroom where he had yet to be discovered. Later when cousin Albert lurched down the stairs, and all the chicanery was figured out, the sisters were apologetic, Mother Rhettie, who never believed it was Coco in the first place, enjoyed a large Mint Julep and Coco was merely pacified. Cousin Albert found himself on the 'off again' list, was ordered upstairs to sleep it off, and a wonderful dinner was had by all."

Bill swayed his head. "I had never in my life been party to such goings on," he said. "I felt like a cast member, with very few lines, out of some drawing room comedy." Bill rolled his eyes and sighed. "*Tres drôle.*

"After dinner," he continued, "Eustacia entertained us with a medley of her own songs, the ending of each accompanied by an unbelievable chord struck by plunging her *derrière* onto the keyboard. Frosty, the fourth sister, swept in on her way to some elegant *soirée*. Actually, Frosty was always going to or coming from an elegant *soirée*, regardless of the hour. She was known as the Queen of the Quarter, where she maintained one of the French Quarter's more elegant homes. In her own words, her home was not nearly as large as Matilda Grey's palatial mansion on the corner of Royal and Esplanade, but the drinks Frosty served were always doubles. So in other words, as Frosty put it, 'they didn't always leave my house impressed, but they sure weren't DE-pressed.'" Bill snickered.

Max had tired of his shrub and lamppost, so we proceeded up First Street, as Bill retrieved another story.

"Frosty had made a very successful name for herself specializing in French Quarter real estate. She conducted her business out of her ground floor living room/office cum desk, in what appeared to be a very glamorous setting. This positively puzzled me to death, because the only source of light in this largish room was a single bulb hanging on a naked cord. Feeling that I knew Frosty well enough to say anything, as *she* was certainly wont to do, I told her it was the tackiest thing I had ever seen in my entire life. She immediately agreed, gave me thirty minutes and *carte blanche* to replace it. At that time, I was working for Charles Gresham through D. H. Holmes, and by my association was entitled to a discount by all the Royal Street antique shops. Since I rather favored Morris Keil, of Keil Antiques, I ran in and chose a six branch Queen Anne chandelier. I grabbed the chandelier and ran back to Frosty's, where she—being the no nonsense person that she was—had an electrician in attendance who promptly hung the thing. This, of course, necessitated many phone calls to her friends in the Quarter and places afar, to come by and have it christened. Needless to say, Frosty's invitations were taken more solemnly than a Papal Bull. A cast of thousands arrived and no one left her home DEpressed that night.

"Of course," Bill quipped with an attitude, "Frosty, noted for five o'clock impromptus, would throw open her six French doors, which opened directly onto Bourbon Street, while all sorts would come and go including an unidentified couple from Iowa, et al who couldn't believe their great luck at being so lavishly entertained in one of New Orleans finest mansions."

This Bourbon Street scene swirled inside my head. I could absolutely imagine myself at Frosty's with martini in hand, and wished that I had been around at the time to have known her. I said this to Bill, but he rolled his eyes and grunted. I knew immediately that the thought of Frosty and me as drinking buddies presented a chaotic picture. I pretended to ignore this and waved my hand for him to continue.

"Frosty and I remained great, great friends," he said with adoration. "Ultimately, her husband Blacky, a habitually unseen and totally enigmatic being, died. But Frosty continued with her real estate and we would see each other socially four or five times a year at functions as diverse as tea at the Le Petit Salon to the Southern premier of *El Cid*, or a boogie night at Las Casa de Las Marinas, New Orleans' MOST decadent and most fun bar. Locals referred to it as DDT, an acronym for debutantes, diplomats and trash."

Bill and I turned up Camp Street with a reluctant Max in tow. Left to Max, we would spend four hours walking one Garden District block. And though I was thoroughly engrossed in Bill's wonderful stories, I needed to walk. So I gave a gentle yank to Max's leash and prodded Bill for more.

"In this city," he readily obliged, "known world wide for carnival, make-believe, jazz and various degrees of immorality, there was one true headliner. Indeed, one Garbage District individual who epitomized it all."

"Bill," I said. "There must be a bezillion people like that in The Big Easy. How can you possibly single out just one?"

"Simple," he said. "She had ALL the qualities."

Rather than asking what he meant by that, I simply waited to figure it out for myself.

"Maude Ellen Farrar." Bill looked introspective. "Maude Ellen died last year. She was in her seventies, and a classic example of a life spiraling into a complex, difficult–to–fathom series of non-events, each as obtuse as they were unnoticed by your average Garbage District elitist.

"Maude Ellen was born into a family with more aristocracy than sense or money, i.e. Jefferson Davis was her great uncle. She was an overly bright, inquisitive and sophisticated little girl who started her education at McGehee, a bastion of learning for future queens and maids of Comus, Atlanteans and such carnival krewes with the most panache. She then finished her high school years at intellectually prominent Newman. While a freshman at Newcomb College, she obediently made her debut and was presented as a maid in Comus. Outwardly, she was a typical New Orleans' *jeune fille* of proper lineage, upbringing, et cetera. But little did her family know that her nights were spent doing mad and frantic dancing in the Greek sailors' bars, which then lined Decatur Street, at that time a seedy perimeter street of New Orleans' famed French Quarter. She was constantly accompanied by largish glasses (many) of Ouzo and every low life in the city, who was not already in jail or going on trial the next day or so of charges as diverse as rape, murder, armed robbery, and an occasional child abuse.

"Actually, Maude Ellen fell so in love with the Greeks and their way of living, that she applied for a Fulbright scholarship to study in Florence during her junior year. While all thought that this bespoke of her quest for higher learning, it was simply a ruse, because getting forth and back to Athens from Florence was a more expedient and less expensive route than shuttling forth and back from New Orleans. She finished her year abroad, returned to New Orleans, reeking of Greek/Italo heritage plus an astonishing grasp of both languages which, when added to her French and English, made her a linguistic natural. After graduating Summa Cum Laude from Newcomb, and spending the ensuing summer months in Biloxi, Mississippi, she decided to enter the work world.

"In the fifties," Bill unnecessarily reminded me, "young ladies of breeding who went 'to work' usually did so in the periphery of New

Orleans' antique businesses, interior decorating, or if possessed of any journalistic flair, *The Picayune*." At that time, *The Picayune*, now known as *The Times Picayune*, was one of New Orleans' local newspapers. "While at *The Picayune*, Maude Ellen became a copy girl."

Without missing a stride, Bill smirked. "At night our young lady of breeding resumed her haunts at the Greek bars on Decatur Street. In fact," he informed me, "it was in the Acropolis Bar where she met her husband-to-be, Rodney Kirkpatrick." Bill's eyes narrowed. "It was— now remember, this was in the late 50s. And I was rather shocked that the introduction between Maude Ellen and Rodney was made by Kitty, a 400-pound Greek transvestite who would just as soon stab you as smile."

That piece of information stirred my curiosity, but there seemed to be no further info on the Greek transvestite, so I was left with horrid images of this creature.

"Kirkpatrick was a dark brooding poet," Bill explained, "who constantly gave the impression that he was about to be swept away by some gloomy malaise. However, all Maude Ellen's friends, relatives and neighbors were delighted at the prospect of her upcoming marriage, as there were many who had been making book that such an event would never take place. After all, she was a oner, with never a fear of entering anything remotely resembling a beauty contest.

"Rowena Buffington, a neighbor, offered her formal rose garden as the sight for this auspicious event, while Row's sisters *all* were casting disparaging remarks about the probability of its ever taking place. There was a series of requisite pre-wedding luncheons, cocktail parties, and *thé dansants*, at which Maude Ellen would turn up in outfits that would set Seventh Avenue back fifty years. Truly in the society column write-up, which in those days *always* went to great lengths to describe the honorees attire, there was nary a word mentioned regarding Maude Ellen's costume of the hour.

"My own grandmother," he laughed, "a paragon of quietude, said Maude Ellen's costumes were never written up simply because no words had yet been invented to describe them.

"The wedding day arrived, unseasonably cold, gloomy and damp. With approximately forty of us crammed into Row's rose garden, we impatiently waited for over an hour for the groom to arrive, which he did—finally. He was riding a Schwinn Flyer bicycle—one leg of his morning suit neatly tucked up with a rubber band—to join his fiancée who was attired in an utterly indescribable get-up.

"Eustacia began playing the piano and the solemn rights began. It was over in a trice. Actually, the wedding lasted longer than the marriage. The catering company that provided for the wedding hadn't picked up their champagne glasses before Maude Ellen filed for divorce. Short-lived as their marriage was, they must have enjoyed a wee bit of intimacy, for when the divorce writ went through, Maude Ellen was eight months with child.

"Kempe was born in a natural manner, but to hear Maude Ellen speak of the event, one would think that she had been a Native American Apache forced to squat by the side of the road, drop the baby, pick it up, and plod on through life to hoe corn.

"This couldn't have been further from the truth. She was lavished upon by every employee at Touro Hospital for at least six weeks, causing this austere hospital to rewrite all its by-laws and rules, as this was the time they were rushing mothers out after forty-eight hours."

Max, having spotted and dotted every shrub and post along the way, was now eager for a bowl of water and slumber upon his large red pillow. But we had another block to cover, so I coaxed Bill for one more story.

He was up to the task.

"I had not seen Maude Ellen in close to ten years," he remembered. "I was a house guest of Ed and Eleanor Curtis who owned The Brass Menagerie in the Quarter. They lived just up the block from Maude Ellen on Chestnut in the old Slue mansion, which is a story unto itself."

"I wanta hear it." I said. "Now."

Bill threw me a severe glance. "Bitch." He then continued.

"When the Curtises moved to New Orleans, their prime, but alas, puerile aim was to appear as landed gentry rather than newcomers from Palestine, Texas."

"There's a Palestine, Texas?" I said.

"Yes. But I've never been. Although judging from those that have, I would venture to say that it's just got to be tacky. You know, not tack-tacky. But, just Texas tacky."

I mumbled something to the effect that I knew exactly what he meant.

"To insure the Curtises of immediate immanence," he informed, "they purchased one of the largest homes in the Garden District, the old Slue Mansion. It was a curious plot, a T-shaped piece of property with large frontage facing Chestnut and the upper part of the T opening out onto both Second and Third Streets consecutively. Most of their new neighbors-to-be, being of the old school, felt that nothing should be done in any way to alter the Garden District's charming ambiance. You can imagine how flummoxed they were when, early of a morning, a house moving company arrived, and with clocklike mechanism, neatly severed the north wing of the house, moved the entire edifice to face Third Street in the upper right hand of the T, thus creating a singular home on its own lot.

"The Curtises set to work at once, repairing the gaping side of the severed wing, tossed up a few columns, and the obligatory shutters, and thus a house was born, which sold for twice what the Curtises had paid for the original house. This also gave them a side yard unparalleled in size by any others in the neighborhood. The top left of the T-shaped property provided them with a residential lot for sale, which did NOT exist in the Garden District, and thus was sold inside a 24-hour span.

"The Curtises then went on to decorate their home which, on the outside, was pure Garden District Federal, on the inside it was Sister Parish In Heat with a healthy dose of Mario Buoatti. Plus strong California current.

"Really," Bill said. "I stood at the foot of the staircase expecting the Rockettes to descend at any moment. The entire concept was garish, overblown, and completely out of sync with anything New Orleanian, and the most divine interior I had ever seen in my life. It just worked.

"And now the house is owned by a former King of Carnival whose daughters have all been feted by dinner dances held in tents erected on the very spot where Mrs. Slue's old half-a-house used to be.

"But back to that day when I was alone in the Curtis' house. Or so I thought.

"The door bell rang. I peered through the peephole, and to my astonishment, there stood Maude Ellen, fiercely swinging an enormous Pyrex measuring cup. Somewhat taken aback, I threw the door open, and with much shrieking, wailing and camaraderie, we reestablished our friendship at once. However, her main purpose of coming to the Curtis home was to borrow a cup of Scotch. She needed to fix a highball for a gentleman caller who was waiting in her parlor. So, after many kisses and more shrieking, she rolled down Chestnut toward home, leaving me standing in the doorway with a three-quarter-empty bottle of Cutty Sark. All I could think at the time was—a cup of scotch? At this point, I turned to go back to the bar when I noticed a gnome scurry through a doorway underneath the staircase. To say that I was shaken would be a positive understatement, because I knew that the Curtises didn't keep gnomes. I mean, they were such high-minded social climbers that even if they had a gnome everybody in the city would have been told.

"Finding myself on the verge of hysteria—too afraid to leave the house and too afraid to stay, I polished off the scotch and went to sit on the front gallery. After a while, Eleanor drove up, and I at once confronted her about her resident gnome. She went scarlet red. 'Oh,' she said. 'You must mean Sally.' At a total loss, particularly since I'd never seen a gnome who looked like a Sally, indeed I'd never seen a gnome before in my entire life. I had been a constant guest of the Curtises for over three years, had stayed in their house alone, and this was my first confrontation with the gnome.

"Well, it turns out that this was no gnome at all, but Eleanor's 99-year old mother, whom they had absconded from her home in Palestine, Texas, and who held the not-so-inconsiderable key to the family safe. Her senility had reduced her to a neonatal existence. She'd been living there for three years, in this gnome-sized apartment, completely hidden from the rest of the house. Her days were spent watching *Ding Dong School, Howdy Doody*, and eating, as I later noticed when her identity was made clear to me, copious cups of curds and whey."

I was stupefied by these tales. Bill caught my astonishment, and in a very blasé manner reminded me where we were.

"This is New Orleans, Pet. It's not real. Think of it this way. Brigadoon has been removed from Scotland and placed squarely inside the Mississippi River Delta."

I pondered that concept, and in a matter of seconds, New Orleans began to make sense. That, in itself, was frightening.

Later that night, awaiting the ten o'clock hour and *Law and Order*, I thought back on the last several days and my recently acquired friend. I concluded that I was now certain of several things. Bill Holcomb was a very learned man, incessantly amusing, he no longer drank, and he was definitely hiding something, and had been for years.

Chapter 2

Several weeks had passed and Bill was now working full-time at Harper's Interiors. I was busy decorating my historic home and putting the finishing touches on my second novel. But hardly a day passed that I didn't stop in Harper's for more animated conversation.

One day in particular stirred my curiosity. Bill was inside one of his fabulous stories when a customer walked in pushing a baby carriage. Bill lurched from his chair in joyous recognition of this woman. He politely introduced me, turned back to the woman, where both dove into reminiscent dialogue. I stood in shadow, listening and marveling. It was clearly obvious that my friend had indeed run with the aristocracy of New Orleans, and had not simply filled me with wondrous tales from an illusionary imagination. This woman was one of the Brennans, a family whose name dominates elegant and lavish cuisine in the entire city of New Orleans, from the famed Breakfast at Brennan's Restaurant on Royal Street in the French Quarter to Commander's Palace on Washington Avenue in the Garden District.

I marveled at the diversity and dichotomy of this man. Bill Holcomb rubbed elbows—or had—with the most elite, as well as low-life deadbeats lurking in musty corners and dark stairwells. It was the latter that I had recently come to know.

There were two bars on Magazine Street where Bill spent most of his evenings. One was The Balcony, a two-story so-so dive that served free *hors d'oeuvre* during happy hour. Though Bill, for the most part, detested the tasteless morsels, they were free and filled his need for nourishment. So along with a Dr. Pepper and the gratuitous eats, Bill spent a good amount of time at The Balcony, chatting with locals. The other bar within walking distance of The Balcony was The Rendezvous Tavern.

There is no doubt about The Rendezvous. It *is* a dive—a two-story gin mill with shabby rooms for rent on the second floor. Although rats and giant roaches claimed it for their own, a few humans seemed to come and go as through a revolving door.

I had heard snippets about Murphy, the owner of this famed saloon, from Bill. It was time to corner him for a more in-depth biography. The potential book that had started rumbling inside my head needed material. I was certain that the life I was hoping to uncover inside Bill's past would not be nearly so entertaining as his stories.

One afternoon, as we settled into our places in my den, the Red Room, I said, "Tell me about this Murphy person." I handed Bill an iced coffee and sat across from him, my vodka and orange juice in hand, eagerly awaiting the details.

"Murphy, the proprietor of The Rendezvous," Bill raised both eyebrows and shrugged his right shoulder, "lets rooms on a weekly basis to a moribund crew of roofers, plumbers, painters and the occasional social security recipient, all of whom he refers to as 'his losers'.

"To the *horror* of the neighbors," Bill inclined his chin at the word *horror* and rolled his eyes, "The Rendezvous has been a bar for some fifty years and is considered to be within the confines of the Garden District. It would take someone holding a Master's in math simply to total the number of times New Orleans' finest have been called to quell everything from fights, shootings, and even once, to arrest an over-zealous couple who decided that the roof of the garage was a fitting place to engage in sexual intercourse—at three o'clock on a Sunday afternoon.

"Now, Jim Murphy is a displaced Chicagoan and has owned the bar for 23 years. The man himself approaches a near mythical incarnation of Fagin. Indeed, one wonders if Murphy *was* a reincarnation, for surely Dickens modeled his infamous Fagin on him. Reputedly worth a fortune, and as more beer is consumed every evening, the fortune grows by leaps and bounds, according to who's had the most to drink. The fact is, Murphy owned another," Bill gasped, "high-scale bar out in Metairie (an upper-crust suburb of New Orleans) a dry cleaning establishment, and enough rental property throughout the city to have accommodated all the Vietnamese who wafted into the city after the fall of Saigon.

"When Murphy first arrived in New Orleans, he spent approximately twelve years involved in business schemes, which were mostly backed by Gotti-esque characters, all of whom would place prominently in the casting of Godfather IV—should Coppola want to film it. Although jovial and friendly, Murphy had managed to retain the first cent he ever made, and was of the attitude that, 'if I can't take it with me, I ain't going.'

"The Rendezvous became Murphy's cash cow. He rented out the eight rooms upstairs, which netted him five-hundred and sixty dollars per week, plus through an intricate system of locking the rear entrance to the rooms, made it necessary for each tenant, wishing to leave, to exit through the bar, where he nailed them for an additional seventy dollars a week, by knocking a quarter or so off a six pack, which they would have had to walk three blocks to buy at a higher price. Consequently, Murphy had built-in cash flow. Also adding to the nefarious allure of the hot spot, were the barmaids. Phineas Fogg could not have conjured up such a crew, if his trip had taken him eight hundred days around the world.

"I started going to The Rendezvous," Bill informed, "around the early 1980s. It was open 24-hours a day, and I usually went to buy packaged liquor late at night when most stores were closed. After about a year, I ventured inside one Saturday afternoon, late."

Bill looked at me wide-eyed. "I felt that I had fallen into a Fellini movie," he said. "In fact, for me, it was so breath taking in its scope of unreality, that I polished off several vodkas. One part of me, my conscience, was crying, 'Get The Hell Out, you know you're weak-willed and easily led, particularly when fueled,' the other part, my hedonistic half, was magnetically drawn to this *outré* setting. But knowing that I had a commitment to the Curtises, my employers, gave me the impetus to leave. On the way home, I looked back over my shoulder repeatedly, thinking perhaps that something I had just seen might still be with me. It was three years before I returned."

I looked at Bill eagerly. "What? What happened?"

Bill turned away with a bashful guise.

"The bar was dark as pitch," he said gravely. "And peopled by a *louche* lot. From the juke box, Patsy Cline was singing loud enough to wake the dead. And the most oft repeated word throughout the bar, which I had never known to be a noun, verb, adjective, adverb, and in some cases, inveigled itself as a pronoun, was *fuck*.

"Someone leaned over and asked me if I wanted to make a score. I retaliated with a rapid, 'no thank you, Sir,' a phrase evidently used here as often as Chinese dialogue, for the offerer rebounded with a bewildered look and then repeated his question. A little addled, I asked him what kind of score he was referring to. Without even a blink of his eye, he offered crack, pot, speed, or himself. Now having imagined *myself* as worldly as James Bond, I suddenly decided that .007 had never been to The Rendezvous. So, I surreptitiously removed myself, and crept out just as the barmaid picked up a guitar and joined Miss Cline in an off-key duet that would have been unbearable even if they had been playing in another parish."

To be perfectly honest, I didn't believe that my newfound friend had felt the least bit out of place that night. But I knew if I confronted him with this so early on, I might never gain his confidence. So I pretended to accept the innocence he portrayed and listened on with sincere interest.

"And the barmaids," he said abruptly shaking his head.

"Wait," I said lunging at his glass. "I want to hear about the barmaids."

Speedily, I made myself another vodka and orange juice, refilled his iced coffee and was back in the Red Room in a flash. I resumed my comfortable position on the leather couch. "Go," I said. "Tell me about the barmaids."

Bill's face lit up and the words flowed rhythmically.

"One night," he began, "Peggy, a faded starlet-type, was sitting behind the bar. It was a slow night, and she was wishing for more customers i.e. tips. In the back of the room, a couple of guys were playing pool. Fortunately, for Peggy, the phone rang. She proceeded to the end of the bar to answer it. Before the words had left her mouth, her wishes for more customers were granted—but not quite in the fashion she would have liked. A Dodge pickup truck crashed through the side wall, coming to a halt atop the stool on which Peggy had been sitting.

"The Mexican driver and his two *amigos* had certainly taken a turn at Tequila Ville, for they were sloshed. The two guys playing pool, after carefully checking out the bed of the truck for anything liftable, decided not, and went back to their game. Peggy called Murphy and the police. Murphy, who arrived long after the police, was absolutely enraged, and for a moment thought he would take justice into his own hands. The police, however, deterred him. After approximately a year of feuding with the insurance company, Murphy had the wall repaired. To my knowledge, Murphy has not served a Mexican patron to this day."

"Keep it coming," I coaxed, taking a large sip of my vodka.

Bill looked across the room and squinted his eyes.

"There was a fellow," he recalled. "The guy had been coming into the bar for several weeks, listening to the ongoing rhetoric concerning Murphy's vast wealth.

"One such rhetoric was when Garland, an upstairs resident, would bellow. 'Hey Murphy, whyja go up on da chips? Wid awe ya money, ya cuda bought Lays and give us all a break.'

"But rather than be assailed by Murphy's usual three-hour dissertation on taxes, criminalism in every branch of public service, and all the other woe-is-mes, Garland slid another quarter across the bar, telling Murphy to go stuff it in his bulging safe in the back office. Which, indeed, does exist. However, all that's in it is Creole mustard and various other condiments that he keeps to embellish his daily snack. A snack consisting of a loaf of French bread, a pound of ham, Blue Plate mayonnaise, the Creole mustard, and topped with an unusual spread of crumpled Zapps jalapeño chips, usually preceded by two containers of bacon and horseradish dip and a package of Frito scoops.

"Now this guy, after hours and days of hearing Murphy's wealth regaled, surely felt that Eldorado lay somewhere behind the bar.

"Because—in the small hours of the morning, when The Rendezvous lay dark and quiet, the man, with saw in hand, proceeded to bore it into the newly repaired wall of the building. No doubt in hopes of reaching Murphy's cache of wealth.

"Unfortunately, for the perpetrator, his saw hit a 220-watt voltage line and in seconds had been fried and ultimately expired. Neighbors, coming home from a late party, noticed this human conflagration and called the police, who in turn, called Murphy. By this time New Orleans' finest had committed Murphy's number to memory.

"This would have been just a minor case of breaking and entering had the chap not come to such an unfortunate demise, but much to Murphy's horror, the deceased's family filed a wrongful death suit against Murphy for not having the 220 voltage wire clearly labeled. Of course, Murphy went into a dead snit, huffing and puffing and letting off steam.

"He wailed, 'should I leave a *fucking* note on my door— Closed. Robberies At Your Own Risk. Suggested hours—2 a.m. to 6 a.m. Watch out for live voltage.'

"Since the flambéed felon had a rap sheet ten miles long, the trial went up in smoke."

"Tell me about Murphy's barmaids," I insisted.

Bill gave me a sharp eye. Then lowering his gaze, he stroked his silver beard in thought. He then raised his head as if a thought had congealed.

"Murphy," he said a wry grin spreading across his face, "adhered to the old premise that a gal behind the bar would entice business, but still managed to miss the boat. Or at least did not quite fathom that having a girl behind the bar had to do with more than just gender— perhaps a smiling face, a modicum of goodish looks, a figure of someone under a size 20.

"And the ability to speak.

"Unfortunately, these qualities were none of Murphy's requisites. Hence, a never-ending parade of barmaids encompassing all such traits as basic whoredom, alcoholism, thievery, drug addiction and just plain old surliness. There was a 32-year old grandmother, an ex-ecdysiast…"

"Wait!" I screeched. "A what?"

"It means whore, Pet. You know, prostitute."

"By whose definition—yours or Webster's?"

"Fuck Webster. It means prostitute."

"Never mind," I said reluctantly. "Go ahead."

"As I was saying. The ex-ecdysiast had three daughters who followed their mother's ex-profession and filled in for her on her nights off. In fact, although no one had a problem with Grandmother, the guys always loved it when one of her daughters was filling in. For she would invariably have other ladies of her profession to come in and amuse the guys. And drink like fish. The poor guys could have been screwed, blewed and tattooed in Manhattan for far less than what was spent on these whores. Their hopes for a hop in the sack were rendered hopeless. These broads, all of whom were lesbians, would order enough doubles to put the poor bastards into a stupor. The guys reached the *non-compus mentus* level. The broads split with their cash. And another fool had fallen."

Bill raised his hand. So I remained quiet while he plunged into another barmaid story.

"Another standout on this long-going roster of Murphy's molls was Insatiable Ingrid. A graduate of Antioch, extremely well-read, above average intelligence, and actually not displeasing to the eye. Ingrid's only mark of detriment toward her character was an insatiable thirst for anything, as long as it had alcoholic content. You've heard of wooden legs? She possessed a wooden torso. She would arrive at work with her own six-pack of 32-ounce Heinekens, which would carry her through until six p.m., exactly one hour later. She had this fascinating way of getting guys to buy drinks for her. It was almost like she cast spells. In fact, I sometimes wondered if she were a hypnotist. I walked in one evening, and she was reading Shakespeare's sonnets to Tom, another live-in, who had never read or heard of Shakespeare—and I would lay my life on the line for this, had never seen a book. Yet, she had him absolutely mesmerized. And for every dollar Busch he would buy, a $2.60 Heinekens would spring forth in Ingrid's hands. As the hour grew late, her toxic level increased. However, Murphy didn't seem to mind. He would graciously offer her a ride home. His recompense—I'm certain—was not in the form of a taxi fare.

"Ingrid's tenure lasted approximately three weeks. A near record.

"Now." Bill took a large sip of his iced coffee and placed it on the side table. "The stunner of this lot was Alex. She was a Swede, born in Bangladesh to Baptist missionary parents. More attractive than her predecessors, this quality was rapidly diminished by her insatiable appetite for food. Any food. All food. Her rapport with customers was virtually nonexistent, for she was also addicted to author Dean Koontz and anyone else that wrote in his genre. Plus, Murphy supposedly purchased a TV for the bar. All the barflies went into cardiac arrest at his munificence, only to find out that one of his tenants had died *in testate*, so Murphy was left with a TV and a closet full of clothes, which were unfortunately two sizes too small for him. He packed them away, making some mumblings about a diet, which no one ever saw him engage in.

"Meanwhile, Alex adopted the TV which she always kept turned to the Sci-Fi channel, assuring all her customers unlimited visions of these nine horn, three nose, green-eyed aliens, et cetera. Alex's downfall, however, came on a Saturday afternoon, when a group of tourists wandered in the bar. They ordered, to her horror, a Tom Collins, Whisky Sour, Bloody Mary, Daiquiri, Singapore Sling, and an Old Fashioned. Alex had no idea how to make any of these drinks and was forced to grovel to the back to summon Murphy. Murphy lurched out with a greedy grin on his face while proceeding to make the aforementioned cocktails.

"The straw that broke the camel's back was that Alex had eaten all the cherries, all the olives, all the lemons, all the oranges, all the celery, and had drunk up all the Bloody Mary mix.

"Alex departed shortly thereafter.

"Then," Bill continued as a twinkle formed in his eye. "There was Marisa, from Utica, New York. She was multi-tattooed, naval ringed, and pierced within an inch of a colander, and had stumbled in after attending Jazz Fest. A holdover of sorts from the hippie days, her studded body and antics turned all our heads more than 360-degrees of an evening. She was unbeatable at the pool table, could drink six Paul Bunyan's under the bar, and had a vocabulary that would make Henry Miller blush. A good sport-type, she got along famously with the raffish renters upstairs, mainly because she envisioned herself as Sweet Charity, meaning that for every three beers one of Murphy's tenants would guarantee, she guaranteed the fourth on the house. It took Murphy several weeks to figure out why his beer cost had soared.

"After all," Bill was quick to remind me, "Murphy counted each sheet of toilet paper before placing the roll in the men's room."

I gave Bill a skeptical look, which he merely ignored and proceeded on with his story.

"When Murphy finally figured this out, and actually caught Marisa in the act of alms-giving, an explosion ensued that rivaled that of Bikini Atoll. Severely chastised, she quickly decided that since she couldn't give away beers, she would have to have something to prove her largesse. This something else was her body. Of the seven living up stairs, I know of but two who didn't engage in dalliance with the charitable Marisa.

"However," he remembered. "I have left out one pertinent fact. Marisa was the live-in of one Noah, a charming schizophrenic alcoholic sign painter, of whom Murphy, at one time, had engaged to repaint a sign which hung outside the entrance to the package goods department of The Rendezvous. The sign was to read 'Package Goods'. After weeks and weeks of waiting, Noah finally delivered the sign to Murphy, and I must say, it was a beautiful piece of craftsmanship—the only wrinkle being, instead of reading 'Package Goods,' it read, with many flourishments and curlicues, 'Watermelons $3.50'. Instead of immediately exploding, Murphy, the eternal tightwad, dashed off to Schwegmans' Market. This being the end of the season, he went to find cheap watermelons. But Murphy was not exactly mollified to find watermelons retailing at $4.50 each. So there went the sign and the watermelon business. Noah put the sign on the back of his truck and left. That was in August of 1998, and I've yet to see a new sign appear.

"Meanwhile, Marisa, having sampled each of the men upstairs, fell madly in love with one, Joe, who also had a room upstairs. She would sneak into his room at night when the bar was closed, or if Joe's room was inaccessible, would simply join him in the back of his Cherokee, where they were interrupted more than once by Garden District Security Police. I'm sure they were quite startled to see a Jeep Cherokee bucking without a sign of anyone in it.

"Their flashlights soon picked out Joe and Marisa in the throes of love making.

"Naturally after several nights of this, Noah, upset that Marisa had not returned home, came to The Rendezvous. Finding that the bar was closed, he scaled the back stairs and barged into Joe's room, catching them *en flagrant délit*. Not given to violence, but possessing a vocal range that would intimidate Callas, Noah shrieked, screamed, threatened, raged, and carried on in a manner heard as far away as Lake Pontchartrain. He then grabbed Marisa by her tattooed wrist, and they vanished into the night.

"Although no one really understood Noah's verbiage toward Joe, Joe obviously did. The next day, Joe was gone, leaving the Cherokee, his television and all his belongings. Not to worry though. Critter, our neighborhood's Artful Dodger, sniffed out the abandoned Cherokee, and within hours, from amongst his other street-wise buddies, had a key made, a damn good imagination temporary license plate, and the Cherokee was last seen chugging down Eighth Street, Critter at the wheel."

Chapter 3

Christmas was nearing and my husband, Des, had come home for an extended stay. We had been combing the haunts on Magazine Street and decided to stop by Harper's Interiors so that he could, at last, meet my new friend, Bill Holcomb. As we entered the doorway, Bill sprang from his chair in a rather awkward fashion. I immediately made the introductions, as Les walked up from the back of the shop. He gave me a stern eye and glanced toward Bill. I didn't need a sledge-hammer over the head to realize that my wondrous friend was drunk.

As Bill used my husband's ear to dive into an obscure dialogue about a particular trust that had been left to him dozens of years back, and a branch of his family that was trying to abscond with it, I pulled Les aside. Well—I was told that this was not Bill's first episode of drunkenness. A few days previous, he had simply fallen into a stupor at his desk. Les, returning from an appointment, walked in to see his em-ployee dead asleep. I gave Les what advice I could; meaning that I told him Bill's conduct was outrageous and detrimental to the business. However, Les did give Bill another chance.

With Christmas only a day or two away, Bill announced that he would probably go to his sister's house in Diamondhead on the Gulf Coast. He then informed me that he wouldn't. I was delighted and in-vited him to our pre-Christmas dinner of Cajun gumbo prepared by my friend and masterful chef, Dale Landry. I also asked Bill for Christ-mas dinner. This invitation seemed to give him immense pleasure, and I was eager for my family—which consisted of my husband, one daughter, a son-in-law, two grandchildren, my son, my sister and her husband, my niece, my nephew, and his wife and daughter—to be regaled by Bill's fantastic stories. But alas, Christmas Eve rolled around, and though a very large Williams–Sonoma gift basket was left on my back doorstep, I didn't see Bill Holcomb for weeks. I heard that he had walked out of Harper's Interiors, leaving the shop unlocked and unattended. Les didn't have to fire Bill. He never returned.

As all recovering alcoholics will tell you, an alcoholic lives in a world of delusions brought on by their own lies. The lies become their excuses and ultimately their reality. They bury the truth as far down inside their pain as humanly possible and live on the periphery. And Bill Holcomb was no exception.

The mystery of this wonderful but lost human being was emerging. And I suspected there was much more to come. Bill was obviously an alcoholic, but I knew that issue wasn't the basis of his torment. I was determined to get to the root of it, even if it meant losing his friendship forever. I am tenacious by nature, so I knew that I would either have Bill fleeing the sight and thought of me, or I would somehow manage to get inside his pain and help free him of the guilt and humiliation I suspected had been eating away at him for most of his life.

All I could think about was the wasted years he had simply sailed through, as though his life were nothing more than a masquerade. The tragedy so obvious to me was that Bill Holcomb's life had been just that, a masquerade spiraling into hopelessness, self-doubt, zero self esteem and would most likely end in a vagrant's death. I could not accept this, but I knew I would have to address this at just the right moment. So believing in fate as I do, I bided my time.

Finally, Bill emerged from his "Lost Weekend" so to speak, and I was pleasantly surprised one day to hear, "Pet, it's Bill," at the other end of the phone line.

"Pet" is the name my cousin, the Professor, William Banks Taylor III, has called me since we were children. Will and I spent most of our youth under draped tables playing doctor and nurse. Not only did Bill remind me of Will, but he sounded eerily like him, which threw me off guard.

I was thrilled and ecstatic when I realized that the caller was Bill, spinning out the lie that he left Harper's Interiors because it was boring him to death. That's not to say that he denied being drunk. How could he? I was there, and besides, I told him he was drunk as a goat. His excuse was that Christmas was always a bad time for him. At that,

I wanted to scream and haul off and slap the shit out of him. I hate lies and excuses and I was getting an overdose of both. Amazingly enough, I kept my mouth shut and my temper at bay, and Bill and I resumed our friendship with continued walks through the Garden District.

Bill was back to drinking Dr. Pepper, iced coffee, or whatever non-alcoholic beverage was available. One night, I had prepared a hot-as-hell-pasta dinner which he devoured with delight, explaining that the tasteless, gratis morsels at The Balcony had abruptly ceased. Possibly the proprietor had come to realize that more people were eating than drinking.

Bill's room in one of the Garden District's Third Street homes did not include the luxury of kitchen facilities. A small microwave was the extent of his culinary appliances. Occasionally, though I came to learn more often than not, Bill would have dinner with his friends at The Rendezvous Tavern. The guys had a broken down barbeque grill on the roof over the garage—the very roof where numerous couples had been caught in the act of fornication. But the guys used it as their private verandah and many a pauper's meal was prepared atop the derelict grill. Bill appeared to feel a sort of luxury when dining inside a real house with food prepared on a newly purchased gas stove.

After putting away the dishes, I suggested that we take Max for his nightly walk. I had missed Bill's company on our walks and was eager for another round of Holcomb's tales of New Orleans' aristocracy/depravity.

This particular night, however, we walked down Chestnut, turned left on Second and proceeded toward Prytania. This was my territory and I couldn't wait to show off with a story of my own. Although Buzz Harper—whose antique shops and interior design talents are legendary throughout the South—was well-known to Bill since he had worked for Les at Harper's Interiors, Bill had only seen Buzz a handful of times. And then only when Buzz would come sailing through the shop and sail out again. So I was proud, eager and delighted to give Bill the full picture of one Mr. Ruben (Buzz) Harper.

"Buzz Harper," I began, "is an enigmatically exquisite, bigger-than-life gentry of a man, who absolutely does not live within the confines of the 20th century. He lives elegantly, grandly and historically in the 19th century, surrounds himself with more gold—color and real—than Napoleon Bonaparte, all the Kings of France and entertains so lavishly to give even royalty pause. He stands six-foot-four, dresses with impeccable tailoring, wears his silver hair in a neatly tied ponytail and often carries a gold-handled walking cane. He rarely completes a sentence but absolutely expects you to know what he means. No wonder that I immediately wrote in a part for him in my first novel."

"And how exactly did you manage to meet Mr. Harper?" Bill said with one raised eyebrow and an attitude. I ignored him and continued on.

"After the 1989 Loma Prieta earthquake rendered our Los Gatos, California home uninhabitable..." Bill twisted his face in horror, but I rapidly continued, not wanting to get into that story at the moment. "Daddy and I happened to be visiting my sister here in New Orleans. I was determined to find just the right chandelier for our newly re-built home, when I happened upon Harper's Antiques on Toulouse Street in the French Quarter. The very chandelier that I had been searching for was clearly visible through the window.

"I yanked my husband off the street and into the shop. To my gasping amazement, I suddenly found myself inside the most glorious room I had ever witnessed. A gentleman who looked like Victor Mature's twin greeted me. His name was Ray Masco, a native Chicagoan who in the 70s and 80s had owned the *Grande Maison de Blanc*, the most posh linen shop on Rodeo Drive in Beverly Hills. His clientele ranged from Ella Fitzgerald to Nicole Brown Simpson to Elizabeth Taylor to Princess Grace and countless others of great fame and fortune.

"It was in Beverly Hills where he met and became long-time friends with one, Verita Thompson. Verita's claim to fame was her lavish culinary skills, owning three of the most popular restaurants in Century City: Verita had bought this Century City complex of town homes from Howard Hughes, put in her three restaurants and leased out the rest to retailers. Her other claim to fame was her lengthy affair with Humphry Bogart, which she wrote about in her book, *Bogie and Me*. This woman knew every movie star of any worth and was best friends with the author, Harold Robbins, and his wife Grace. Her restaurants were filled to the brim every night with everybody who was anybody.

"But as the 1980s drew to a close, taking the economy with it, Ray and Verita left Beverly Hills and landed squarely in Natchez, Mississippi, of all places. They purchased an historic Victorian home directly across the street from one, Buzz Harper. And so, a fast friendship between Buzz and Ray ensued. Eventually, Buzz, having owned practically every bed and breakfast and antiques shop in every historic Southern town from Natchez to Vicksburg to Savannah to Charleston, decided that the small town life was a way of the past and promptly moved to New Orleans. Verita and Ray followed suit. Ray went to work for Buzz and Verita opened a bar called Bogie and Me on Rue St. Louis in the French Quarter across from the famed Antoine's Restaurant. This is where the Gennifer Flowers Kelsto Club is now.

"My house on Washington is the first house Buzz and Les had in New Orleans," I proudly informed Bill, who gave me a pleasant smile and kept walking. I reached out and jerked him to a halt. We were now standing in front of 2507 Prytania where, until recently, Buzz and Les and their friend Ray had lived.

(Two brothers who have houses all over, from San Francisco, to Laguna Beach to Palm Springs and now New Orleans, bought it from Buzz. And they are interested in buying more homes in New Orleans.)

"Now Buzz," I was quick to mention, "has lived in more houses than most people do in a lifetime. But he doesn't make his money buying and selling houses. No prospective buyer is capable of viewing a Buzz Harper home without wanting every piece of furniture in it. He's in the antiques business, not the real estate business," I told Bill.

Bill flipped me a look that assured me he was well aware of Mr. Harper's occupation. So I quickly moved on with my story.

"After Buzz and Les left the house at Washington and Chestnut, they bought a grand old place on Chartres Street in the French Quarter. This would be their first encounter with the restless ghosts and evil spirits of the Vieux Carré. There was a vile monkey and an angry vanishing woman who could be heard pounding her high heels across the attic floor, dragging who-knew-what. There was absolutely nothing in the attic for anyone, ghost or mortal to drag, so the new occupants on Chartres suddenly found themselves in a restless, unnerving environment.

"Ray once saw the ghostly image of the woman, but thought it was merely someone trespassing on their property. He swung his cane at her. Ray, though certainly not prone to any manner of violence, watched as the cane sailed through the air and—through the woman! She instantly vanished, leaving Ray in a morbid state of shock."

It seemed that I had now captured Bill's attention, and with Max enjoying an intermediate rest, I zealously continued.

"Now this monkey thing," I informed Bill, "is actually documented. It seems that some time in the 19th century, young women would be lured off the third story gallery to their death by a six-foot monkey wearing a red pill-box hat, sporting large brass buttons, a red satin tux and an enormous smile."

Bill let out a howl, rolled his eyes, and gave me a look of disbelief. I moved on with another ghost story.

"One day Buzz and Les were in the bedroom. Ray was gone and no one else was in the house. The bedroom doorknob suddenly began to turn, followed by an urgency for whoever was on the other side to get in. Knowing that Ray was gone and that it was virtually impossible to get inside this structure without a key, Les reached for his gun from the bedside table. The commotion abruptly ended and neither Buzz nor Les could find anyone anywhere inside the entire house.

"The next incident," I said, "was the worst of all. One day Buzz was coming down the winding front staircase, when he suddenly felt a heavy push to his back and found himself sprawled at the foot of the stairs. I had returned to New Orleans for a visit and was to attend Sunday Mass with Buzz and Les at St. Louis Cathedral. Buzz was sporting a most handsome gold handled walking cane, which he used from time to time. But this time I could see the cane was more for function than show. He refrained from mentioning the true cause of his fall until a few years later. It wasn't long after this incident that they sold the house and moved to Royal Street. The wife of the couple who bought the house on Chartres grew ill only days after their purchase. She only began to recover after they sold it. They moved to the country for a few years and now rent the penthouse in my apartment building on St. Charles Avenue."

"So," Bill asked. "Did Buzz and Les free themselves of the ghost?"

"Those ghosts," I replied, ready to move on to the house on Camp Street where Penelope had the run of things. "Little did Buzz and Les and Ray know that they would, yet again, encounter the disturbing antics of New Orleans' restless spirits. As far as I know, there were no disturbances on Royal Street. But the house on Camp Street had once been the Delachaise Plantation. It later became a home for Protestant widows and orphans. Who knows," I speculated. "Maybe Penelope was one of the orphans not fortunate enough to be adopted, remaining in the only home she'd ever known."

"Maybe," Bill said, an edge of sarcasm rumbling.

"Whatever," I said. "Anyway, Penelope wasn't a particularly angry ghost, but probably a very sad and lonely one. She spent most of her antics opening and slamming doors and even once yanked the canopy off the wall in the upstairs bedroom where I usually stayed."

Bill pivoted with an abrupt, "What? You were in the bed when this happened?"

I was immediately incensed that I could not answer that question with a yes.

"I have been fascinated with ghosts since childhood," I told him. "I write about them, read about them and haven't missed a ghostly or eerie movie of any credence ever. But I have never had the good fortune to encounter one. So no," I admitted. "It was friends of Buzz and Les'—a couple who live in Los Angeles and own Monmouth Plantation, now a five star hotel/bed and breakfast in Natchez, Mississippi. They were sleeping in the ill-fated bed that night when the canopy was ripped out of the wall and came crashing down, missing Lani and Ronnie by inches. And Peaches," I remembered. "She's Buzz and Les' long-time housekeeper and cook—Peaches heard Penelope all the time, and swears that Penelope attached herself to her back one day as she was leaving the house and didn't release her for six blocks.

"Ray used to get so irritated with Penelope's rantings that he would scream mild obscenities at her to stop. And she would.

"The incident that galls me the most is yet another example of how these restless spirits seem to take pleasure in eluding me.

"It was in the middle of the night. My daughter, Ashley and her two children were sleeping in an adjoining bedroom. Alice, my friend from Atlanta, was sleeping in the twin bed next to mine. A low-grade moaning woke Alice from a deep sleep. Not quite sure of who or what she was hearing, turned to find me dead asleep. After a few minutes to gain courage, she left her bed, cautiously entered the sitting room only to run into Ashley who had also been awakened by this ghastly sound. Alice and Ashley quickly conferred that no, they were not hallucinating, and yes, they were scared out of their wits. But by the time they rousted me from my slumber, the moaning had ceased. Yet again, I had not been privy to the ghost on Camp Street. Or any other ghosts for that matter."

"Don't push it." Bill groaned, turning his attention to the imposing Greek Revival house in front of us. "When did they buy this house?"

"Oh, about the time I moved into the St. Charles Avenue property," I replied. "Around March of 1996."

"Any ghosts hanging around in there?" he wanted to know.

"Peaches says yes," I told him. "But then Peaches says they're ghosts in my house on Washington. Who knows? To my knowledge, Buzz never complained of any." I looked through the tall gray wrought-iron fence. "All I know about his house is that I've probably had the most lavish dinners imaginable inside those walls. The finest champagne, exquisite *hors d' oeuvre*, accompanied by lovely piano music, opera singers who sang the Lord's Prayer while the guests were seated at the 20-foot dining table.

"And dancing with my Uncle Buzz in the ballroom."

I was suddenly overcome with reminiscences of those glorious times, experiences that most people could not even dream of. And I felt fortunate to have the opportunity to be a part of Buzz Harper's world of elegance.

Bill was now looking at me in a stupefied state. "Buzz Harper is your uncle?"

"*Mais bien sûr*," I replied ever so anxious to show my erudite friend that I too, had a working knowledge, though minute, of the French language. He didn't seem the least bit impressed, so I proceeded as though I didn't expect him to be. "Since putting him in my novel as Uncle Buzz," I explained, "I sometimes forget that he's not."

Bill threw up his hands and did an awkward version of a pirouette and landed himself in front of the mansion Buzz had recently purchased, which stood directly next door to his former house. Bill knew absolutely nothing about the history of this house and I knew very little.

"What I know about this house," I said, "is that Anne Rice purchased it, adding to her already bulging real estate collection. Quite a while back the house had been converted to a Catholic church, Our Lady of Perpetual Help. Through the years, it had fallen into termite-infested disrepair. When it was offered for sale and ultimately purchased by the Queen of Gothic herself, the Garden District parishioners went into a raging snit."

I released more line for Max since he had zeroed in on one of his favorite shrubs. Curling my fingers around one of the many spokes of the massive fence, I gazed at a masterpiece in progress.

"You would have thought that Dracula himself had made the purchase," I said, remembering the absurdity of it, "and planned to hold court for the purpose of claiming more victims. Poor Anne was talked about in every parlor, drawing room, tabloid and news program throughout New Orleans. What they were expecting the novelist to do within the crumbling walls of this once-beautiful private home, I can only imagine. But rumor had it that some were of the mind that she was planning all sorts of Voodoo goings on with devil effigies lurking in dark corners of their once sacred edifice."

Bill only shrugged his shoulders. He too remembered all the hulla-baloo after Anne's purchase had become known.

"What do you expect, Pet?" He threw up his arms and swung them around in a frenzied gesture. "Those are the same people who believe soap operas are real."

I thought about that for a minute, which brought to mind when my granddaddy Taylor would reproach my grandmother for undress-ing in front of their television. He was absolutely certain those people could see her. I remember trying to explain to the best of my ability how television worked. I was all of 15 and had been on Dance Party, a local TV show in my hometown of Jackson, Tennessee. But being of such a young age, I was not very convincing. My granddaddy pushed his fat cigar into his mouth and said, 'Well, you never know about those things.' I dropped the subject and never discussed it again.

"Regardless, they can stop stewing now," I told Bill. "Buzz Harper is turning it into the Sistine Chapel of New Orleans."

Bill lifted his right shoulder and cocked his head my way. This re-mark had caught him off guard. Bill was an on-again-off-again devout Catholic. I knew this because there would be times when he and I at-tended Mass on a regular basis. I knew he often went as a daily ritual. This, of course, was his crutch for staying sober, which never works when you are determined to keep your demons buried and your ad-missions at bay. And Bill Holcomb had more garbage buried than the entire city of New Orleans. To admit any truths about himself was out of the question. So how could God help this man when he wasn't ready or willing to help himself? I wanted to tell him this, right then, right there, in front of that once-beloved chapel. But something told me that the time was still not right.

"Sistine Chapel?" Bill was waiting for an explanation.

"Aside from all the 18-carat gold leaf moldings and furnishing," I informed, "Barrie Tinkler," whom Bill knew and had painted life-size portraits of my husband and me, "will be painting the ceiling in the front parlors. And I can tell you, without a doubt, it will be of reli-gious connotations."

"Is Buzz a Catholic?" he asked.

"Devout," I said sharply. "There have even been masses held in his parlor." I pointed to his former house. "He and Miss Mary Harper are very devout Catholics," I said, hoping to pique his curiosity.

"Who the hell is Miss Mary Harper?"

"Miss Mary Harper is 18-years old. She's totally blind, totally deaf and has more recamiers and portraits of herself than any long-haired Chihuahua that I know. She once had her own credit card."

Bill gave a quick snicker, lowered his head and we turned back toward home.

Chapter 4

It was early spring and Bill and I hadn't see each other for several weeks. I suspected, or should I say, I knew damn well why the absence. But I also knew that the perfect moment to confront Bill had not shown itself. So I went about finishing my second novel, decorating the upstairs of my house, which consisted of painting, gold-leafing and sewing. Les had done his masterful wonder of draping my downstairs windows, some of which were floor to ceiling. So thousands of dollars later, my penurious husband announced that he would build me a professional cutting table on his next sweep through New Orleans and give me a budget within which I was expected to stay.

I have never followed a budget in my entire life, which has caused me great stress, and led me directly back to Daddy (calling your husband 'Daddy' is a Southern thing and needs no explanation) to beg for large credit card payoffs. However, I have finally seen the light and have made a rather impressive New Years resolution: I will not ask Daddy for another payoff.

I focused on staying within my means and dumping most of my allowance into my credit card debts, which are considerable and will not be revealed. So—I worked the credit card mambo, consolidating and transferring my balances to one card at a 2.99% interest rate. Since I continually receive offers of this kind, at the end of their introductory period, I transfer to yet another low rate credit card. So far, this has been working to my advantage.

Daddy, however, was finding that even with my free labor, it cost a fortune to decorate a house, especially a 146-year old one with windows as tall as flagpoles.

Harry's is our local Ace Hardware store and blissfully convenient when not wanting to cross the river to "The Depot." "The Depot," as Daddy calls it—that's with a short (ĕ)—has become my second home. I found treasures there that most people think cost a fortune. These treasures, like my credit card debt, are absolutely no one's business.

One day while I was on my third trip to Harry's, I saw Bill crossing Magazine Street. He spotted me and gave a big wave. Later that day he called. And again, I invited him over for dinner followed by another jaunt through the Garden District.

The night was dark and overcast. We strolled down Chestnut, turned left on Third and came to a halt at Coliseum. I could see immediately that he had something grave on his mind. He dove into immediate dialogue.

"As much pomposity, grandiosity and ribald humor that is associated with the Garden District," he said looking just beyond me, "there is also a tragic side, which I hesitate to elaborate on, as it sort of throws a pall over the hilarity that accompanies most of my tales."

Though I sensed a dire story ahead, my curiosity simmered, and I looked on with guarded interest.

"You see that big house?" Bill pointed to a sprawling Greek Revival masterpiece.

I saw it all right. In fact, Max and his now-deceased father, Jocque and I had once stood in front of that marvelous home, chatting with the owner. I had told him how much my husband admired his home. He immediately offered to sell us the house, leave the impressive structure, move into the equally impressive attached guest quarters and live happily ever after. I relayed this offer to Daddy—we were still living in our apartment building on St. Charles Avenue at that time. Daddy entertained this offer with interest for a while. Of course, my anal-retentive, ever penurious husband decided to pass on the opportunity. The mansion sold two years later for over $2 million. That's a massive figure for New Orleans.

Bill was now staring across the grounds at this glorious piece of architecture. "At first glance," he said. "It certainly does give off an aura of being very grand and indeed it was. The family who occupied this property for years and years and years, consisted of a father, fabulously wealthy—one of the few people ever to completely corner two markets at the same time, both cotton and pork bellies—his wife, born of New England gentry, and their four impeccably raised and educated children.

"The oldest daughter was betrothed in the '50s to a young man of equal rank. After a typical Garden District wedding, the young married set out for a European honeymoon. The third night on the continent found them at the internationally famous, *Vier Jahrezeiten*, on *Maximillian Strasse*. This hotel in Munich has played host to the international set for years. After checking into their suite, the groom insisted that his young wife bathe and get dressed for dinner. When she was finished, he told her to go downstairs to the bar, where he would join her for a drink before dining. She waited long after a reasonable time had passed, and with newlywed nervousness, went back to their suite to see what was keeping him.

"He wasn't in their room.

"Stopping to get a sweater from the closet, for it had turned quite chilly in the lobby, she threw open the closet door, screamed, and fainted away. When she came to, the hotel staff, which had been alerted by her scream, were busily applying salts, et cetera. After an investigation by the Munich police, the file was closed and their press release read as follows: American honeymooner commits suicide in the *Vier Jahrezeiten*.

"This is but one of the tragic tales," Bill said gravely. "But to me, the strangest part was that the widow returned to New Orleans and took up her merry old life, as if what had transpired in Munich was but a bad chapter plucked out of an otherwise fascinating book. Actually, I never heard her mention her marriage, the demise thereof, her deceased husband…it was as if it had never happened."

"You know," I said, "I have friends who know that family and that's not exactly the way I heard the story from them."

Bill simply looked back toward the house. "And then," he said, pointing to the left wing of this glorious mansion, "one evening, one of his other daughters put a gun to her head there in the parlor—right in front of her father—and pulled the trigger."

"I know," I said as we turned away from the house and headed toward First Street.

"All right," he said. "Let's go ahead and exorcise all the demons. See that house on the corner with the beautiful gallery?" He pointed to a sort of Italianate Villa. "The young lady who resided there with her parents was a rose amongst roses. In fact, she was the only person in New Orleans invited to Truman Capote's Black and White Ball, one of the most prestigious affairs of its kind.

"As a debutante, she had been presented in New Orleans, Washington D.C., and London. A more fastidious background could not even be imagined. She was beautiful and possessed of a certain *je ne sais quoi*. She was courted by a young man from the Mississippi Delta whose father had been editor and owner of one of the South's most liberal newspapers. In fact, his stand on anti-discrimination in the pre-integrated South caused many of his ilk to look on him as a traitor. However, this did not daunt the gentleman. He continued to write in this vein, and was awarded the Pulitzer Prize. No one knows, I suppose no one ever shall, what conversation, manner, movement, precipitated the young man's action, but he walked out on that upstairs gallery," Bill pointed as though to the very spot. "He pulled a small Beretta out of his jacket pocket and promptly killed himself. Again," Bill lamented, "it was like another scene that had fallen on the cutting room floor. It was the talk of the town for two days, only to vanish into obscurity."

Bill and I turned away and walked toward Louisiana Avenue. As we approached the corner of Ninth and Prytania, he stopped.

"See that old sort of French Gothic house? It was the last home of a daughter of perhaps one of New Orleans' greatest entrepreneurs. He started off in the early 1900s, pushing a fruit cart in the French Quarter, and due to diligence and long, long hours, built one of Americas largest fruit importers. This man, while head of a monstrous conglomerate, never lost his old-world humility, or his dignity. All of his five children were finely educated by the good sisters of Sacred Heart, and all married up into life, except for one.

"This young woman absolutely had a streak of paganism running through her. Papa didn't ask for much, but the '60s, with their dissolvement of social mores, were too much for him. The daughter, while never in trouble of any sort, cultivated as her friends a group of intellectuals ranging from French Quarter beat poets to graduate types from many of New Orleans' universities.

"On Christmas day, in the early '60s, Papa went by to pick up his daughter for Christmas luncheon. When no one replied to the bell, he broke the door down. There sat his daughter fully dressed for a luncheon party; the only thing awry was a small neat hole in her right temple. Her hand lay on the sofa, Colt revolver still in it. Again," Bill said. "While causing comment among the Garden District's populous, this, too, became a forgotten act in but a matter of days. Except for the fact that the child's mother was never seen in public again. Indeed, the House of Bultman buried her in a closed casket some years later."

Chapter 5

Again, Bill seemed to fade away. I had not seen him in days, so I decided to stop by the house on Third where I knew he rented a room. He was not at home and his landlady was of no help whatsoever.

I left a note and heard from him that night.

Bill was jubilant, announcing that he was working for one of the cruise lines at their office down by the Mississippi River next to the Convention Center. I was thrilled with his news, because I knew that if anyone was world traveled, it was Bill Holcomb. He had worked for Thomas Cook Travel and American Express Travel for years and years and had spanned the world.

One incident of spanning was when he went on a drunken binge, and, with American Express in hand, landed himself in every major city throughout Europe and the world—none of which he could remember well enough to write even a passing review. Three months later, Bill came down to earth. When sobriety set in, he found himself without a job, no place to live and an Amex bill in excess of ten thousand dollars.

Hearing this revelation from a seemingly sane person who I have actually witnessed buying clothes from thrift shops, I turned to him with a gasp.

"You what!"

Bill casually turned his head with an ignominious shrug and said. "But of course. I flew front cabin. If I was going to bugger off, I was going to bugger off in style."

With style, he did. But style had now become an unattainable factor in his life of discourse.

With the cruise line position, I had great hopes that Bill might, at last, find himself and crawl his way back to sobriety and become a useful part of society. But nothing could have been less likely, and nothing was going to help my friend until he could admit denial, and accept Bill Holcomb for who he was—and to hell with who and what society and family thought he should be.

Bill informed me that he had given up his cruise line position. I accepted his reason that he was utterly bored with this rather menial position, accompanied by equally menial pay, and decided that he'd rather just drink and hang out at The Rendezvous.

Bill Holcomb had fallen yet again, succumbed to his wretched pain, and was back to idle days and morning walks down Magazine Street to purchase beer at the A & P.

It had occurred to me that beer was not an item one was allowed to purchase with food stamps. I knew the room he rented was somewhere just under $300, and I wondered how Bill was managing rent and non-food stamp necessities when losing, after only a short stint, one job after another.

So one day I simply asked. 'Bill, how in the hell do you pay your rent, buy your beer and have money left over for thrift store purchases?' And that's when I learned about the tragic accident caused by an inexperienced intern at LSU Eye Clinic.

Bill's doctor was to perform routine cataract surgery. Bill still remembers hearing the words leave the intern's mouth, "I can't insert the lens." To which a doctor answered, "Make the wound deeper." At this moment Bill's retina suffered irreversible damage. Not even extended laser surgeries to repair the damage could save Bill's sight. He was rendered blind in his right eye. His compensation came to an unimpressive $3,000, which of course he drank away in a matter of months. I later learned that he had boasted of a twenty million dollar settlement.

Needless to say, Bill was apprehensive when forced to undergo the same surgery on his left eye. But the option of living with no sight in his right eye and diminished sight in his left from the cataracts gave him little choice. An experienced doctor performed the surgery and Bill came away with decent sight in his left eye.

For someone who lives inside crossword puzzles and an endless stream of books, the ability to see is imperative. For Bill, sinking like quicksand inside that abyss of hopelessness, these pastimes were the only real joy he had managed to hang on to.

So it was the loss of his eye that now provided him with a whopping $614 a month Social Security disability benefits. And this was what kept Bill from landing squarely in the middle of homelessness and ultimately a vagrant's demise.

Since Bill was still in the ranks of the unemployed, I readily snatched him up to accompany me to the matinees at The Palace Theatre. I am a movie lover and was thrilled to have someone of his intelligence to toss critiques back and forth.

We were on our way to The Palace to see *The Bone Collector* when a conversation we had had the day before came to mind. There was a word he had used (he was always using words that I had absolutely no idea what they meant). "Remember yesterday," I said, "when you mumbled a word and I thought you had said 'enema'?"

Bill let out a yelp, immediately overcome with laughter, and dove headlong into another group of quirky stories.

"The word enema," he suddenly recalled, " brings back some raucous memories of living on the Mississippi Gulf coast.

"We lived for two years in Long Beach, Mississippi, crammed into a teeny house embedded with great historical background. None of which was ever disclosed to us. As a matter of fact, Count Frederick Joohris and his wife, Jeanette, had owned Old Chimneys, a lovely West Indies-type cottage directly on the Gulf of Mexico. They had fled Europe in pre-Nazi days and came to America with their fortune intact. As they were up in years, they decided to settle into the then-bucolic atmosphere of the Mississippi Gulf Coast. They were both fascinating, and their home contained an astonishing accumulation of altar pieces taken, over the centuries, from plundered cathedrals throughout Europe.

"My mother was quite taken with the house, and my father, whose abacus eyes were already subdividing the forty adjoining acres, whipped out a contract, and in a matter of hours, Madam Holcomb was the chatelaine of Old Chimneys. The Joohris zipped off to Europe. Indeed, I visited them myself some years later in San Juan Cap Ferrat, where they were ensconced in a villa so filled with antiquity that they had not one but two chapels. The better to show off all their religious tableware."

"What does that have to do with enemas?" I asked.

"Don't bandy with the beauty of the benighted bag," he scolded.

"Bill," I said. "What the hell are you rambling about?"

He turned his attention out the window and proceeded with another outrageous story.

"Our house in Long Beach, Old Chimneys, was exactly two blocks from Gulf Park College, which is now a branch of Mississippi Southern University. Keep in mind," he said. "This was in the late '50s. Gulf Park was considered to be a junior college of the finishing school caliber for young ladies supposedly of breeding and high station. The breeding we'll get to later. But the high station, if that's the way to rank it, for the yearly tuition must have been that of Columbia.

"My good friend, Anne Marie, attended as a day student, and of course, in her Pied Piper way, attracted all the girls in her class who thought it just great to have a friend who lived off campus. As a matter of point, I can remember one weekend when Anne Marie had 38 houseguests, all of whom were boarders at the college. Anne lived two houses down from me with her grandparents. The house had indeed seen better days. But its vast columns and sheer girth, when seen on a moonlit night, were extremely impressive.

"Now Anne Marie was the first person to greet me when my family and I first moved into Old Chimneys. She came barreling up the driveway in her lavender Ford convertible named Capone. You see," Bill, informed me, "all the girls named Anne Marie's car that because she brought more bootleg liquor onto the campus than old Scarface took from Kiln, Mississippi, to Chicago. She shrieked her introduction and told me to hop in the car. As we roared out of the driveway, she announced that she was going to launch me into Gulf Coast society."

"I'm waiting for the enema bags," I reminded.

Bill raised his left eyebrow. "I'm not stopped up yet. We'll get to that part in due time."

Not the least bit consoled, I turned my attention back to the road.

"In the course of one afternoon and early evening, this soigné, young (seventeen) hedonist, had introduced me to 36 bars, *all* of which were conveniently having happy hour i.e. four drinks for a buck." Bill cut his eyes toward me. "The '50s, remember."

I immediately explained to him that, though he was a mere one year older than I, strong drink at the age of 17 was *not* in my repertoire of societal doings. With practically lethal clarity, he informed me that it had been an integral part of his daily life since somewhere around eight years old.

Knowing this man as I had come to, I had no reason to believe that what he had just told me was anything but gospel.

"I also met," he continued, "everybody who was anybody on the Mississippi Gulf Coast. When Anne finally dropped me off later that night, I stumbled into the house, ran into my mother, my father conveniently out of town, and announced that I had been *launched*. Mother looked at me and said, 'Yes, like you've been launched into a vat of '69.'

"Several days later, Anne arrived with three of her classmates from Gulf Park—Rooster, Greer and Susie. Accompanied with three thermoses full of martinis and a copy of *Peyton Place*, we all went out on the pier to sun. Anne Marie, in the role of Athena, proceeded to read from *Peyton Place*, a book about which I knew absolutely nothing, except that my mother had told my three sisters and me that if she even heard of us looking at it, we would die a cruel death. I think my older sister had already read the thing, which meant my other sisters and I wouldn't be far behind. When Anne Marie reached the part about where young Norman, such a mama's boy, would race home from school every afternoon to run into the arms of his dear Mamma, she, upon seeing him, would be so alarmed at his agitated state, would immediately give him an enema to calm him down.

"All five of us, much fueled by the martinis, began shrieking and squealing as if it was the funniest thing ever written. After we calmed down and started talking about this, we all decided that 'enema' was a word we had all known, but no one had ever really said it or even remembered seeing it in print. So this set off another round of shrieking, at which point we just rolled off the pier and into the Gulf.

"I shall never forget that day as long as I live," Bill howled. "And that's the day the Enema Club of America was born."

The Palace Theatre was drawing near, so I begged Bill for at least one quick enema story before we arrived. With a profound lack of hesitation, he plunged again headlong.

"All during the second semester, the young maidens of Gulf Park were one by one selectively seduced to become members of the Enema Club. By mid-semester it had practically become a cult, and those who had not been asked to join, lived in fear of social ruin. Although there were approximately 50 members at this time, the school year was running out, so the movers and shakers, of which Anne Marie was *the* leader, decided to have a year-end enema blow out.

"No pun intended.

"So as to be the charming democratic young ladies that they were, they decided to extend an invitation to the entire student body.

"Some months before, Dean Ryan, Dean of Women, had been receiving reports that some of her virginal charges had been seen slipping out of those ivied dormitories and vanishing into the bowels of the night—also known as Elsie and Lannie's Bar and Grill, which featured the longest happy hour known to man. It ran from twelve noon to twelve midnight. Dean Ryan decided that along with three of her fellow teachers, she would put in an appearance at Elsie's one evening, just to prove that Gulf Park girls didn't hang out in such dives. As fate would have it, the night of the infamous enema bag ball, being held at Elsie's, was the same night Dean Ryan had chosen for her foray. Naturally, yours truly, who had been named mascot of the ECOA, was there sitting on the bar with a twenty foot long enema tube, which Anne Marie swore had once belonged to Paul Bunyan. All about the bar was the entire student body of Gulf Park College, doing the Bop. Each girl had pinned to her breast a miniature corsage consisting of a tubeless gold lamè enema bag with a carnation in its throat.

"At the moment that these frenzied enema-ites were reaching a pinnacle of hedonistic joy, Dean Ryan entered, attended by three of her school's elder teachers. The entire tableau turned to stone. She simply stood there swaying a bit, eyeing every girl with a look that said, 'I have seen you and I will not forget you.' She then turned and left with her attendants, leaving the girls in a state of either mad hilarity or morbid terror.

"Unfortunately for Dean Ryan, it seemed there was not one of her errant flock that she could castigate, because included in this lot of ECOM members and guests, were: Miss Gulf Park College for the year, plus the already selected and alternate, salutatorian and valedictorian of the senior class, and the Daughters of the American Revolution's Daughter of the Year, an honor annually given to the girl with the best school spirit, and the right stuff to be a model for America's young ladies. Footnote: Although the ECOA enjoyed only one year of notoriety, to this day, it is mentioned by those game enough to bring it up. However those who were told of it, think the whole tale is sort of a Hieronymus Bosch dream."

With an image of Bosch's discombobulated work swirling inside my head, Bill and I finally arrived at The Palace. However, I learned quickly that he was not particularly fond of gory thrillers. In the middle of watching *The Bone Collector*, Bill announced, "I have to go to the bathroom." He then mildly screeched, "For a week!"

I was certain that I would not see him again until the movie had ended, and I was headed out the front door of the theatre— but he did return and guardedly watched the rest of the movie.

Again, knowing that Bill would probably attach himself to the wasteland of renters at The Rendezvous, I informed him that dinner would be at seven. He had yet to turn down even one of my dinner invites and this was no exception. I prepared one of my famous pots of scathing hot beans, popped a tin of Jiffy corn bread in the oven and tossed a salad, which I topped with my homemade vinaigrette.

That night, setting out for Max's nightly walk, we somehow ended up some six blocks from home.

"Moosey!" Bill shrieked stopping dead in his tracks at the corner of Jackson Avenue and Prytania. "Now this one predates even me," he announced, practically ranking it with the time of Egyptian hieroglyphics. He thrust his arm into mid air and vigorously pointed to a combination raised cottage, and subject of many architectural revisions. "Somewhere around the mid '30s," he said. "Moosey, a little short of ancient, but well beyond the *demoiselle* years, lived there with a flock of family. Now Moosey will be remembered, if not for the raffish way she managed to make the news, but her sheer determination to assert that she had 'made it.' Being very theatrical by nature, it would be hard to believe that she didn't spend but a little time on planning her *first* suicide attempt.

"According to *The Picayune*, on March 17, somewhere in the '30s, La Moosey tied herself in cascades of silk moiré, opened her dormer windows on the second floor, and much to her glee, saw Jackson Avenue filled with people. After an unheard soliloquy, she cast herself off the balcony, and landed just inside her yard.

"Since very few defenestrations are…"

"Hold it!" I barked. "What was that word?"

"What word? Defenestrations?"

"Yes, Willie, that word. Is that another Holcomb word?"

"It means suicide, Pet."

"Muh, huh," I simply replied.

"Anyway, as I was saying, there are very few successful defenestrations when jumping out a window only 18 feet above ground. Poor Moosey suffered only a broken arm. As for her audience gathered on Jackson Avenue, they were all totally absorbed in the St. Patrick's Day Parade, and nary a soul saw the fair lady fall. Her family, although not possessing a drop of Irish blood, was celebrating with such intensity that—even though they did see poor Moosey sprawled amongst the hyacinths, and certainly knew, due to obliquely dropped hints by Moosey herself, that something was *up*—did not rush to the rescue. After a family council, now mind you, this was a two full days later, and bearing in mind that their grounds would be open to the Garden District Walking Tour, they thought it best to remove Moo.

"The family explained that her broken arm was the result of a croqueting incident. However, after Moosey's limb was set, she was quietly deposited into DePaul's Mental Health Facility. Six months later, a mentally rehabilitated Moosey was again holding court in her Jackson Avenue *Hôtel Particulier*. While outwardly appearing to be afloat on society's seas, her mind-set was that of a Pollyanna Borgia. After about six months hiding behind a facade of good health and mental station, she began planning a dinner party for a newly engaged cousin. In Moosey's mind, it would be the *fête* of the pre-Christmas season. Scheinuk's Florist and the Prytania Liquor Store had virtually no stock left, and added staff members were hastily advised of all the nuances, which they were expected to perform, making Moosey's party divine. Moosey's Machiavellian scheming would take first place in this evening's events. At half hour before the first guests were to arrive, she persuaded all the staff, both personal and rented, to go into the rear garden and take a break before the long evening ahead.

Moosey was nowhere in sight as people began to arrive, so her family descended into the entryway to greet the guests. Moosey's father, noting the absence of both Moosey and lack of libations for the guests, made his way to the kitchen. Pushing open the swinging door, he faced, what in later years he would refer to as a scene out of a *très mauvais film noir*, a recamier had been pulled from the sun porch and artfully arranged in front of the open Chambers oven. Reposing upon the recamier was none other than Moosey, attired in exquisitely hand-tucked georgette, her head lolling about in the oven's gaping mouth. So unnerved by this tableau, her father suffered a mild stroke on the spot, emitting enough noise to cause the gathered guests to dash into the kitchen, where they all were exposed to this ghoulish drama.

"The amount of gas Moosey had inhaled did little more than upset her sinuses. One story had it that she had gone to spend the winter in Scottsdale, Arizona, where the lack of humidity would settle her nasal complaints. When, in actuality, she spent four months languishing at Menninger's, the renowned mental treatment center in Lawrence, Kansas.

"Poor Moosey." Bill smiled and shook his head. "You couldn't keep her down. She returned to New Orleans shortly before Carnival season and went on a social tear reminiscent of Berlin before the war. She was seen at every ball, cocktail party, brunch, lunch, and *thé dansant*. Indeed, twice at some, 'cause she had picked up a curious habit of slipping out from a party with one man, only to return later with yet another, and looking ever so mussed.

"In a city where anything goes—Moosey had went.

"Various rumors swirled around her. It seemed she would go from an alpha of effervescence to an omega of despair. Often occurring two or three times daily. Or sometimes even hourly.

"The continuous round of parties, much imbibing, even though done in lavish and decorous salons of the city, could not obscure this fact from her. Something heinous and fatal was growing cancer-like inside her poor bemuddled mind. In a state of alarming clarity, Moosey beseeched her parents to return her to Menninger's. All arrangements were quickly made. Moosey was packed. Tickets had been bought, and the trip was set. On an early morning in May, Moosey, her mother, and father were driven to the Carrollton Station, where she would board the Sunset Limited. While their driver unloaded her baggage, Moosey wandered off on the levy of the railroad tracks. The Sunset Limited could be seen approaching the station at a leisurely pace, when without a word or backward glance, Moosey ran toward the approaching engine and placed her head on the track in an Anna Karenina paradigm."

Chapter 6

Patrick and Chuck, two friends who lived with me at the time, were busily helping with my upcoming Garden District cocktail party. Patrick prepared the food, while Chuck and I made sure the old house looked up to snuff. Rosa, my housekeeper, stood a mere five feet tall, and I did not want her teetering on high stools and unstable ladders, which left certain parts of the house out of her reach.

Bill was overjoyed at the prospect of a Garden District *soirée* and asked if he could bring his friend, Brian.

"Of course," I said, wondering how Bill was going to transform this man into a reasonable picture of acceptability. Brian had been living at The Rendezvous for somewhere around forever and had less than the basic necessities for living.

Bill had taken Brian under his ever-so-caring wing and these two lost souls had begun an even deeper descent into oblivion. Patrick and I escorted Bill to one of his favorite thrift stores to find Brian, appropriate clothing—clothing other than ragged cut-offs, seasoned thongs and tattered shirt. Bill picked out a pair of trousers, white shirt, tie, and a sports coat. The entire ensemble came to $9.50. Brian was now set for his very first Garden District cocktail party. Possibly even his first *real* cocktail party. I asked Bill to make sure that Brian wash his hair and groom himself as best he could.

Bill promised.

The night of the party rolled around and sure enough, Bill and Brian appeared in their finery. Bill looked absolutely marvelous and Brian, dreadfully shy, probably had not looked so perfectly coifed in his entire life. If Brian said more than two words throughout the evening, they were not within my earshot. What I remember of his presence is a slight of a man who seemed in the throes of excruciating self-consciousness, shrinking and fighting an urgent need to get the hell out of a most awkward environment. Bill, on the other hand, held court with his sophisticated wit and vast knowledge of every living soul who had once lived—and those who still did—within the confines of New Orleans' Garden District.

One particular group of guests that night had, but a few months previous, arrived in New Orleans. They were entranced as Bill began his diatribe.

"Not that I am by any means," he so elegantly informed, *"le dernier cri* with regard to society, as it is known and totally misunderstood in New Orleans. However, much to the horror of even my own illustrious ancestry, society in New Orleans simply ceased completely around the year 1867.

"Our vast metropolitan mixture of French, Italian, Spanish, Irish, German, and Negro blood enthused and diffused whatever segment even referred to itself as being social. Of course, this does not mean that cafe society *nouveaux riches* and just plain old multi-moneyed people don't exist. They do, and most certainly provide an element of raffish refinery, wit, and gaucheries so genuine and fun that even the most hard-boiled mainliner from Philadelphia must somewhat envy the manner in which we function and malfunction in The City That Care Forgot.

"First of all, those that claim parentage descending back to the city's earliest *arrivants*, would never admit that achieving the station in life they occupied would have been possible but for their Negro slaves and other minions, domestics, et cetera who literally ran things homewise while their uppers paraded into St. Louis Cathedral on Sunday and in and out of each other's salons with nightly frequency. The inevitable sexual intermingling of the gentry and their underlings produced children of different hues, bearing the same names as the very families they served.

"The arrival, *en masse*, of German, Italian, and Irish immigrants further expanded this blending of races, behavioral manners and mores to the point that one simply became a New Orleanian. Not a Creole, Frenchman, Spaniard, German, Italian or Irish, but a New Orleanian.

"So much for society.

"Now that I have the floor," Bill expounded. "I might as well go for broke and shake up that old myth of Mardi Gras."

And so he did.

"Back in the late 19th century, New Orleanians, heavily populated by Catholics, began to celebrate Mardi Gras, which translates from its lovely French vernacular as Fat Tuesday. Mardi Gras is an unexplainable madness; yes, a miasma that settles over the entire city, totally obliterating any rhyme or reason and leaving its celebrants in a state of exhausted euphoria.

"A custom carried over from France, Italy, and Spain celebrated the day before Ash Wednesday, which is, of course, the traditional beginning of Lent's forty days of fasting, penance, and richly deserved peace. Starting twelve days after Christmas, on Twelfth Night, the city becomes a slowly simmering vat of mad partying, parades, and balls which come to an end at the stroke of midnight on Fat Tuesday. All of this necessary nonsense is ruled over by the various krewes or clubs, consisting of the men belonging to these organizations with names like Osiris, Proteus, Atlanteans, Comus and finally on carnival day, Rex, the Lord of Misrule.

"My father once told me that he would rather be lame than endure a membership in any of these krewes."

Several of my guests who had wandered into the second parlor said in unison, "Your father has a point."

"Yes," Bill agreed. "But I, thinking that belonging to one, was akin to beatification, asked him why he thought this. I was told that everyone knew that the men who ran these (in his words) tawdry goings on were old nannans (a French term I could never find in any French dictionary). But his vilification in saying this marked my memory to never become either a nannan or a krewe member."

Other seated guests throughout the parlor nodded agreement. Others seemed offended. But no one left the room. They seemed entranced with Bill's performance whether they agreed with his take on their traditions or not.

"Some of these krewes," Bill didn't miss a beat, "had lavish parades which ran nightly, starting about two weeks before Mardi Gras day. For the most part, the parades would start around Napoleon Avenue and roll down St. Charles toward Canal and would involve as many as 20 or more floats. They would float their way down St. Charles Avenue to Canal Street, loop-de-loop Canal and end at the auditorium where the Bal Masque would be held. The whole lot gave an ethereal feeling as these enormous floats, ridden by masked and costumed members of the krewe, sailed down the avenue lighted only by *flam-beaux torches* carried by masked and dancing Negro men.

"The riders all threw trinkets to the crowds, who stretched their arms screaming, 'Throw me something, Mister.' Alas, your life was in mortal danger if you tried to interrupt the path of one trinket hurled from the float to a particular person. All this glee, accompanied by bands, marching clubs, and general hoi polloi is what children growing up in New Orleans remember. Once it was said that even the worst speller in the city could spell Czechoslovakia, as the trinkets thrown for years were beads with a tiny tag that read Made in Czechoslovakia.

"The highlight of all this merry-making and mayhem was Fat Tues-day. The first parade to roll that day is Zulu Pleasure and Culture Club, consisting of some five hundred males, mostly black, dressed in Zulu attire, who with mad abandon, tossed gilded coconuts into the crowd. Its king was a black male who had made major civic contribu-tions to the city, or was well known in the arts, such as Louis Arm-strong who served as King in the '50s. After this impressive but rag-tag—I say ragtag, because Zulu, up until a few years ago, never fol-lowed a set route—the Majesty of Majesties, Rex, also chosen from the elite in the civic, business, and commercial fields, proudly rolls out from his den on Claiborne Avenue to begin his ride up St. Charles. Rex is followed by any number of parades, guaranteeing you four or five hours of non-interrupted viewing. The city is literally packed. Carnival day is one of wild abandon, whisky and beer practically inun-date the city, whose populace is arrayed in costumes, ranging from Bo Peep to the most *outré*. It's a day so out of control that even the halest welcome the 40 forthcoming days of Lent.

"One of the most unpleasant memoirs of this *sans souci* season was one I had the questionable privilege of sharing with my divine friend Maude Ellen—muse of madness. It seems that about a week before the carnival parades started rolling, she suffered an inflamed skeeter bite on her left buttock—which would be to most other people a trifling unpleasantry, but caused Maude Ellen agony just short of Mimi's in the last act of *La Bohême*. It seemed that the inflamed buttock would render her inoperable, thus missing the parades completely. Unless she could prevail upon some poor charitable person (you got it, coach—the dupe was me) to escort her up the long road to St. Charles Avenue (one and one half blocks) to watch all this nonsense pass by.

"Now Maude Ellen was a great believer in costumes, feeling it necessary to costume from January 6 to Mardi Gras day. But her costumes were by no means run up by the old seamstresses of Town and Country and the Liberty Shop who outfitted all manner of queens, kings, maids, jesters, and socially-connected drunks throughout the season. Sadly, Maude Ellen's entire wardrobe, which could be hidden under a St. Joseph's aspirin with room yet for St. Joseph himself, consisted of snippets of ribbon, large wilted organdy flowers, opera-length gloves, and the odd lavaliere. Her assortment of footwear would have caused Emelda Marcos' instant demise, and this is not even to mention hats, hairpieces and veils, ranging from Thessalonican times to Lilly Dache.

"Actually, the evening of our first sojourn to watch Momus (The God of Mirth) roll pass, she was covered from neck to toe in a caftan of dubious origin, although quite diaphanous. Topping this off was a frayed half domino, and upon her (at the moment, for she was forever dying or re-dying her hair) sepia-dyed tresses, and at a rakish angle and under-chin strap, a pie plate filled with a cabbage, two roses, a turnip and a black banana. The whole effect was that of a dipsomaniacal Carmen Miranda fleeing Yasser Arafat. Now, if I neglected to tell you earlier, Maude Ellen had a vile aversion to any type of under clothing. In fact, in her home and, as I soon found out, anyone else's home, preferred to go without clothes. Period.

"When I arrived to pick up Maude Ellen, she suggested that we have a *soupçon* of French vanilla ice cream to fortify ourselves against the low February temperatures and the rising winds. Of course, her idea of fortification was dropping the entire half pint of ice cream into the Waring blender, filling the lot with bourbon and giving it a whirl. Thus, positively stink-o, we staggered up to the Avenue. All thoughts of a bitten buttock being left behind.

"Shrieking, squealing, dervishly whirling about the crowds, screaming, 'Throw me something, Mister,' Maude Ellen jumped to heights unparalleled by Shaquille O'Neal's pulling two for the Lakers. The winds had picked up to nigh gale-like proportions, and in one swoosh, raised her caftan over her head, dislodging one very old turnip and exposing a completely uncovered Maude Ellen—except for the Band-Aid protecting her butt bite left by the skeeter. I wished myself to be in Addas Ababa where caftans stay close to the floor, but managed to re-cover this barren body by pulling down the caftan and making mention of more vanilla and bourbon.

"That was the first night."

By now my parlor was filled with laughter. If anyone *had* been offended by Bill's satirical rantings, his humor had won them over.

Bill performed a 40-degree *pirouette* and threw up his hands. There was no doubt about it. He was *on*.

"The following evening as the sirens announced the oncoming parade, Maude Ellen, rapt with the thought of a performance to outdo last evening's, did away with all thoughts of vanilla ice cream, poured two stout glasses of bourbon, tossed both back, handed me the near empty bottle, indicating that I down it, and bellowed, 'Let's roll!' This time Pushwah, her adopted dog, an improbable mix of French poodle and warthog, accompanied us.

"Pushwah, a former stray who had spent the last years alternating between handouts from Christ Episcopal Church and chasing automobiles down Jackson Avenue, had been taken in and treated by Maude Ellen as if he were a Westminster winner. One day Pushwah escaped from Maude Ellen's ministrations and went tearing on the loose in the Garden District, only to run up against a Manny's Sanitary Supply Company truck in the middle of Magazine Street. Maude Ellen, in hot pursuit, witnessed the accident and threw herself on the ground wailing and keening like a Sabine woman.

"Such an uproar lured all the neighbors out into the street where Maude Ellen tearfully remonstrated Pushwah's dilemma. Pushwah meanwhile, prudent though wounded, had crept out of the road and collapsed under a clump of aspidistras.

"Thus began the biggest manhunt since the Lindbergh kidnapping. The local police, the harbor police, Salvation Army, and a group of Seven Day Adventists trying to proselytize were pressed into action. They danced up and down, calling for Pushwah. At this crucial moment, Bonnie/Miz Scarlet, she of questionable genre, appeared sashaying down Magazine encased in a gold lamé jumpsuit, gone quite green at the seams. An air of superior knowledge surrounded her somewhat Delphic visage, and she loudly announced to all, accented by Pernod-induced hiccups, that she alone knew where Pushwah could be found. And for the price of a bottle of Pernod, would gladly tell. Anxious to get this rag tag posy out of his road, one Garden District fellow gave her five dollars on the spot to tell.

"Pushwah was found, poor hound, but he was lacking an eye and had innumerable breaks and cuts and was in near trauma. I borrowed Maude Ellen's car and drove him to the vet. Maude Ellen, fortified by numerous snorts of bourbon, caterwauled, sounding like the entire cast of *The Trojan Women*. No small feat, coming from the back seat of her Volkswagen Rabbit. Pushwah's stay in hospital lasted three weeks at a cost of what it had cost me precisely to stay at *Val d' Isere* last.

"Upon his release, *sans* one eye, and walking with a rather hesitant motion, we overnight became one of the Garden District's oddities. Being blind in my right eye and with Pushwah likewise in his left, I at once purchased his-and-hers eye patches.

"We would swashbuckle through the District twice daily. My only regret was the lack of a parrot on my shoulder, a ring in one ear, various tattoos depicting Jolly Rogers, jug-breasted babes and Johnny jives referring to mothers, broads and other dark thoughts. Pushwah, while on our perambulations, had a most irritating habit of never voiding his bowels until we stood directly in front of one of the District's most prominent homes. And nine times out of ten, only if the owners were in the gardens, or arriving by car. Such a show off. I, feeling more paranoid by the day, took to wearing dark glasses, one of Maude Ellen's three-thousand hats, and began entertaining ideas of asking Bonnie to loan me one of her least flamboyant numbers. I refused to be known as the defiler of the neighborhood. If this kept up, Pushwah would have to be given free run of the District, Manny's Sanitation or no.

"This evening I, being convinced that Maude Ellen had become the queen of carnival, decided to stay five steps behind her as lessers in royalties' entourage were bade to do. On reaching St. Charles Avenue, Bacchus, one of the more lavish and lengthy parades, was already rolling. I, feeling the jolt of the bourbon, slipped underneath a large oleander bush, where I was perfectly content to squat and watch Maude Ellen's shenanigans from a distance, lest I be thought of as her escort. As usual, as the floats passed, and the krewe members tossed out their favors, Maude Ellen leapt into the air as if propelled by an overactive pogo stick. Each trinket she caught was then thrown at yours truly and Pushwah as we cringed deeper into the oleander's foliage.

"Some wag, and believe me, the parades were full of them, had filled one of his bags with condoms, and Pushwah and I both took rumpled umbrage when Maude Ellen deposited an arm load of Tropic Night Ticklers into our laps. Bacchus, the longest of all parades, save Carnival Day's linking of Rex, Mid City, and Elks, lasting forever. Pushwah and I were roused out of a small slumber and were taken back to the house by Maude Ellen, shaking like a pudding and weighed down by scores of beads, masks, bikini panties, plastic cigars, and all the other tacky doodads she had caught. Pushwah and I, feeling a tad tawdry with our gross or so of Tropical Ticklers, followed behind her. When home, we found it positively necessary to drink everything in the house as fast as possible. This necessitated dog and I to leave for K & B Drugs to replenish the proverbial empty well.

"Maude Ellen was the past master at having guests for cocktails who, upon arrival, found that they had to wait while she passed the Pyrex alms-borrowing cup around the neighborhood. The few guests who possessed the fortitude to make this their second scrape with Maude Ellen's hostess-with-the-mostest ambiance had learned to brown bag their own booze.

"As Pushwah and I set off to the store, I glanced over my shoulder to see Maude Ellen in the act of blowing up the psychedelically printed prophylactics. Between puffs, she squealed how divine the house would look the next day—Mardi Gras day. This year, it seems, her theme for her annual party would be of a tropical nature, the condoms being printed with waving palm trees. The last words I heard were something referring to an old sarong and Dorothy Lamoure, and for the life of me, I think she muttered something about a ukulele. Having not succumbed entirely to drink, in the fuzzy distance, my thoughts were finding a way of escaping the party. Indeed the whole day."

A frequent guest at my house and an old New Orleanian shouted from the hallway door, "Hey, Bill. Tell them about our debutants."

Bill swung around, threw back his head and gave a hearty laugh. "Drama, debutantes, and dilemmas," Bill announced with a great deal of on-stage presence. "Since New Orleans is one of the last cities to honor these gifted and gilded young ladies upon their entrance into society, I feel it absolutely unnecessary, yet fair, to denote a few thoughts and observations about this ever so misunderstood phenomena.

"As we glance backward in time, there has always existed in man's society a certain rite, rather like coming of age, in which the treasured daughter is formally introduced to society. From the days of the cave man, I am certain these Alley Oopers taught their not-so-frail daughters to succumb gracefully at the slightest tap of a club rather than resist and be turned into pulp. While sounding a bit harsh, I feel that these *jeunes filles* of the ice age or whatever had a rather easier time of it than their modern day sisters.

"Of course, to debut in New Orleans one must be of impeccable lineage, well-educated, and bear either a modicum of physical looks, or be so effusive in personality and belonging, that if outwardly she resembled a witch, which many do, it remains unmentioned.

"Parents possessing level heads and lots of money, if unfortunate enough to have spawned a daughter who is just not going to make it, immediately enroll her into the most expensive schools and colleges. Preferably in Europe and I'm sure, if available, somewhere in a lunar orbit. When queried if their daughter was coming out this year, they could very righteously reply that their cherished daughter was so keen on acquiring further education that she would pass the season and continue her studies at the University of Cairo where she was writing a thesis questioning the water level in the blocks used to build Cheop's memorial."

Bill lifted a languid hand and waved his finger somewhere toward the ceiling.

"Mind you," he informed with a roll of his eyes, "all this highfalutin' education is being undertaken by a girl whose past four years of high school had earned her laurels in group games and social dancing, accompanied by such pre-deb functions as *Les Pierretes, Les Écolieres*, Youngers Set, and Eight O'clocks, where looks were not really important. The captains of these balls would simply blow a whistle and a hundred young girls dashed out onto the dance floor—all in identical costumes—and proceed to cavort.

"Years ago carnival reigned supreme over the debutantes. While the Grandmother Tea at the Orleans Club was still *de rigueur*, there was no such thing as a cotillion or debutante club. The grandmother, the mother's mother, would let the Orleans Club, a magnificent edifice on St. Charles Avenue, for a tea honoring the debutante. From two to four, all the mothers, aunts, and various other female relatives and friends would arrive, hatted and gloved, to pay homage. It was rather grand with much curtseying and hopeful bravado floating about concerning the child's future, (read that husband) and how much filthy lucre would enter into it."

Bill winked at a seemingly bewildered and spellbound woman who slumped inside the curve of my French sofa. By the look on her face, you would have thought she had succumbed to a surreal sort of plague. This only fueled Bill's soliloquy and he plunged ahead with more rhetoric.

"The carnival krewes, remember the old nannans, would then take over. Gentlemen who belonged to these krewes and had daughters of debut age were asked to have their beauties appear as maids in the court or as queens. Now being a maid is usually within the budget of every father, and these girls, so designated, will be presented at court during the fanciful tableau. Thus they are more or less socially launched. Many is the woeful daughter who never knew that her father had been asked if she would reign as queen and had steadfastly refused. This was done simply because of the expense involved in having a daughter who would be a queen. By the time PaPa shelled out for the dress, the limousine, the Queen's Supper and all the other unexpected accouterments, the poor PaPa stood to be poorer by amounts ranging from twenty-five to one hundred G's."

Bill twirled and sent his arms off in various directions. I suddenly saw this gent upon a stage performing in his own one-man play. He had managed to capture the attention of most of my guests in the second parlor and others were trickling in from the front parlor and hallway. This fueled him.

"Back in the '30s—" Bill looked toward the ceiling. "Our great democratic society gave birth to a group of young ladies who decided to start the debutante club. It would stage its own ball either at the civic auditorium or the Imperial Ballroom at the Fairmont, *né* Roosevelt Hotel. A group of 12 to 20 young ladies, all attired in nuptial white, long kid gloves and bouquets, would be introduced as they stepped through a floral arbor accompanied by tunes such as *Thank Heaven for Little Girls*. They would then twirl around, finding their fathers' arms for an opening waltz. This was all so twee and pat.

"On the sidelines the guests would sit, applaud and watch as the girls' escorts for the evening would oblige the doting fathers to relinquish their daughters to them. After dancing the evening away with a wash of copious amounts of carefully chosen, inexpensive, unrecognizably-labeled champagne, all would repair to wherever the Queen's Supper would be held.

"No light affair, this. The breakfast would be several lengthy courses of viands such as grillades, the inevitable broiled half grapefruit with the only cherry in the house resting in its middle afloat in grenadine.

"All of this was yet again accompanied by an ever-flowing bar issuing such libations as ramos gin fizzes, sazeracs, and yet more champagne, a better vintage as the bottles were set on the tables with easily readable labels. At the head table, the queen, her king, her maids, and their escorts ensconced themselves after taking part in the grand march around the dance floor. After hours of festive dancing and foolish drinking, this *fête* would come to a close around three a.m., thoroughly denying anyone a day of work, school or whatever.

"In fact, so disabling was all this, that in the '60s some of the families of the up-and-coming deb crop found themselves debilitated by the sheer number of parties which necessitated more gowns et cetera. One of my favorite tales is that of a young girl whose family was not above a little penny pinching and soloed through the entire season with one elegant bouffant, peaudesoi skirt and thirty interchangeable bodices.

"The social schedule for one coming out would consist of, particularly on weekends, a day starting with breakfast at Brennan's, followed by a brunch at someone's home, a luncheon at the race track where the more rakish of the hosts would have suede bags of silver dollars at each place so that the honorees and their escorts could bet the ponies. With, say an hour or so to rest, the momentum would start up again with a *thé dansant* at the country club after which anywhere from four to six cocktail parties would ensue.

"Then to top the day off would be a large buffet supper dance. To say this could be a bit tiring on the girls would be enough, but the parents were becoming slightly manic at these excessive doings. Everyone had to honor the daughters of their friends for after all, their thinking was; we have our own daughters coming out soon. And God forbid they should only be honored with some paltry little parties."

Bill had become so enthralled with this theme that he had taken to almost dancing about the parlor. I stood next to the French secretary and watched as more people gathered around, thinking that his antics were as amusing as his verbiage.

If only, I mused, his talents could somehow become his protector, his provider, his reason for living. He was a masterpiece in motion and I couldn't bear to think of this extraordinary human being wasted in alcoholism, depression, and despair. I desperately needed to understand the man and his source of destruction. Still, he, not I, had to be the one to conquer his demons. Even so, I was determined to give him that extra push, bit of encouragement. I leaned back against the wall in thought. Bill's words spilled out over the ever-gathering crowd like a verbal work of art.

"After the season reached proportions of madness, as to the amount of scheduled events, even the most dedicated daughters started taking sabbaticals from college to keep up with this social suicide. A group of parents whose daughters were coming of age decided to start a new venue, and *Voila, Le Debut des Jeunes Filles de la Nouvelle-*

Orléans was born. This was to be *nec plus ultra* of debutantism. All the members of the *soigné* set would take their bows at one huge affair and the girls participating would be allowed only four other parties during this season.

"All of New Orleans went into a frenzy. This was to be an event so grand, so chic, and so costly that only Marie Antoinette in heat could have conjured it up.

"To be held at the Fairmont's Imperial Ballroom, the finest of champagnes (labels recognizable), Lester Lanin's orchestra, and Costa Rica's yearly national output of roses and carnations were requisitioned. The ball was set. It was a dazzling triumph, landing one of the debutantes of questionable Canadian ancestry on the cover of *Life* magazine, followed by a dutiful recalling of the event in Jane Howard's column, *Life Goes To A Party*.

"However, all this splendor incurred astronomical costs, while the parents were happy overall with the affair and the rules surrounding, the number of parties allowed each girl caused financial chaos, which was only bested by Malcomb Forbes wee gathering in Morocco.

"Hence, the following years, after checking their cash reserves in the Whitney Bank, they decided that in order to defray costs, more girls should be included, and raised the count to sixty. Private parties went up to eight per debutante. This meant a minimum of four hundred and eight parties starting with the small season, which was Labor Day week, and culminating with the large season, Thanksgiving through Christmas. Of course, this is not to mention the Bachelors' Club Ball, Mid-Winter Cotillion and the Pickwick, Boston, Louisiana, and War of 1812 Clubs presentations to be followed by six weeks of nightly carousing to the tunes of Mardi Gras season. Thus the gentry had doubled the amount of affairs to reckon with and some of the more staid and less well off among the swells began to have reservations about the whole situation. The Debutante Club tried a dismal resurrection. Impeccable sources tell me that Quack, *The Times Picayune* society arbiter, didn't even attend and there were only six girls trotted out in the shabby finery of the Jung Hotel's ballroom.

"As the years passed, the debutante's dilemma had cooled down somewhat. But occasionally some stunner will strike it hot and be featured on the cover of *Town & Country*, or be honored with an invitation to some glitzy affair, albeit promising proper press coverage. However, as the younger ladies tend to concentrate more on decorum and diversification rather than Dior, we can only sit back and muse whether these undertakings are, by design, a ruse to present themselves as shrewder, more educated and worldly, so to perhaps snag a husband with enough urbanity and untold cash to ensure their daughter a fabulous coming out year."

Chapter 7

Bill and I had finished another of my blistering hot pasta dinners. The sky had opened up, letting loose torrential downpours and flooding most of the streets in the Garden District. So we were forced to forego our nightly walk and settle into my Red Room for a late evening chat. I wanted to hear more about a colorful creature who inhabited several blocks of Magazine Street. I didn't hesitate to inquire.

His eyes widened, rolled, then narrowed into mine. "Good heavens," he said, scooting further into the leather wing chair. He reached for his sweet cigars as though he needed one to calm him, but he knew how I felt about smoking, especially anywhere on the premises of 1237 Washington, and stuffed them back into his pocket. "Why ever do you want to know about her?"

"You've got to be kidding," I said. "I can't wait to hear. Now get on with it."

Bill snickered slightly and moved to the edge of his chair.

"Well," he said a bit disdainfully, "I never was really formally introduced to Miss Bonnie. But no one walking past Jackson Avenue on Magazine Street could have possibly missed this apparition, unless they were dependent upon a white cane or a German shepherd. For starters, this Bonnie, whose affectations brought to mind a darkish Miz Scarlet, whose real name is Herbert, and if one could look southward from his waist, would have to acknowledge that either Miz Scarlet had a large tumor or, as they say on the streets, a bulging basket.

"Never mind Bonnie/Scarlet's proclivities, she knew everyone in the streets and also knew something ever so juicy about each. Not to matter if you hadn't a shred of scandal about you, Miz Scarlet would make up something. This guaranteed that each and all who were ever so remotely connected with her would be members of the same squalid sorority.

"Several years ago, a onetime friend of mine descended upon the city after a long and mysterious absence. We walked down to the Rue de la Course for ice coffee, where we engaged in hours of lying to each other about how far up life's ladder each had climbed.

"Now Ben had been a portraitist of no small note, and had bummed around the scruffy rims of society. His grandest moments were spent in regaling one with antidotes about his closest, dearest, most divine friends, all of whom had last names of at least 26 letters. Prefaced by Vons and de La's and such. In other words, Euro trash's dreckiest output. I, of course, pretended to be overawed by all this grandiosity and practically went into a swoon, wondering how many years in hell he would spend in atonement for these atrocious lies.

"With a trace of a sneer, he deigned to inquire what I had been up to these last years. Knowing that whatever I answered would pass onto deaf ears, I simply told him that I had invested in a string of small towns throughout New Hampshire and Delaware and was lazily sitting back and clipping coupons. In reality, I was in a mad heat to get to the Salvation Army to buy a pair of already-walked-in shoes.

"As we left this emporium of the world's highest priced coffee, we ambled back up Magazine Street. Ben clutched me by the arm with all the artfulness of a boa constrictor and pointed down the road toward this aberration gliding toward us. He quietly stage-whispered in my ear. 'Have you ever done Jack?' Naturally, I asked. 'Jack who?' That's when this *doyen* of café society retorted in his best pseudo-Jacki-O accent. 'Not Jack, fart breath. CRACK.'

"Now--the only thing I knew about crack was that it was a drug that homeless black people, huddled together in condemned houses, smoked until they were all dead or had been arrested. I never realized that the mention of this heinous delicacy would cause him to froth at the mouth. He then told me that the apparition approaching us could manage to put an hour of absolute glory in our hands if we could depart with forty bucks. Twenty dollars seemed okay to me for an hour of as yet undreamed ecstasy. So Ben and I ran to the apparition, who turned out to be Bonnie *né* Herbert. To say Herbert was streetwise would be an unkindness, for he—she—had been around longer than the wheel. Not in years, mind you, but in streetwise.

"After cooing, giggling, and a lot of oh-girl-have-mercies embellished with a lot of divines and other ornamental garbage pretending to be refined camping, the deal was struck and Ben and I hauled ass down to his *unparticulier* hotel in Coliseum Street.

"Once when in my teens, and all my contemporaries were smoking grass, I tried with all my heart and soul to do the same. Indeed, if I had strived as hard to be President of the United States, as I did to conquer marijuana, I would be squatting in the oval office as we speak.

"When Ben and I arrived in his home, he started taking what he called a few precautions. After double-locking all the doors and windows, pulling all the draperies and shades shut, and turning off all the lights, he explained to me with a martyred tone, that if we were to be caught doing this, we could end up with life in the joint at best, but probably would both end up saying our adieus as lethal injections flowed through our veins. I felt this to be troublesome, not because of the joint or even the injections, but simply because I knew that with my luck, we would be strapped to side by side gurneys, and the last thing I wanted to hear before meeting my maker was Ben's voice shrieking out good-byes to all those fake dilettantes he had never known.

"Anyhow, after he had gathered cigarette lighters and an empty beer can (which I thought odd, as he had led me to believe nothing of less importance than Dom Perignon ever passed his lips) we crept into the basement to SMOKE CRACK. The trick was, to make an indentation with a hole somewhere alongside the beer can. This was, I found, called a bunt. One then would place a minute quantity of crack into the indentation, hold a cigarette lighter to the crack, ignite it and inhale like mad on the opening at the end of the can. This was to be sheer glory."

At this juncture, I wanted to say all sorts of things about drugs and the kind of company Bill was allowing himself to associate with, but I knew it would only fall on deaf ears and probably make him mad. And besides, I wanted to hear about the drugs as well as this Ben character. So I remained quiet and listened with great interest and intensity.

"Well," he said with much exasperation, "I never sucked, slobbered, and coughed so much since an asthma attack when I was four years old. The fruition of all this was nothing but a taste of slightly flat Budweiser and an uncontrollable desire to sneeze.

"So this was glory?

"For twenty dollars I could have had Eggs Sardou at Gallatoires on Bourbon Street.

"Ben meanwhile continued to push and prod, fiddling with the bunt, rendered one Bic lighter fuel-less, and somehow managed to acquire a sort of meek euphoria. I shortly thereafter departed, telling him in a repentive tone that I was going to go home and think about how close I had come to inhabiting the joint or succumbing to a lethal injection. And that I must atone for my ways. Since, although still rather meek, he was bordering on *non compus mentis*, I slid out into the street and up Magazine toward home, only to pass Miz Bonnie slinking down the street, obviously in search of another mark.

"I *ran!*"

Running from this creature was not a bad idea where Bill was concerned. Still I eagerly awaited my introduction to Miz Bonnie. I couldn't imagine that I had missed her these past four years. But then, I probably wasn't looking her way.

Bill suddenly took to boogying about the Red Room and then segued into a downbeat camel walk. Then, with highly intoned inflections, plunged into another Bonnie *histoire*.

"Now—Miz Bonnie, lest her ink-black soul be forgotten, was trying to vamp Abdul, the Moslem owner of the Jewel Store, an interesting boutique of delicatesse. The Jew, as we locals called it, featured such tempting items as eleven-year-old tins of Spam, the odd mildewed tomato, innumerable cut-rate cigarettes, and my favorite Bic-type lighters which sold three for a buck—my only interest.

"The Jew did have the most dazzling array of whiskies and liquors available since Sherry's in New York closed. The only disconcerting note was that no one had ever heard of any of the brands Abdul carried. I often thought that perhaps he and his brother, Ramfis, had these potables produced in Mecca or wherever, then shipped to New Orleans where some demonic sign painter labeled them. The logistics of this was rather forbidding. I mean, being Muslim and all, but it made for a rather catchy story.

"Bonnie had a great proclivity to drink, when not in the throes of spasmodic, but short-lived inhalations of crack. One day when I went into the Jew to buy my cheap lighters, Bonnie was behind the counter scrutinizing the booze with Abdul hot behind her—obviously on the lookout for gaping sleeves, loose waistbands and such orifices into which a bottle of Old Voodoo vodka could be slipped and then whisked away without so much as a by your leave at the abacus. And, yes, he did use an abacus, then would tilt the cash register on its side and push the emergency open button to make change. The register, already passing middle age when IBM was founded, let out a distressed sound when opened in this way. I think in its younger years, it emitted a shrill sort of alarm, which by now had been reduced to a gurgly plea.

"Bonnie, ravishing in a pink satin mini skirt, and a voluminous artist's smock, replete with a huge bow at the neck, and voluminous sleeves, finally circumnavigated Abdul and the counter, placing two fifths of an evil looking Pernod down with two fives. At one point she belched with all the refinement of a walrus, and the odious fumes that escaped were enough to kill every fly in the store.

"Mesmerized by this transaction, I watched Abdul bag the booze, and Bonnie set off mincing toward the exit. The fact that she was more than inebriated was complicated by the torturous way she was walking. Both her legs and feet held tightly together, she sort of shuffled out an inch at a time. Critter, who had earlier confiscated the bucking Jeep Cherokee vehicle across from The Rendezvous, happened to be coming into the Jew, held the door for Bonnie. Bonnie made it to the sidewalk when another belch began rumbling up through her. This inner exertion must have relaxed her tension somewhat, for in a thrice, a whole fifth of Seagram's Crown Royal dropped from between her legs and exploded onto the sidewalk. Bonnie, at a speed previously obtained only by Olympic track runners, vanished into the depths of Josephine Street.

"Critter and I were holding each other up to keep from folding over with laughter. And Abdul, whom I had really thought to have a devout Muslin upbringing, was ranting on about the lack of a father in Bonnie's past and some other snide critiques on the wholesomeness of her mother.

"Critter asked Abdul to give him a pack of Trojans, and I sort of looked away demurely, then I walked him out to his Jeep Cherokee, which he had looking like a bright new penny. Tossing the box of Trojans from hand to hand, he said, 'Me and this car, tonight—I'm gonna get...' And then he sailed into a soliloquy of women's parts and what his intentions for all of them were and how soon he hoped to do it.

"I wished him the very best of luck, while thoughts of the clap, AIDS, and unwholesome bodies flew through my mind. He rolled the window down with a wink and said, 'Ain't that Bonnie sumpin'?' He said that the only thing Bonnie couldn't hide "up there" was a Harley, and swore that she had once walked out of Schwegmanns' store with four quarts of Busch "up there."

Though the hour was late—Max had already collapsed beside the leather sofa and I rarely stay up past nine—something was said about the various obscure classes of New Orleanians that sent Bill into an in-depth description. As usual, I settled in for another round of entertainment.

"Tacks and Yats, and NOCDs.

"While much has been said about New Orleans as a melting pot, and the abrupt demise of society *per se*, one should never for a moment believe that our city does not still have its small and idiosyncratic grouplets of unexplainable societies. The N.O.C.Ds (not our class, dearies) constitutes those persons, mostly salt of the earth types, who are invisible. These perfectly happy but thought-to-be-denied citizens, are those who happen to simply live in New Orleans; let's say an engineer whose firm moves him and his unsuspecting family to New Orleans to work at Michoud, part of NASA, or the nearby Stennis Space Center in commutable Mississippi.

"These people, truly necessary to the structure of our economy, move to New Orleans, buy a three-bedroom-two-bath house in a per-fectly fine area that no New Orleanian has ever heard of, enroll their children into (gasp) public schools and even join the Lions Club or such. For them, New Orleans may be the first or perhaps the fifth re-location required by their companies—thus reducing their existence to a somewhat nomadic trek toward the 401K. Rather than sinking to anonymity, these people, made of staunch stuff, get into the commu-nity, scout groups for their children and one of New Orleans' ten thousand churches. Even a few tend toward the political. Until they realize that anything political in New Orleans is akin to federal investi-gations, scandal and a more than likely stay in the slammer.

"They gleefully embrace our food, our Big Easy attitude, Mardi Gras, and all the other *fraibole* involving the Crescent City. They are soon numb to the fact that every thoroughfare in the city has at least nine potholes per block, and that our crime rate rivals that of old Shanghai. But in reality, they may as well live in Sheboygan. They sim-ply *are*. And I do not honestly know anyone who has actually known *them*. They're simply relegated to the ineffectionalness of N.O.C.D.-dom.

"Yats and Tacks are absolutely divine. If asked to choose between a group of Yats drinking Abita beer in a Ninth Ward saloon, or high tea at the Vatican, I would go flat out for the Yats. Yats are a curious amalgamation of New Orleanians, mostly laying claim to Chalmette (also called Chalmations with due respect to the fireman's dog) and the lower Ninth Ward as their place of origin. They speak a rarefied *patois*, every sentence usually ending in a preposition i.e., 'where YAAT?' instead of 'how are you?' One of the YATS self-felt testimonials arrived quite innocently when the Hyatt Corporation opened a hostelry in our city, causing all YATS to proclaim the 20-story building as the tallest YAT in town—the Highyat.

"Predominately claiming French, Italian, and Irish heritage and peppered with an infusion of slobs, the YATS are not without their culture pertaining to their own carnival capers, church celebrations, and other forms of blue collar hell-raising. All looked askance upon and envied by those not quite able to let go and roll. Even the most ethereal Hindu mystic, hearing a YAT speak but once, would never have trouble recognizing the source of that accent.

"Tacks are a harder nut to crack. I deem it highly probable that tackiness exists in every level of mankind. Not to blame are those various underlings, who in actuality haven't the vaguest notion what tacky is, yet, are the seminal personification of sane. There's tacky and there's TACKY. Low class tacky might consist of someone, usually a YAT, buying a Barq's Root Beer and a bag of Planter's peanuts. This seems innocuous enough, but the true Tacks will then empty the peanuts into the bottle of root beer, shake it up, and proceed to partake of this gourmet creation with all the verve of a wine connoisseur enjoying a *soupçon* of Chateau Y'Quem.

"Other rankings in the table of Tacks usually involve the manner of dress effected by these unknowing persons. Anyone would look askance at a woman wearing long black nylon gloves with obviously *faux* diamond bracelets and rings worn over them. This is high tack and falls right into the realm of men wearing white socks, brown shoes and shiny blue suits.

"My only question about the rules of Tack, in reference to dress is, who makes them? New Orleans as a City that Care Forgot, stopped caring about what it wore late in the 1800s. The men, in summer, resembled a faded Seurat painting, their wrinkled seersucker suits and boaters. Uptown ladies obviously buy from flea markets and in nearby Mississippi, to obtain dresses once worn by Shriners' wives at conventions in Hazelhurst or Hot Coffee. The immediate effect when espying a male and female together in their finery would encourage nudity at the very least.

"Tacks have things as dreary as Tupperware parties in Gentilly, and all-woman carnival krewes, where they appear to have such fun that a friend of mine who had a seamstress belonging to one called The Mystics of Marrerro—Marrerro being a drab little suburb beyond YAT territory—got her seamstress to sneak her aboard one of the floats.

"Well, she had such a ball that, with all her children married and her husband succumbing to nannanism, she upped and divorced him, moved to the West Bank (not prudent) and opened a bar which became The Mystics of Marrerro's Krewe Club Room—the scene of nightly revelry never imagined by her former uptown friends. The really fine line of true Tackiness, in my mind, can only be explained by two events which, while being early tacky to the nth degree, both were perpetrated by two of our city's supposed uppers.

"First, you must remember that poor unfortunate bride whose husband committed suicide in Germany several years back. Her family had passed on, and she alone occupied the family home, slightly larger than the Pentagon. By chance, I was reintroduced to her one evening at a Garden District bash. After the introduction, she imperiously asked me where I lived (not meaning house or trailer). But in what social district. I replied that I was simply visiting the city, a white lie but necessary rather than admit that I stayed where paid. In turn, she murmured something about being domiciled in a wee cottage on Coliseum Street. Well, this paid-to-stay dude had more than once traipsed across the threshold of this wee cottage in Coliseum Street as a guest of her younger brother. And had also had the good fortune to partake of her father's good whisky due to the parents being out of town. Also, one evening with Paul, the brother, both under the spell of peppermint schnapps, sneaked two ladies of questionable virtue into his mother's boudoir and, we thought, seduced them with great panache.

"This lady's downplay of her legitimate wealth and palatial home was nothing short of tacky in reverse. Perhaps she thought of it as *noblesse oblige*, but I felt that she didn't oblige anyone.

"The second person to hit the finals in tackiness was an admiral's wife who was bizarre and personable enough without having to be tacky. With more money than Croesus, she had the nerve to send her servants over to my grandmother's house every evening as the dinner hour would come to a close. This was done primarily to see if we'd by chance had watermelon for dessert. It seemed that she had a fetish for watermelon rind preserves. But as no one in her household could stomach watermelon, she relied on her neighbor's slops to keep her pickling going. My grandmother, not above an occasional dip into tack herself, became infuriated because Marie Elise Du Guey Riggs never sent her a smidgen of preserves, and, being too lazy to make it herself, was denied the fruit of her own garbage."

Chapter 8

Late one morning, Bill stomped up my stairway and lunged into my bedroom suite, where I was putting a second coat of paint on the bathroom vanity. He plopped the toilet lid down and positioned his small ass onto its surface. I was certain he had something of great importance on his mind. And I was equally certain I was about to hear it. By the look on his face, I wouldn't have been surprised to learn that he had just hit the slot machines at Harrah's for an enormous amount of money.

"What!" I said turning from my painting creation. Bill had captured my attention, not only by this aura of glee, but the pure sight of him sitting on my toilet was priceless.

"I can't believe it." Bill giggled and snickered and sent his arms afloat. "I practically had to lift myself off the floor."

I carefully lowered my paintbrush, leaving it to rest atop the paint can.

"What are you talking about?" I said, turning back to an even more vibrant Bill Holcomb sitting upon my toilet seat. He then latched on to my confusion with his ever-so-squinty grin and proceeded to tell me from whence he had come.

"Cafe what?" I said. And then it dawned on me. "Cafe Atchafalaya. Yes, I've been meaning to go there. It's up on Louisiana."

"Louisiana and Laurel," Bill confirmed. "I heard they had an opening for a waiter. So I thought, oh hell, I can do that and decided to apply."

"And?" I couldn't imagine he'd be in this much of a tizzy over a waiter's position—and as it turned out, he wasn't.

"Well," he said with more arm swinging and various other contortions. "I walked through the door, was immediately greeted by a woman with very short gray-blonde hair and a long skinny cigarette held between her thumb and forefinger. Before I could utter my reason for being there, I heard her squeal.

"'Why William Lafayette Holcomb, what are you doing here?'

"Since I had never seen this woman in my entire life, I practically lost control of my limbs, which would have landed me on the floor in a not so gracious heap. But since I had come to apply for a job, I managed to contain myself and held on to a small slice of dignity. Wondering how or what this woman knew about me was alarming, and the odds of securing a waiter's position was narrowing with rapid expediency. I wouldn't have the chance to fuck this one up, I thought. My track record has already preceded me. But I pulled from what remained of my genteel resources and inquired as to how she knew me.

"'I could tell you were a Holcomb,' she responded. 'And I can tell you right off the bat, you won't be waiting tables here.'

"Before this could register, she stated that she needed someone to help her. She and her partner had just split and she could only pay me a hundred dollars a day. At that, I practically went into a coma. My mind was in fast forward. Suddenly I had risen from an applicant for a servile position to a hundred dollars a day management position. Of course, in hindsight, I thought—something sounding too good to be true usually is."

"Stop!" I gave Bill a stern look. "I don't want to hear any of your pessimistic ramblings. What happened?"

Bill threw his chin to one side and squinted his eyes. "Well, Miss Iler and I immediately sat down and began discussing seven trillion people we knew between us.

"It seems she had grown up all her life in Drew, Mississippi, a little bitty town just south of Clarksdale, my father's hometown and where my parents still live. And, to top it off, my grandfather had been her dentist. I asked her why she felt the need to drive to Clarksdale to go to the dentist."

'Oh,' she said. 'Our dentist in Drew was a friend of my father and just a drunk old bastard. I loved him to death, but you wouldn't want him in your mouth.'"

I thought this to be hysterical. It was also tragic. Here I had a drunk sitting on my toilet seat telling me all of this. But confronting that issue at the moment was out of the question. I was certain that Bill could see the disdain in my face, but he slapped the empty space in front of him and continued.

"Anyway, after several hours of bantering forth and back, she asked me to join her for dinner at Dick and Jennie's, a smart little uptown bistro on Tchoupitoulas Street."

"That new restaurant across from Sav-A-Center?" I had been meaning to try the place since they opened. "So how was it?"

"Fabulous, you'll love it."

"And how did it go with Miss Iler?" That's what I really wanted to know.

"Couldn't have gone better. We had wonderful food and nonstop conversation. She drove me home, said see you tomorrow at nine and sped away.

"The next morning I arrived sharp as a tack, went through the introductions with all the staff, then went to market with Iler to buy what the restaurant needed.

"As the first luncheon customers arrived, among them was an antiques dealer from Columbus, Mississippi, an old friend of Iler's whom she asked to join her for lunch. I, at my own request, was working the floor surreptitiously, standing behind her wait staff as they took orders, then turned them into the kitchen, so as to get the feel as to how her restaurant ran. After about five minutes, Iler beckoned me to come and join her and her guest. This little luncheon lasted two hours, at which time Iler announced that she was going home to take a nap and would drop me off so I could do the same and to be back at five on the dot.

"Five o'clock, I was back and overseeing the restaurant's preparation for the dinner crowd. Traffic was rather slow that evening, and at about seven, a cousin of Iler's from New York, and her friend, arrived for dinner. Iler told me that she wanted to sit with her friends and enjoy dinner. I told her to go ahead, that I most certainly could look after the restaurant. After five minutes, Iler sent one of the waiters to fetch me to her table where I was again invited to join. She had already ordered dinner, and I must say that it was divine. But right at that point, I started thinking again—this is too good to be true. Whoever heard of being paid a hundred dollars a day to eat and be witty."

"Oh, shut up," I said.

Again, he slapped his hand through mid air and laughed. "Well, I felt that if my wit was such a talent, I should be paid a thousand dollars a day for my impromptu performances."

I gave Bill a slight smirk.

"Anyway," he continued. "Everything seemed to be going swimmingly. When her guests left, she announced to me that she and I had spent enough hours at work, and that she was going to give me a ride home immediately. Since I only lived a few blocks from the restaurant, I demurred, saying it was too much trouble, which she came back saying, 'Goddamit, if you lived in Metairie, you'd have to walk. But you're only three blocks away, so get your ass in the car.'

"When we pulled up to my apartment, she handed me a hundred dollar bill. I said, 'What is this for?' She said, 'I pay my help.' I then retaliated with, 'I didn't do anything.' She said, 'Never mind. I'm going to work your ass off Saturday and Sunday.' Which meant, with this being Wednesday, I would have two days off. A quick mental arithmetic on my part still came up with, five days of work, hence five hundred dollars. Still too good to be true."

I decided not to comment on his pessimism and told him I couldn't wait to meet this Iler person.

Sunday mornings, I often go to my favorite church, St. Peter Claver. It's a Catholic Church with a predominantly black congregation, and if you've never been, you've never lived. My dearest friend, Renée Dedini, a native Campbell, Californian, had also succumbed to the inexplicable seduction of The Big Easy. This was her third visit, and she eagerly awaited the St. Peter Claver experience. Since the services didn't begin until 11:30 a.m., we decided to stop by Cafe Atchafalaya to see how Bill was faring and to meet Miss Iler.

The minute we walked in the door, I knew I had to immediately request the nonsmoking section. *Everybody*, including Miss Iler was sucking on cigarettes. Renée and I plowed through the smoke and up the stairs to the nonsmoking section, where we were the only occupants. Bill joined us and within moments, Miss Iler deposited her cigarette and appeared at our table.

The very sight of this woman, before even opening her mouth, was arresting. It was as though my insanely crazy Aunt Maggie McGill, who had died years ago, had quite suddenly reincarnated herself into this woman. Miss Iler not only looked like Aunt Maggie, but, learning from Bill that Iler was a lesbian, brought home years of suspicions surrounding my Aunt's unorthodox life.

Maggie McGill was married to Dill McGill. They had a farm outside of Gibson, Tennessee, a town so small it had but one stoplight—and if memory serves me, it only blinked. My cousin, Will Taylor, my sister, Tomi Sue and I, spent many a memorable week with our Aunt Maggie and Uncle Dill. Will swore that on their numerous fishing trips, Aunt Maggie invariably peed while standing. In fact, Will even swore that she could hit a mark far more accurately than he. To be quite honest, I believed every word of this. And still do.

Aunt Maggie was most certainly the black sheep of her family. Mine and Will's grandmother's younger sister, she smoked unfiltered Pall Malls, drank copious amounts of bourbon, could shoot a rabbit or squirrel through her kitchen window, dress it and have it ready for dinner that night. She loved to play cards—not some Christian sanctioned card game—but poker, although, she and I played many a game of canasta while smoking our weight in cigarettes. Of course, all of Aunt Maggie's questionable characteristics horrified her older sisters, one of whom was my grandmother.

There is no doubt in my mind that when that Jersey bull killed Aunt Maggie's husband, his death was a tragic loss for her. And though I believe with all my heart that she loved her husband in her own way, I also believe that if she could have lived the life born to her, she too would have chosen a lesbian lifestyle. But this was hardly the way of the world in the '20s, '30s and '40s, so our Aunt Maggie simply did what society expected of her. Still, she did it with a flair of her own making, while snubbing society in its face.

Although Miss Iler was the spitting image of Aunt Maggie, I did not ask her if she practiced the art of standing while peeing. This was far too personal a question to ask so soon after our meeting. In fact, I quickly came to realize that I need not ask much of anything other than, "keep the stories coming, Miss Iler." She, like Bill, was a born storyteller. The hordes of cigarettes she had inhaled over the years had left her with a deep, raspy voice that only added to the flavor of her stories, one of which took place when she was a mere twelve years old.

Iler's mother had gone out of town leaving her daughter and her mother home alone. Grandmother's chauffeur was also out of town, and being that Grandmother had never driven a day in her life, she found herself stuck at home with an urgent need to go to Memphis, which was some 80 miles away. So Grandmother turned to her granddaughter.

"Iler," she said. "I want you to get in the car and drive it around the yard." Iler, being the tomboy that she was, afraid of nothing and more than ready to tackle the automobile, obliged her Grandmother's wishes and took the car for a whirl around the yard. Grandmother, ever pleased with Iler's driving skills, then told her to take the car to downtown Drew. If she didn't hit anything, her grandmother said, she would be driving the two of them to Memphis the next morning.

Iler, thrilled at the thought, took the car to downtown Drew, drove it around the square and back home again without so much as smushing a squirrel crossing the road. The next day, twelve-year-old Iler drove her Grandmother to the big city of Memphis, Tennessee, had a wonderful day of shopping and drove back home safe and sound.

When Iler's mother returned from her trip, she was apprised of what her mother and daughter had just done. Iler's mother went into near hysterics, screaming at her mother that that was absolutely the stupidest thing she had ever done.

Time was running short, and Renée and I had to get to St. Peter Claver for the 11:30 service. I couldn't wait to return for another chat with Miss Iler.

That night, Will Taylor and his new bride were at the house and I was eager for him to meet Bill. The two reminded me so much of each other and I knew they would dive into scholarly conversations and immediately become fast friends.

Wrong.

Will and I and Chuck, who was still living with me at the time, were all in the kitchen engrossed in Will's opinions on various things. Chuck was going back to North Carolina to law school with aspirations of becoming a professor. He and Will, who is Professor of Criminal Justice at Mississippi Southern, were now in zealous conversation regarding Chuck's future when the door opened and in came Bill.

It only took a second for it to register. Bill sauntered into the kitchen and stood before us in a dazed stupor. I suppressed the urge to kill him, and introduced him to my cousin.

My curiosity, however, preceded my anger. I had just seen Bill that morning at the cafe and everything seemed to be going splendidly. I couldn't imagine that he had slipped a drink while on the job. He was too ecstatic about his new position; he adored Miss Iler and enjoyed the restaurant. So what happened?

The next day I searched Bill out for his version of the truth. I pulled him from The Rendezvous and brought him home. It was obvious that he had already had his morning beers, but he was coherent enough to tell me why he had arrived at my house drunk as a skunk the night before.

"After you and Renée left that morning," he informed, "Iler and I made a trip to Sav-A-Center to buy some snap beans and other essentials. Back at the restaurant, I found myself doing little to nothing. I sat with Iler, talked Mississippi Delta talk and smoked a gazillion cigarettes. At one point in time, I did have to make a martini for a customer."

Bill had once owned a bar and restaurant and could do a very credible Tom Cruise *Cocktail* performance.

"I really impressed the customer," he said. "Flipping the bottle of vodka in the air and turning out a perfect martini.

"After the last luncheon guests left, Iler asked me to take a walk with her. We strolled outside. 'Bill,' she said. 'I'm just so sorry. But this is not going to work.'

"She then slipped me a fifty, which I tried to give back to her. That's when I told her that I knew exactly what she was saying, and that if I could be of any help to her in any capacity, just feel free to contact me.

"As I left the restaurant, I was really sort of amazed with myself. I wasn't upset, because I felt, even after our somewhat short conversation, that Iler was never going to relinquish her hold on any aspect of the restaurant. The few small changes I had lightly voiced as possibilities, she immediately threw the damper on. So I actually felt that had I stayed, I would merely be another lackey, which was the position I had wanted in the first place. So—big deal. And besides, I knew Iler was gay, had just recently broken up with her partner, and I know so little about gays and their way of life. There was probably a lot that I just didn't understand.

"I also had three hundred and fifty dollars burning a hole in my pocket, and my need for reward, I mean, after all, I did have to listen to her for four days. I skipped over to the A&P and purchased a bottle of vodka. I went up to Brian's room over The Rendezvous. He was always happy to have a drink delivered, and we had at it. Like most drunks, my thinking was, Iler, whom I had really enjoyed, and sat great stake in, became with each slug of vodka: mean, petty, overly authoritative, and just plain tacky. Brian, delighted to have his drinking buddy back and unemployed, helped me to forget the debacle, and assured me something else would come along. Which shows, no sage he."

I sat quietly listening to Bill's account of his last day at Cafe Atchafalaya. I had but his side of the story, yet some of it made sense and some of it didn't. But the part where he had made the statement about his lack of knowledge of gays sent me into a fit of exasperation. The hell he doesn't know about gays, I thought. But again, I didn't feel that perfect moment had arrived. I only knew it would.

I saw Bill from time to time as I passed The Rendezvous. Often he would be sitting inside this dark haunt drinking ice water, sometimes coke and sometimes beer. One night Daddy and I stopped in to see if he was there. Sure enough, he was. And I actually think he was drinking a coke that night. He introduced Daddy and me to all his buddies as well as the infamous Murphy himself.

While Daddy played a game of pool with Brian, Bill took me upstairs to see his room. No longer allowed to stay in his rooms on Third Street, Bill was now among the raffish crew atop The Rendezvous. He owned no furniture, hadn't for years, no appliances, only a scattering of clothes. His room consisted of a twin bed of sorts, a shabby nightstand, an equally shabby bookcase and a small refrigerator that seemed to work. He shared a bath and shower with the other renters, as well as hordes of roaches and an occasional mouse. When he showed me this squalid excuse for a home, I wanted to gag. Instead I just said as many positive things as I could and went back downstairs. I could not believe that my friend had allowed himself to land into such a perverse condition. How could he possibly stomach the idea of living in such filth with people who couldn't come close to his intelligence or breeding?

I thought about this for a while and came to the conclusion that Bill must have the lowest self-esteem possible and being among those who could never hope to measure up to his attributes gave him that much-needed yet false sense of self worth. With his extensive knowledge of the English language, enough French to intimidate and world traveled, Bill Holcomb reigned supreme.

I had a hard time accepting his explanation of why he had to leave his rooms on Third Street, so I yanked Bill out of The Rendezvous one morning, brought him to my house and insisted that he tell me the truth. And I didn't want the same lie he had told me earlier about his landlady's taxes going up, which was forcing her to sell the house and move back to Honduras. I had figured that to be a lie the first time I heard it.

Bill hung his head. "All right," he said. "I'll tell you.

"There was this guy I met at The Rendezvous. His name was Scott, and he had lived there several years back. He was a sign artist by profession and told me that he would be able to illustrate a children's' book I had written about a mouse. Of course, all of the chatting forth and back was accompanied by copious quaffs of vodka. Indeed, after the conversation was over, I sounded more like Louis Carroll and Scott was coming off more like Beatrice Potter. I staggered my way home to my celibate cellar and collapsed. Around two-thirty or three in the morning, I heard the bars on my window rattling. I jumped up, threw on the light, only to look out the window to see Scott's weaving form. I went to the door and let him in where he proceeded to collapse on my bedroom floor.

"I immediately went back to sleep.

"The next morning, Scott still lay there, immobile. I walked out front to smoke a cigarette, for I was not allowed to smoke in my rooms. My landlady and her son asked me if I had heard any noise in the night. Immediately sensing something was afoot, I asked them if they had heard anything. Well, the upshot of it was that poor old drunk Scott, not knowing exactly where I lived, had rung all the other tenants' doorbells. In other words, had practically awakened the block, before he discovered my window. Realizing at this point that the truth would be better; I told my landlady that indeed a friend of mine had come by looking for me in the night. That I had let him in and as we spoke, he lay snoring on the floor in my bedroom.

"Poor Mrs. Del Valle went into a 90-minute lecture about the sanctity of her home, the evils of gin and other *faribole*, and immediately informed me that she would be leaving for Honduras in approximately a month and that I would have to move out during her absence.

"At first, I was furious with Scott for causing such a commotion, got him out of there—as far as the Parasol Bar—and tried to explain to him why I couldn't smoke, drink, or have company where I lived. He apologized profusely. I went back home to plot how I could forestall my eviction. Mrs. Del Valle and I had always gotten along famously in the past, and I saw no reason for us not to in the future.

"I knew that Scott wouldn't turn up again for fear of death, so I thought that everything would be copasetic. However, knowing Scott's proclivity for booze, I decided, just to be safe, I would stay with my friend Brian for a while at The Rendezvous in his expandable chair. After about three days, I went back to my apartment and ran into my landlady who said that a young man had been beating on my door for the last three nights. I knew that it wasn't Scott, for the simple reason Scott never, under any circumstances, shower or sleep, took off his Stetson hat. I then told her quite truthfully that I couldn't imagine who it could have been, and that if he turned up again, feel free to call the police. At this point, I pretty much had Mrs. Del Valle wrapped around my finger. That afternoon, I was resting on my bed, and there came a rapping at my window. I shot out of bed like a bolt and hollered, 'who's there?' The voice on the other side said, 'I'm looking for Ben.' At this point it all fell into place. I immediately told the guy that Ben had moved to Guatemala. He hadn't, of course, but it was a grand thought.

"With that, he replied, 'I got eight hard inches and need forty bucks.'

"Well, since this was not on my *ordre du jour*, I told the guy to Fuck Off! That evening Mrs. Del Valle came to my rooms and informed me that she was leaving for Honduras, that she was placing the house on the market, her taxes were too high, she didn't know whether she was coming back, she was so old and so on and so on, a never ending litany of grief and horror. In other words, she wanted my ass out of her house.

"And I wanted to tell her that I wanted my forty dollar poinsettia back that I had given her for Christmas, or that it would turn into a man-eating plant out of *The Little Shop of Horrors*. However, I didn't. Just moved down a step on the social ladder and cast my lot into The Rendezvous.

"I now found myself amongst American's most wanted. I suddenly felt as though nothing in the world could happen to me. The old Frank Sinatra song, *That's Life*, came to mind. I've been a boozer, a bastard, a *bon vivant*, and a king; I've been a borrower, a bum and a real ding-a-ling. But I know one thing. That's life. And that's it. Life."

"Yeah, life," I said. "Did Scott ever show up again?"

"Well, as I mentioned earlier, good old Scottreaux (rhymes with fido) was partially to blame for my being evicted. Affectionately or somewhat cheaply referred to as my Honduras haven, my little flat fitted me to a tee. And my Honduran landlady, who spoke six words of English, no weemen (broads), no cigarillos (cigarettes, hemp or otherwise) and no *agua biente* (booze) and I got along rather well.

"After Scott showed up in the middle of the night, dead drunk and

louder than a klaxon, I felt my days as a pseudo Latin lessee were num-
bered. This feeling was more than a little compounded by the look of
sheer disdain la Madame Manague shot me the next afternoon. Poor
Scott, he actually believed he had simply paid me a social call. And
even my ranting about social callers not falling into drunken stupors,
and sleeping on their hosts' floors for eons, did nothing to change his
mind.

"Months passed, and I was spared his social insignificance. One afternoon, shortly after release from DePaul's Chemical Dependency
Unit for the zillionth time, I had to go to the druggist and have prescriptions filled. Now these prescriptions were supposedly paramount
to my total recovery from fifty years of the most entertaining sorts of
alcoholism and debauchery. One was a puce colored pill which did absolutely nothing but squat somewhere in my bowls, and wait for the
moment when I would ingest anything with a millimeter of alcohol in
it—Old Spice, scotch or sterno. The meeting of the ingested matter
and this puce pill would guarantee a cataclysmic affect in my interior
and brain, enough to make me deathly ill, comatose or dead. Having
never seen Missouri I needed no proof, I simply abstained.

"Pill number two, was a multi-vitamin, which was supposed to
give me a physique comparable to Schwartznegger, and an athletic
prowess equal to Mohammed Ali. In actuality it caused me a lingering
and loud case of excessive flatulence.

"Pill number three was a cure-all tranquilizer that had been the
center of medical dispute some years previous. The only effect it had
on me was to make me swallow yet another glass of water. This made
three goblets of chlorinated Mississippi River water—I've never been
able to take more than one pill at a time—which practically caused re-
nal collapse by noon. I wouldn't dare darken my church on Sunday, as
the only men's room was attainable by crawling over the altar, and I
somehow felt this action drew away from the focal point, which was
inevitably some high mass, replete with Te Deums, benedictions and
the like, being intoned by all God's creatures.

"Also, I found this tranquil substance very disturbing for one who
would wantonly bust out of his shorts at the mere sight of naked flesh,
because I now suffered from a noticeable and much missed tumes-
cence. Actually, it was the lack of, that was running through my mind,
along with the fantasy of skipping this tranquility for a few days, if only
for a fair chance of whacking off when I looked up and saw Scott.

"He wore his Stetson hat and cowboy boots—neither of which I've seen him without—and fairly permeated the air between us with an oh-so-melancholy odor of scotch and Marlboros.

"I must have struck him as a born-again dude with my fragile sobriety, dapper mustache, and starched but still butt-sprung Levis.

"He asked me where I had been for the last six weeks, and I flatly, no nonsense, told him I had been a guest at DePaul's. He said that this was marvelous, immediately clueing me in that he did know that DePaul/Tulane was a drying out situation, or that they didn't exactly take "guests." Then he suddenly asked me if I had a picture ID. I wanted to tell him, if he so needed my image, he should go look on the post office wall. But taking into consideration his unsteady gait, felt that a trek to the post office would only land him under a car or bus. Not having the spiritual need for any more guilt at the moment, I let that go.

"It seems that he was awaiting a Western Union money order from his sister and had no picture ID to present. I told him that I would acquiesce. So he called and had the money wire sent in my name. As we were waiting for this speedy (NOT) transaction to take place, he explained to me in seventy-proof syllables that he had asked his sister (he had told me he had no family) if she would like to buy a parcel of his acreage in Idaho (some months earlier his acreage had been in Wyoming) which he had placed in trust for his daughter (he had also told me months earlier, that he had gone through a vasectomy when he was fifteen) and that his sister had agreed to buy a little piece of his property for two-hundred dollars. I bit my tongue to keep from inquiring how *little* a piece this must have been, when bingo, the wire came through, he tipped me ten dollars and wandered over toward the questionable brands liquor counter (read that as cheap).

"Exit my old friend Scotteaux, forever practicing midwifery on his imaginary ponderosa."

Suddenly, during gut wrenching laughter, I had a myriad of visions floating through my head—each one more distasteful than the last. And William Lafayette Holcomb was smack dab in the middle of it. I felt horribly guilty for laughing at all this misery, and exasperated that Bill had become so tangled up in it.

"Having happily disencumbered myself from this lowlife Lash La Rue," Bill said, "I headed toward home, only to run into Garland. You remember Garland."

Yes, I thought. I surely do remember Garland.

"He's The Rendezvous's bestest guest. At least the only one who has been in and out of jail 32 times in his seven years of residency. He looked rather spruced up. And, as if he had just received a cable from Scott, employed me to advance him ten bucks for a bag of really super-duper grass, which I had no doubt was super-duper, for neither of Garland's feet were anywhere near the sidewalk. After hastily explaining that I had an agonizing twitch in my colon, I raced home, immediately swallowed another tranquilizer, kissing my notions of masturbation good-bye."

Chapter 9

My memory serves me well as to Bill's rapid decline. I had seen him seven or eight times walking along Magazine Street in all sorts of dysfunctional modes. The Rendezvous had taken him, and was extracting the last bit of dignity he possessed. By the next time he arrived at my back door, a sort of moribund acquiescence had replaced dignity.

Bill Holcomb was unwittingly crying out for help. And I prayed that I had the words and wisdom to rescue my forlorn friend. I knew I had the determination.

It was early spring, and the weather was beautiful. Bill sat at my courtyard table, mildly intoxicated and deeply depressed. He was mumbling incessantly about his friend Brian and how much he cared for him, and poor Brian this, and poor Brian that.

This irked the hell out of me, because the only thing wrong with Brian was laziness and a morbid array of distorted attitudes. Of course, Bill had taken on the role of the co-dependent, which only exacerbated his own condition. But I listened with sincere and earnest compassion, while he poured out his pain.

I had always felt that when the time was right, I would know it. And there was no doubt about it.

That time was now.

"It's all right, Bill," I said placing my hand firmly around his arm. "It's all right to love Brian. Those feelings are normal. Stop hiding them. Look at me," I said. "Tell me how much you love Brian."

Bill's eyes flitted back and forth. "He's my best friend. I love him."

"And what's so wrong with him being more than your best

friend?" I released his arm. "Why do you have such a problem with loving another man? What makes that idea so impossible for you?"

Bill jerked his eyes squarely into mine.

"Why?" I prodded "For God's sake, Bill. Tell me. Say it. Just say it."

I have never had anyone look at me with such intensity in my entire life. When he finally looked away, I honestly didn't know what to expect.

Bill laid his hands flat on top of the wrought-iron table, lowered his head and began swaying to and fro. Finally he started to speak, but the first word, though I could tell it was "I," hung inside his throat. With each swaying motion, it was as though his body needed to regurgitate what his mind refused to release.

For 30 eternal seconds, I waited, prodded silently, and prayed.

"I—I—I'm gay." Bill all but collapsed onto the table.

"Yes, Bill. You're gay," I said. "So what? Why do you have this overwhelming problem with that fact?"

He looked at me with blurry eyes. "I love Brian. I can't tell him. He's not gay. But I love him. He's the only man I've ever loved. But I could never tell him how I feel."

This confession only frustrated me more. Whether Brian was or wasn't gay was not the issue. Brian was using Bill; this was something I already knew. The fact that Bill thought he loved this guy only further complicated an out of control situation.

Ten minutes had not *even* gone by before Bill was fervently denying his homosexuality and spewed out a litany of ridiculous reasons why he wasn't. I became so frustrated and downright exhausted listening to this, that I told him to shut up and help me edit my novel. He seemed thrilled with the idea. We left the courtyard and headed upstairs to my office.

I sat at the computer to continue writing, and handed Bill the first 20 chapters. I was hopeful that editing would keep him busy while I figured out just how to approach his obvious homophobic condition.

It was either the second or third word of the prologue that started the whole thing. He couldn't merely edit, he had to completely rewrite, run every point into the ground, not once, but again and again. Nothing I could say or do would shut him up. Then, after his third trip downstairs to get himself a glass of water or orange juice, I turned to him.

"Bill Holcomb," I spouted, "You are drunk."

I immediately pulled him from his chair and somehow managed to descend the 23 steps to the first floor with him in tow. We went into the kitchen, and there it was, sitting out on the counter: Daddy's

Bombay Sapphire Gin.

Bill swayed unsteadily and announced. "I'm not going to lie. I drank it." And he lurched for another swig.

"Damnit, Bill!" I grabbed the bottle from his hand. "You come into my house and behind my back sneak downstairs and drink my husband's liquor."

Bill swayed again. "I had to have it," he said. "I need it. I don't like gin anyway." He staggered then bent down toward the liquor cabinet. "Do you have any rum? Please, Pet. I just need one more. Just one."

I pulled Bill from the liquor cabinet, put my hand around a bottle of rum and slammed it onto the counter. "There," I said. "You might as well drink yourself into oblivion here rather than God knows where." I took a small glass and poured a hefty shot. Bill downed it. "Now get your ass back upstairs."

Bill cowed slightly, angled himself toward the dining room and lumbered toward the hallway and tackled the stairs back to my office. After positioning him firmly into his chair, I settled in front of my computer without so much as a glance toward the screen. I looked Bill straight on.

"Bill, listen to me. You're living in some illusionary world. And you're either too scared, too embarrassed, too stubborn, or just plain too lazy to admit it. Listen to yourself. One minute you admit you're gay, the next minute you're not, the next minute you're bisexual and the next minute you don't give a shit about any of it. You just want to run away—do and be what you want to do and be. Let me tell you something, my friend. There hasn't been a place created where you can hide. I don't care where you go, Bill Holcomb will always be there. Always be inside fighting like hell to get out. And if you don't come to your senses, he will destroy you from the inside out. Then it won't matter any more. And that's just about where you are, Willie boy. So start talking to me. Now."

As I was firing these mini sermons right and left, Bill seemed to wither. His hands shook, his eyes bloodshot and pooled with tears, and it seemed every muscle in his body had succumbed to spasmodic fits.

Dear God, I thought. What am I doing? I'm tampering with something I know absolutely nothing about—this man's mind. And that's way out of my league. But I had seen enough movies and read enough novels to give me that ounce of encouragement not to flee the scene. I decided to not back down but to hold fast. Bill needed to see my confidence, not my self-doubt.

I leaned forward and placed my hand on his knee. "Talk to me, Bill. I want to hear what all that pain is about. I'm not here to condemn, or judge or condescend. I'm here because I happen to care. There is nothing you can tell me or confess to me that could ever change that." I then leaned back in my chair. "In fact," I said smiling, "there is nothing you could possibly tell me that would give me the least bit of a shock. I've lived a life too, you know. The only difference is that I have accepted it as a very valuable lesson, and have left the guilt and shame in the gutter where it belongs. Guilt and shame are normal reactions. It's when you let them hang around that they and you become abnormal and torturous. And another thing while I'm philosophizing. The most dangerous of all is when you allow others to place the guilt."

When the words shot from his mouth, I almost fell out of my chair. But I tried to stay calm.

"I was sexually molested!" he blurted.

"All right," I said, a bit stunned. "You were sexually molested. So tell me about it."

Bill hung his head, his hands shaking violently.

"How old were you?"

"I was four."

"Now tell me exactly what happened. Don't leave out any details."

The idea of telling this horrid story seemed to sober Bill, if only slightly. He left his chair and began pacing the floor.

"Dean. His name was Dean. A friend of my father's. A Navy buddy. He—he and his wife had come to Clarksdale, Mississippi, to work in the real estate business with my father. One day we had walked down to the Sunflower River to feed the ducks. When we returned, it was about time for dinner."

"Did he say anything or do anything while you were feeding the ducks?"

"No. He always treated me like a contemporary. Not like a little boy. He would say things like, 'you can have two pieces of candy. Just don't tell your Daddy.' I remember that he winked and laughed a lot."

"All right. Go on."

"After we got back to the house he said that he was going to take a shower and wanted to know if I'd like to take one with him. And of course, I said yes. I was only four years old and I guess it struck me as being an equal."

"Go on."

"In the shower we were playing and making soap bubbles. That's when he said, 'Look, look at what I have.' I saw that he had gotten this huge erection. He asked me to put my hands on it."

"And? What did you think?"

"I thought that there was something wrong. But since it was Dean, my friend, my father's friend, I couldn't understand what. But then he asked me to kiss it. And the next thing I remember was that he was sticking it down my throat. I didn't know what the hell was happening. I thought I was going to choke. But then it was suddenly over with and we got out of the shower and dried off. I can remember him telling me that it would be our secret."

"How did you feel about keeping this secret?"

"Obviously I just knew what he meant about keeping a secret. I never told anyone until now."

"Then why are you telling me now?" I asked.

"I'm telling you this now because you seem to be of the opinion that I am hiding a multitude of horrendous memories."

"Are you?"

"No, I'm not. I really have nothing to hide."

"Then why did you hide that all these years?"

"It's not exactly something you pop up with in Sunday school."

"No, I wouldn't think so. But shouldn't you have told someone?"

"I don't see where it would have benefited anyone. Really, after a lot of self-analysis, I realized I would have ruined a friendship between my father and Dean. Besides, in view of other situations and circumstances I found myself in, what's sucking a dick? I mean, I've never felt that this caper could be faulted as cause for my drinking or not too badly hidden promiscuity."

"All right. Then what do you feel has caused your drinking?"

"Very simple. I'm stubborn, and do what I want to do."

"I guess I should ask, why do you want to live your life as a drunk?"

"I don't particularly want to be a dunk. But, I'd be very happy to remain sort of mellow. I don't want to hurt anybody. I just want to be left alone to do what I want to do and not have to answer to anyone."

"That sounds like a good life to me," I said. "Then what happened?"

"Unfortunately, money raises its ugly head again."

"What does that mean?"

"Well, every now and then, I have to go back to work somewhere in order to finance the treks to the bar."

"So, what you're saying is that all you really want to do is drink all day and when you run out of money to do that, you are forced to find work?"

"Well, not all day. Just starting around mid afternoon."

"So that's all you want from life?"

"No."

"Then let's talk about what Bill Holcomb really would like out of life and what he's willing to do to get it."

"My feelings are: if I had access to enough money, I would be very happy."

"You can be assured, if I had enough money, I would be very happy, too. Most people would. But, most people are out there working for it. Why do you prefer to stay in the morbid alcoholic state?"

"It's like, money can't buy happiness, but it sure can alleviate unhappiness."

"Most people agree with that. That's why they're out there earning their way. Why can't you?"

"To be very honest, if I had a job and was clearing $200 per week, I would be the happiest that I've ever been in my entire life. I don't want a whole bunch of stuff. All I want is the means to live my life, the way I want to live it. This includes, yes, cocktails in the afternoon, cavorting with the people I want to cavort with, even (society throws up their hands at the mention of same) though they be drunks, philanderers, sycophants and users."

"All right. Then if this is the life you want, why haven't you done what it takes to realize it?"

"I could pull it all fucking together, and I could work off-shore, make two thousand dollars in three weeks, have two weeks off, and indulge myself in any decadent way I wanted. Unfortunately, at my age, I doubt that I could make three weeks. And that's the only kind of fast money you can make around here. Unless you want to get into drugs and stuff like that, and I'm too much of a coward."

"Then why didn't you do what it takes years ago to live the life you say you want? What happened there? You were once very young."

"Because then I still cared about what people said, what I wore, where I went, and all the other foolishness connected with society today."

"Okay, I understand that. But it seems to me, you have only yourself to blame for that. Are you saying that attitude is what has landed you where you are today?"

"Yes, it landed me where I am today, because I never stopped caring about the aforementioned. And now, I realize that while these things maybe important to some people, to me they are totally superfluous. I mean, I don't want to be a Jack Kerouac, but to use the punch line of a joke I can't even remember, I'd sort of like to be at a large formal dinner party and get up and wiggle my dick in the mashed potatoes."

"There's certainly no problem with that at my dinner parties. You are most welcome to do that."

Bill threw up his hands. "I can see you now, making a mental note, *never* to serve mashed potatoes."

"Let me ask you something," I said. "When will all of this society stuff and imposed etiquette finally release its hold on you to the point that you are no longer defensive about it? It seems to have more of a hold on you than *it* or anything should."

"I already have."

I looked at Bill skeptically. "Oh really?" I said, and decided to drop the conversation for now. I then asked him to tell me about the time he went to visit his aunt and uncle in Los Angeles.

He closed his eyes with a hefty sigh, then obliged my request.

"When I was twelve going on thirteen, I wanted to go and visit my aunt and uncle who lived in a suburb of Los Angeles. Feeling that with my lifetime ambition of acting, Hollywood would surely sweep Billy off his feet. I fantasized myself being in movies and after all Los Angeles was a million miles away from Clarksdale, Mississippi. My father told me that he would not send me to Los Angeles, at which point I told him that I would send myself. I immediately got an after-school job, clerking in a drug store. I managed to save enough money to buy a round-trip ticket on Greyhound Bus Lines from Memphis to Los Angeles.

"My aunt had a good friend who did screenplays for MGM and my father had an old flame who was married to the head of music at Twentieth Century Fox. So, I had sort of an entrée for studio tours and hobnobbing a bit with the Hollywood crowd.

"One day I had a tour planned to MGM Studios. My aunt drove me and told me to call her when I was finished. Wanting to appear very worldly, I told her that I knew how to get back home on the bus. This was no big deal, because their house was only two blocks off Wilshire Boulevard. After a fascinating three hours at MGM, I struck out to catch the bus.

"While waiting at the bus stop, a man pulled up in a Cadillac and asked if I wanted a ride. Everything I had ever been told in my life about talking to strangers and accepting a ride with same just vanished.

Here I was not yet thirteen years old, I had just been royally shown through MGM, and here appears this dude in a fancy silver Cadillac offering me a ride. My first thought was not that of accepting rides with strangers—but—to hell with the Wilshire bus. So I promptly opened the door and got in.

"The man was very personable, in his 20s or 30s, and made much of the fact that I was from the South. Although I noticed we were not returning the same way I had arrived and thought nothing of it. What did I know of LA?

"After a bit, the man drove up into some hills and then parked at the end of a cul-de-sac. He was all over me so fast that I didn't even have time to reflect. He had my pants opened and was kissing me all over. He then pushed my back up against the seat, then he raised my legs and started going down on me."

"What were you thinking then?" I asked.

"I thought it was great. I was getting head for the first time. And I liked it."

"Did you think then, that you were a homosexual? Or did it even cross your mind?"

"All I thought was here's this dude giving me head and I'm getting ready to come and I didn't know if I was supposed to come in his mouth or what. Obviously I was, 'cause I did and WOW—HOW!"

"Then what happened after that?" I asked.

"I don't know. I guess the haze of orgasm prevented me from closely following his movements. Because the next thing I knew, he had my pants off and had lifted me up higher against the seat and with one shove pushed his dick up my ass. God! I don't think I have ever had anything hurt that badly in my life. And I think I must have half-fainted. I kept yelling at him to take it out and he just kept pushing and pushing and slobbering all over me. When he had had his way, he pushed me aside and tore away from the curb. I was pulling up my clothes in a frenzy when he, without another word, dropped me off at the bus stop on Wilshire Boulevard.

"Welcome to Hollywood, I thought. God, I hurt. If this was what one did in Hollywood, I'll take Mississippi any day. I remember taking the bus and somehow getting off at the corner where I could walk up to my aunt's house. Then I went next door to Chris's, my aunt's neighbor where I had been using the swimming pool."

"Wait," I said. "Tell me exactly how you were feeling. Mentally that is."

"I don't remember feeling like anything, really. I just felt numb. My ass hurt like hell."

"Okay. Then what did you do?"

"I remember seeing, in the dressing room at Chris' pool, a bottle of Seconal."

"What's Seconal?"

"It's a very, very strong sleeping pill."

"How did you know about Seconal?" I asked.

"Because I had just read a book by William Gibson called *The Cobweb*. It was a story of nuts in a mental asylum in which everyone was gobbling Seconal and knocking themselves out."

"So, is that what you wanted to do? Knock yourself out?"

"Yes. By all means. Forever. I practically took the entire bottle. Well, at least as many as I could hold."

"Then what happened?"

"I went back to my aunt's house and into my bedroom and went to sleep. Then, the next thing I remember is my aunt and uncle trying to wake me. I mean I was really out."

"What did they do?"

"They called a friend of theirs who was a nurse. And I guess she managed to get me to say that I had taken something."

"What did you say about your reason for taking a bunch of sleeping pills?"

"I don't think I said anything. I just remember being marched around a lemon tree."

"Then what did you say later?"

"Just that I had read about these and wanted to see if they really worked."

"Then you had no intention of telling anyone what this man had done to you?"

"Hell, no."

"Why not? Because you felt guilty for enjoying part of it?"

"Perhaps. But I simply could not just come out and say that this guy had screwed me."

"Not even to your father?"

"God no! Him the least."

"Why did you feel that way about your father?"

"All right." Bill turned to me with a look of utter exasperation. "He was so fucking pious that the very thought of his *only son* engaging in sex with another man would destroy him."

"But Bill," I said. "This man raped you. There's a difference. You don't think your father would have understood that?"

"My father never understood anything unless he instigated it, had done it, or expounded on it."

"So you really feel that if he had known you had been attacked and were injured, he would simply have—what?"

"He just would not have believed it. He would have simply put it out of his mind."

"So did your aunt and uncle call your parents?"

"Yes. My father was in New York on business and he immediately flew to the West Coast."

"So. What did you tell your father?"

"I didn't tell him anything. It was never mentioned. It was as though it had never happened. The next day we did the whole tour of Los Angeles, had lunch at Martha & Alfred's, then flew out that night for Las Vegas."

"What did you do in Vegas?"

"I drank seven-thousand dollars-worth of ginger ale and saw all the shows while he played the tables. After two days, we returned to Clarksdale as if we were two guys who were simply returning from a trip."

"Did your father tell your mother?"

"I guess so. Frankly, I really don't know."

"So nothing was said and you went on with your life as usual."

"More or less, as usual."

"What does 'more or less' mean?"

"The whole summer sort of had a shattering effect on me. I didn't want to see anyone, go anywhere, or do anything except read. And go and see my grandfather often. Because he always fixed me a bourbon."

"And the bourbon made you feel better?"

"Yes. It made me feel mellow."

"So you were twelve going on thirteen and drinking bourbon most anytime you felt like it?"

"Yep."

"Were you also allowed to drink at home?"

"Not really that openly. But if there were parties or people over, I'd fix a drink and no one would say anything. And that's when I decided I preferred scotch."

"But what about your parents? Didn't they notice or become concerned about your behavior? I mean it really wasn't like you to just hide away in your room—was it?"

"No. It wasn't. Hell, I was usually on stage, so to speak, most of the time. But that all seemed frightening now. I just wanted to be left alone and drink bourbon at my grandfather's."

"Then what did your parents do?"

"My father's doctor suggested that I go up to this mental clinic in Memphis called Wallis Sanitarium. They didn't know what the hell else to do. So we went to Memphis, where at great costs, Wallis embraced me as one of its own. Since I didn't know what the hell the shrinks were talking about, even though I appeared quite sophisticated, the doctors seemed to think, I guess that my head needed a little rattling, so they gave me insulin shock therapy."

"Insulin shock therapy? What the hell's that?"

"They wake you up at four o'clock in the morning, give you a hypo full of insulin, enough to induce shock, and supposedly either the shock causes you great recall, or total forgetfulness."

"What exactly did it do for you?"

"I don't think it did either. I still remembered everything and the more I remembered, the more I was determined not to ever tell anyone about it."

"Did you at this point feel any guilt about what had happened?"

"Not anymore. It was something that had happened. And I guess I was just numb to it. Frankly, the insulin shock treatments were worse than getting fucked."

This was not Bill's first account of California or Dean. It was the third.

When Bill first told me these things that day in my office, he was shaking, and had a look of haunted madness in his eyes. And when I asked him why he was telling *me* after all this time, his answer was that he didn't feel that I was condescending, or that I was judgmental.

And, I suppose, in his drunken despair, he had also arrived in the right place at the right time and possibly with the right person to let go of something he had long since buried deep down inside him.

And his first account of the last incident was not told with such honesty. He presented this as a horrible rape, pure and simple. The oral sex was not mentioned. His second account was similar. It wasn't until a few weeks later when I asked him for the third time, that the oral sex and his enjoyment during it, was admitted.

Bill was in a state of helplessness and despair, however, he did seem, though guardedly, to want to do something about it.

So with my mind made up, I asked him how long at any given time be had managed to stay sober. His answer was from June to November a few years back. Then I asked him how. Antabuse was his answer.

Antabuse is a drug that blocks the body's ability to metabolize alcohol normally. It causes a rapid buildup of toxins when a drink is ingested. Violent nausea, headache, a sudden drop in blood pressure, and intense fear of death occur very quickly. In behaviorist terms, the drug provides strong and immediate negative reinforcement for drinking—punishment, in other words.

Bill truly seemed at wits end with his drinking, as well as living too many years of a wasted life. I felt that he was genuinely ready to take the steps needed toward sobriety. Yet I knew that sobriety teetered precariously. Bill Holcomb must confront the emotional cancer that was devouring him. But why couldn't he find the strength and determination to face it? Was he afraid to wake up and find himself alert, lucid and healthy? And if so, what was it inside reality and awareness that frightened him? Like a slow dying of hope, each year a little less than the previous, until finally, hope had faded into obscurity. I wondered how much ugliness still remained, locked up inside Bill's conscience. What evils had crawled inside his soul? I wondered if I would be able to exorcise them.

I picked up the phone and called my doctor who, coincidentally, is also Bill's doctor. I told Dr. Johnson about the situation and asked about Antabuse. He said to get Bill into his office immediately, that Antabuse was not a drug to prescribe without tests. Dr. Johnson knew all too well Bill's history with alcohol.

Stuffing Bill into the passenger's seat of my car, we were at Touro Medical Center within four minutes. That's the wonderfully convenient amenity we have, living in the Garden District. Almost everything is minutes away and Dr. Harry Johnson is one of the most caring doctors I've met. I would even venture to say that if we had needed him to come to us he would have. This man is like no other and we were fortunate.

I sat Bill in the waiting room and announced our presence to the receptionist. Within moments Bill was ushered to an examining room for tests, and I was shown to Dr. Johnson's office. I relayed what had transpired the last several hours and asked for advice. The advice was quick and forthright. Bill must check into DePaul/Tulane Behavioral Health Facility. He simply could not do this on his own. And after several minutes when Bill's EKG and blood pressure results were revealed, there was no doubt about it. He needed to get to the hospital and begin detox. And we needed to go immediately.

Thank God for Medicare and Medicaid. After several phone calls to DePaul's, we had an appointment to meet with a counselor who would ultimately commit Bill for treatment. Bill asked that I drop him back at The Rendezvous so that he could gather a few personal items and said that I could pick him up around three-thirty. Our appointment was for four o'clock and it was only one-thirty. I knew exactly why he wanted that time alone. For one, he was desperate for a few beers to take the edge off. Two, he wanted to see Brian. Though I hated the idea, I obligingly dropped him off. As much as I wanted to stay with him, help him gather his clothes then whisk him away, I knew that the decision to get help had to be his. Maybe he would be waiting for me when I returned.

Maybe he wouldn't.

That was the chance I had to take.

Chapter 10

The Rendezvous' door was closed, but I pulled my car up to the curb and honked. I'm not sure if I was prepared for him not to appear. Perhaps I was a little numb to the possibility. So when the door opened and I saw Bill walk out, I let out a sigh of relief and thanked God.

The first positive step.

I had left him in that pit of a place where sloth and booze, drugs and sex run rampant, and he was actually waiting for me to take him to the hospital. That was positive. But I wasn't so naive as to think that the road ahead would remain equally so. I hoped I was capable of handling the challenge.

Naturally, Bill had downed several courage-seeking beers to face yet another round in rehab. He was no stranger to the vast rehab programs and hospitals. And why did I think this time would be different? Well, I suppose it was my own stubborn idealistic dream, that I could put Humpty Dumpty back together again.

After arriving at DePaul's and checking in, we were shown to a small counseling room. A man in his late 30s or early 40s entered and introduced himself. It was then that the questions began. One after the other, firing in rapid succession. They came so fast and so direct that Bill, his hands shaking, his eyes glazed over, his speech slurred, could barely keep up with the answers.

And there I was, sitting on the couch while making damn sure that Bill wasn't twisting his answers into his own version of the truth. At least what I, at that point, believed was the truth. I could only imagine what deeper truths lay buried inside. But I knew I had managed to pull some of the garbage from him that day, and felt encouraged while Bill relayed the same to his counselor. He shook and stammered as he pushed the words from his mouth.

Another positive, in my view of things, was the counselor. Like Bill, this man was a Catholic, an alcoholic, and gay. The challenge was to enlighten Bill as to how this man had put his life in order and come out the other side. I hoped that hearing his story, which he freely expressed, would give Bill an optimistic and confident outlook for the future. But I knew the pieces were not going to fall into place quite that easily. The larger challenge still lay ahead.

After escorting Bill to his temporary home, I bid him farewell and drove straight to The Rendezvous. He had gathered none of his personal belongings while there, only consumed more beer. So I scaled the iron stairs behind the building and entered this pit of squalor to find Brian. He sat in his room, which has nothing resembling a door, just a large blanket partially covering the gaping hole. I informed him that I needed to get into Bill's room to gather a few clothes and toiletries.

Brian expressed his appreciation for what I had done. I thanked him, but reminded him that Bill's recovery was Bill's, not mine. Brian and I threw several articles in a plastic A&P grocery bag and I quickly left the premises. If I never entered that dive again, it would be too soon.

Three days later Brian and I were allowed to visit Bill. His blood pressure was seriously elevated, so they had put him on the tranquilizer Librium. It had rendered Bill to nothing less than a walking zombie. Our conversations, though Brian and I said very little, were focused on Bill's account of his treatment to lower his blood pressure. With Bill's proclivity for gab, he slurred through copious soliloquies of how and why this treatment was taking place. Brian and I listened patiently, giving him our support and promised to visit him as often as allowed.

As we left the building, I remember thinking that the only difference in Bill since first admitting him was his lack of aggression. He still slurred his words with unfocused eyes and swayed when he walked. The whole scene was horribly depressing. I had never been through anything like this—only seen it in movies where the reality didn't exist. But this was far removed from the comfort of a theatre. I thanked

God that neither my family nor I had ever experienced it.

My friend, Renée, mentioned earlier, succumbed completely to the mystical spell of New Orleans and decided to pick up her life in California and move it to 1237 Washington Avenue. I welcomed her with open arms. Renée and I had known each other for over 20 years, taught aerobics together, designed clothes and sewed together. Her second wedding had taken place in my home in Los Gatos.

Both her marriages had been mentally abusive with alcohol playing a major role. During the second one, she was suddenly stricken with a hefty dose of what doctors called panic disorder. An overwhelming feeling of *déjà vu* triggered an onset of physical symptoms. Immediately following the *déjà vu*, she heard familiar music and smelled familiar scents. It felt as if she were having a past life experience. She also experienced severe nausea, dizziness, and disorientation.

In the beginning it was so overwhelming that she would end up on the nearest floor in the fetal position. Being of strong will, she did her best to recover and not empower the attack and move on. It took approximately one year of monthly attacks for her to self-diagnose these seizure-like episodes. With this knowledge and a deep personal conviction to grow, Renée absolutely refused to let this nightmare take control. The panic attacks continued on a regular basis and on Father's day, took a turn for the worse. The day began with an extreme panic attack in the midst of preparations for a family gathering, and it took her an hour to recover. Shortly after, she pulled herself together to greet her guests and achieve the impression that all was well. In the middle of a conversation with her parents, her husband made a derogatory statement with the sole purpose of humiliating her in front of her family.

Somehow, driven by a force beyond her control, she was able to appear calm and gracious throughout the rest of the day. Later that evening, after they had gone, Renée quietly escaped to a place where she could be alone and feel safe. She was overwrought with feelings of anger, revenge, remorse, and fear for her sanity. When her husband came check on her, she did not hesitate to give him a large piece of what was left of her mind.

She proceeded, with self-righteous anger, to come clean with every morsel of how she felt about the way she was being treated. With a blank look on his face, and like a dog with his tail between his legs, he swiftly returned to the house. She was alone now, hysterical for three hours.

Renée continued to feel confused and afraid. She questioned whether or not she was emotionally stable to trust her own intuition and thoughts. The cliché, am I losing my mind, suddenly became less of a cliché and more of a consuming reality. It became immediately clear that she was physically unable to go outside.

As the days went by, she frantically researched her course of action. She contacted her family doctor, whose response was to have her breathe into a brown paper bag. Hysterically, she grabbed the phone and called her insurance company. Thank God, the representative was a compassionate man who understood that she needed help. He reassured her that she would be seeing a psychiatric specialist later that week.

Patiently she struggled with each day until Friday. Every morning she sat on the front porch to fight the looming cloud of agoraphobic thoughts that imprisoned her. As each day passed she would complete new challenges, walking to the end of the driveway, then the end of the block. By Friday she was up to driving the car to locations that were close enough for her to make an emergency run home.

It took all available courage to drive and walk into the shrink's office to ask for help with an illness that you could not describe or see. After waiting for over an hour, the receptionist came to the conclusion that the doctor was not coming in, and canceled her appointment.

Back in her car, the anger and confusion returned. She became hysterical and hopeless once more. It was Friday and another weekend of family gatherings lay ahead. The last thing she wanted was to reveal that she was not handling her marriage well, and she could be blamed for a second failed marriage. She begged her husband to call for help, and he was able to get her back to the family physician. This time she instructed them as to the correct medications based on her research. They disagreed, but did give her enough tranquilizers to make it through all the social functions of the following weekend. Ironically enough after locating and visiting a qualified doctor, she was eventually given the medications that she had originally requested.

During the mid'70s, Renée had become the queen of self-help and home remedies, cooking up her own concoctions of various illegal drugs found in The Whole Drug Manufacturers Catalog by Chewbacca Darth (like chew back a Darth—from the movie *Star Wars*). That knowledge helped her to formulate her personal recovery program. She developed her own prescriptions to manage her attacks and learned to be a shrink-on-a-budget. Her personal recovery program included abstinence from alcohol, so for the seven years before moving to The Big Easy, she had been alcohol free.

Woe be to those who succumb to the seductive spell of *La Nouvelle-Orléans,* where the cocktail hour begins anywhere from 10 a.m. to 7 p.m. depending on the situation. Renée has yet to miss even one, though, true to her fashion, she developed her own survival kit.

One day, I caught her on a return trip from the local Walgreen's (across the street from A&P on Magazine Street). She was in high spirits, proclaiming that a trip to Walgreen's beat the hell out of Las Vegas.

She probably spent two hours there, rummaging for just the proper drug combinations to achieve a balance of high energy to counteract the effects of our nightly drinks. Talk about drug concoctions. She found a budget blend of Excedrin and generic Metabolite to achieve that drug high legally. As further evidence of her total confidence that she really is okay with her new life-style, I caught her at ten o'clock one night, posing alone in her room, dressed in nothing but a pair of painter's overalls and full face make-up, seductively posing in front of her camera, tripod setup and all.

As I've said, nothing in New Orleans is real, so I turned from her doorway, maneuvered my feet so as not to stumble over Max, and the two of us silently retired for the night. The next morning, having completely wiped the incident from my mind, Renée confessed what she had been up to the previous evening. I was still not certain that what I witnessed was nothing more than illusion, but she swore she had film to prove it. I then suggested that I might pull on my painter's overalls and join her for a few shots. She loved the idea—and we did.

Renée's first aid kit for surviving New Orleans: Wake up no earlier than 10 a.m.— stagger into bathroom for a heavy dose of water, antidepressants, her legal concoction of uppers, (yet to be divulged) vitamins and, of course, birth control pills. Mosey out for some exercise along Magazine Street, possibly a cup of strong coffee, return home in time for an afternoon nap and, of course, reading from her latest cache of self-help books. Later, around cocktail hour, magically appear dressed for an evening of libations and Paulette's blistering hot beans. Afterwards, retire to her boudoir to polish off the evening with her own personal blend of tranquilizers, Excedrin P.M. and another self-help book.

Having Renée close by was a godsend. She knew firsthand the perils of living with an alcoholic and understood, through her own experience, the trappings of a mental disorder. And she was more than generous with her advice and support. She was well aware of what we faced when Bill's hospital stay ended. I, on the other hand, was not.

After a trip to Memphis, my sister, Tomi Sue, spent a few days in New Orleans with me, so I dragged her along when I went to The Rendezvous to collect Bill's personal belongings. This was prefaced with a warning of the conditions she was about to witness—though nothing really prepares one for such things. The smell alone was nauseating. I hoped that Brian would be there, and sure enough, as I pulled up beside the building, Brian leaned against the upstairs railing, his morning beer clutched in his hand. A buddy sat on the steps doing the same. Tomi Sue and I scaled the iron stairs, announced our mission and followed him into this squalid dungeon. We stuffed Bill's few things in plastic A&P grocery bags and prepared to get the hell out—but there was one more piece of business to attend to.

Before Bill had left for the hospital, he had given Brian his food stamp card. Poor Brain, who is afflicted with various degrees of laziness, could not seem to get himself down to the food stamp building. So he grabbed what bit of money he could doing odd jobs for Murphy at The Rendezvous and helped out a friend that does, I'm not sure what, at the cemetery on Washington Avenue across from Commander's Palace. There was some problem with Brian's food stamps, so he opted for an easier method of survival. Lately, that survival had been looking up—in the form of Bill Holcomb. Bill was a wealthy man compared to most of The Rendezvous' raffish renters. This of course had put Bill on an elevated level of superiority, which fed his low self-esteem, and much desired social status. He would throw his money around freely, buying drinks for The Rendezvous' motley crew. He had also fancied that he was in love with Brian and now had someone to mentor—again giving Bill that surge of superiority.

However, it was time to ask for Brian to return Bill's food stamp card. When I did, he paused, then offered the pitiful stall, 'Oh, I was going to go to the A&P and buy ribs for everyone.'

It was Memorial Day weekend and Brain was going to barbecue on that relic of a grill still teetering on the much-fornicated-upon garage roof. When I appeared unmoved by his tale of woe, he reached for the food stamp card and handed it over saying, 'I guess I just won't eat.'

Excuse my French, but this royally pissed me off. However, being the softhearted dufe that I am, and after loading all of Bill's things into my car, I decided that since Bill wanted Brian to have his card, I would drive him to the A&P and let him buy what he needed for his Memorial Day barbecue. But—*I* now had control of the food stamp card.

After depositing Brian back at The Rendezvous and before driving away, I told him that Bill must never return to this God-forbidden place or associate with any of its occupants. Bill needed a clean start and his goals set toward a more productive life. Brian said that he agreed, wished me luck and quickly vanished, with groceries in hand, into his doorless digs.

As we pulled away, my sister made the comment that she hoped to never again experience the depravity she had just witnessed.

Bill's clothes smelled like smoke, filth and neglect. His suitcase had been stolen, so I retrieved my husband's leather suitcase from the closet. I dumped all of Bill's washable clothes into the washing machine, washed them, dried them, ironed them, folded them and packed them into the leather suitcase. On my way to the hospital, I stopped by Stein Mart and bought a leather toiletry bag, which I filled with various items, such as an electric beard and mustache shaver I purchased at Walgreen's.

At the hospital, I turned over these things to the nurse, since I was not allowed beyond the door. Then that I caught a glimpse of Bill down the hallway. He looked forlorn and lost. The Librium had reduced him to a meek and submissive human being. I gave him an oblique wave of my hand, knowing that he couldn't possibly recognize me at that distance. Frankly, I doubt he had any idea there was anyone there at all.

Driving back to the house, I did manage to smile at a pleasant thought lingering in my mind. This was by no means a first-time visit for Bill at DePaul's Behavioral Center and he was thrilled to find that one particular nurse would be caring for him.

The very sight of this woman would cause one pause. She was a bull dike from the word go, and like all the counselors and nurses, a recovering addict. She was capable, at even a hint of trouble, of picking up a very large person and rendering him helpless or dead. Bill had bonded with her during his previous stay at DePaul's. Another nurse that Bill came to truly like was a transsexual named Robin. She was effeminate and delightful. It lifted my spirits to know that people Bill trusted and genuinely liked surrounded him.

Since there was no way I was going to return this man to that upstairs garbage dump at The Rendezvous, I decided to prepare one of my guest rooms. The eight days of detox, I was told, consisted of lowering his blood pressure, weaning him from the Librium, and filling the hours with group therapy. Shortly, I was informed that Bill was ready for release with the stipulation that he was to attend their four-week outpatient program. He was also given a roster of AA meetings throughout the Uptown and Garden District areas and was urged to attend often.

At the hospital, I was greeted by a young woman who had been his counselor. She explained what one should expect when living with an alcoholic—the lies, denials and all the trappings an alcoholic is capable of. If Bill was seriously prepared to stay sober, she said, he must faithfully attend the outpatient program as well as one AA meeting each day. And without fail, he must take the Antabuse and the Prozac.

When she finished, she had Bill join us. I then proceeded to inform Bill that what I was doing was a one-shot deal. He would be staying with me under these conditions:

He was to turn his $614 Social Security check over to me. I would take $300 out for room and board, and open a savings account where I would deposit the remainder. As for spending money for personal needs, he could use his food stamp card to pay for part of our groceries, and I would then reimburse him in cash. This arrangement was agreed upon and we left the hospital to start his new life of sobriety.

We drove home, stopping by Walgreen's to fill his two prescriptions and buy several packs of his sweet cigars. He seemed very appreciative of his new home as we unpacked his clothes. He would be responsible for cleaning his own room and bathroom, I told him, plus certain chores, such as taking out the trash at home as well as the apartment building on St. Charles. I showed him how I wanted my outside plants and garden watered and offered to do the cooking if he would do the clean up. This seemed agreeable, so we set about the business of living.

Bill had some urgent dental problems and a credit card that was robbing him at a rate of 20% interest, I took his $400 balance, transferred it to one of my 2.99% cards and made an appointment with my dentist. As I mentioned, living in the Garden District has its advantages. My dentist, like my doctor, lives within four minutes of my house. Dr. Dov Glazier is a rarity, and though I was prepared to pay in full for Bill's treatments, Dr. Glazier knew of Bill's situation, commended him for his sobriety and obviously charged him far less than the standard fee.

So Bill was now on his way to recovering his good health. He made an appointment with the eye doctor and showed a sincere desire to take his medication. He read the paper every morning out in the courtyard, smoking his sweet cigars and using a small tin can for an ashtray. He announced that this can was molded from some rare metal that I can't even pronounce—which of course it wasn't. If memory serves me, the can had once held anchovy-stuffed olives. So, between the *New York Time's* crossword books I bought him and *The Times Picayune* crossword puzzle, he was mentally stimulated and doing what he loved.

I had by then decided to write Bill's story.

Each morning I crawled out of bed between 6:30 and 7:00. Max, after lengthening his body into a full stretch, pranced behind me to the head of the stairs. I could always tell if Bill was up. His bedroom was directly behind mine, which often played havoc with my sleep when Daddy was in town and had been partying the night before. With Daddy on my left and Bill behind the wall to my right, I was often engulfed in a storm of snores. There were times when even Max, asleep atop his red-fringed pillow, fell into restless dreaming, emitting indescribable noises.

As Max and I reached the stairs, I coaxed him down with promises of his morning treat. I started the coffee, which is by the way, the freshest coffee possible since my sister and her husband own Carpe Diem, the most fabulous coffee and teahouse in Mobile. They roast their own beans, a large bag of which is delivered to my house every month.

As the coffee brewed, I prepared Max's breakfast of a prescription diet dog food, chopped carrots and three pills hidden inside a bit of cheese. As he gobbled his gourmet feast, I'd turn on the *Today Show*, retrieve the paper from the front porch and place it on the courtyard table for Bill. I would then pour my coffee and settle in for the morning news.

Bill usually appeared about this time with a cheery *bonjour*, went into the kitchen, took his Antabuse and Prozac, poured his coffee and headed out to read the paper, smoke his sweet cigars and master yet another crossword puzzle. Around 8:30 a.m., I drove him to outpatient treatment. While Bill was in treatment, I ran errands and wrote on our book. When 4:00 p.m. rolled around, I picked him up, stopped at the A&P for groceries then headed home for more writing until 6 or 6:30. Bill usually took the car to the nearest AA meeting while I prepared my nightly vodka and orange juice and began the evening meal.

This is my absolutely favorite thing to do. I light all the candles, whip up a screwdriver with my preferred Sky vodka and begin creating inside my kitchen. Don't ask me to go anywhere once I've started this ritual. I won't go. And heaven forbid that you fly in for a visit and expect me to pick you up at the airport past 7 p.m.

I won't.

You'll have to take a cab. Just ask Daddy or any one of many who have made the mistake of asking. Once I've had my first drink, which is usually between five and seven p.m., it is virtually impossible to pry me from the house. There are but two accounts that I can think of. One was the birth of my first grandchild; the other was when Buzz and Les were hosting a charity event at their home. Les was bored to tears and called me after my second drink. I think I arrived within thirty minutes of his call. But then, all I had to do was throw on a elegant dress and walk three blocks. As I have said, living in the Garden District can be delightfully convenient. It was this party where I met a certain lady by the name of Shirley Angelle. I have now hosted many charity events and have found that, since I would rather stay at home at night, it is a perfect way to give of myself and meet the movers and shakers as well as New Orleans' society.

When I first mentioned to Daddy how much I enjoyed these parties, he was quick to point out that I had never been this joyous about hosting parties, and seemed baffled by it. I had no problem reminding him of *who* it was that ended up with the majority of the work when *he* wanted to throw a party.

Bill and I held true to our routine for four weeks of outpatient treatment. After that, he was released and we now had full days of writing and living ahead of us.

They played out this way.

About half way through the *Today Show* I'm ready for my cheese and jalapeño sandwich. I realize that this is not your typical breakfast, but I've not been typical since the day I was born, and I have grown perfectly comfortable with my strange and enigmatic breakfast habits.

Out in the courtyard, while Max lounged and Bill worked his crossword puzzle, I hid away in my upstairs office and worked on our book.

When 11:30 rolled around, I changed to my workout clothes and popped the Tae Bo tape into the VCR. This is NOT something I particularly want to do. I taught aerobics for eight years. I'm tired. But I'm also extremely vain—and have a husband who also has a hefty dose of vanity. So Tae Bo it is.

After that I hop in the shower, then do the hair and make-up thing, summon Bill from the courtyard and we'd retreat back into the office to go over our book.

It was during our collaboration that Bill's life began to unfold. However, I knew that the truth was something that Bill was seriously unfamiliar with and hung somewhere between fact and fiction. He had lived inside his lies for so long, that there were times when not even *he* understood where the truth was buried.

Remember Ed and Eleanor Curtis? They were the ones with the gnome from Palestine, Texas, that Bill saw that day scurrying from under the stairway. Ed and Eleanor now live in Palm Beach, Florida and their son, Edward, and his wife, Kathy, have The Brass Menagerie once located in The French Quarter. It is now next door to Harper's Interiors on Magazine Street where I first met Bill.

Kathy and Edward have known Bill for 35 years, so naturally I asked Kathy to come by one morning when Bill was still in treatment. Kathy is just about the cutest little thing you've ever seen. She's from Mexico City and has the most adorable accent. She is all of five-feet with blonde hair and possesses an array of clever hats.

Kathy doled out words of appreciation as well as severe warnings. She and Edward had lived with Bill through years of destructive behavior, endless lies, and empty words of contrition. For two hours she enlightened me with pathetic stories of a life gone out of control. Though there were many, three really telling ones come to mind.

One day Kathy and Edward, finding themselves at wits end, threw Bill out of the house. It was the dead of winter, and trust me, New Orleans can be soppy cold when she wants to be. Bill ended up sleeping inside the Curtis' shed, under the house and God only knows where else. Then one day he appeared at their shop and presented them with a note, swearing to the heavens that he would absolutely never drink again.

This affirmation, like all others, was short lived. He soon returned to the bottle, fell back into the abyss with weeks and months of excessive boozing, whoring and deprivation. After this bout of madness wound itself down, a contrite Bill Holcomb came crawling back to his friends, Kathy and Edward. And again, they opened their hearts, took him back, gave him work, and attempted to find a semblance of control for their friend.

Since these bursts of sobriety are short-lived, Bill soon pulled another disappearing act. Weeks passed without a trace until one day when he came stumbling into the Brass Menagerie wanting money. He was filthy, he was drunk, and his upper bridge was missing, leaving him virtually toothless. He immediately began weaving some outrageous tale of falling on the sidewalk while trying to catch a bus for work.

Work! You've got to be kidding.

So—Kathy, jaded by his lies and tall tales, adamantly refused him one red cent. This sent Bill into a raging fit, during which he plowed a very heavy object into the glass counter.

Still, Kathy and Edward took him back.

Then there was the time when Bill had come to know a man who was a recovering alcoholic and fancied that he might save Bill from the evils of booze. The man still hung around the local bars without so much as a drop of alcohol passing his lips. And it was the bars where he first encountered Bill. They struck up a relationship and before long, Bill found himself living with this man. The man had an apartment on Magazine Street, which was dreadfully convenient to all of Bill's haunts. Bill, with no intention whatsoever of embracing a life of sobriety, played havoc inside this relationship. One day he called Kathy stinking drunk, ranting that he was not about to be this man's wife.

Remembering Bill's Los Angeles experience, I had a pretty good idea of what he meant by not wanting to play the part of wife.

He screamed his conviction to Kathy again and again and again, until she simply hung up the phone. Soon after that, the man called Kathy and told her that Bill had gotten stinking drunk and trashed his apartment. While in this stupor, he crashed into a table, sending it and a glass ashtray hurling to the floor. A shard from the shattered ashtray pierced Bill's back and blood gushed. The man insisted that Kathy get Bill out of his apartment and strongly suggested that he be taken to

Charity Hospital, which she did.

Bill was released from Charity after a couple of days. Kathy picked him up only to find that his clothes were missing and all he had were hospital greens. She was given several prescriptions and directions as to the appropriate care for the gaping wound in Bill's back. After days of dressing and redressing this oozing wound, it finally healed, and Bill was available to continue his maddening excuse for a life.

As I watched Kathy drive away that morning, I leaned against the back door and wondered what the hell I had gotten myself into. I had kicked one alcoholic/drug addict out of my life. His name was George. He was a very tall black gay man who had once been married, had a wonderful daughter and ex-wife whom I met when in San Francisco. I, too, had been a casualty of loving a gay man, so I understood that situation perfectly. George eventually left the closet and became involved with a professor and scholar. Their personalities and goals were at opposite ends of the universe, but they seemed to love each other, so who am I to judge?

George became my dog groomer, maintenance man and house sitter during the times I was in San Francisco with Daddy. Max and his father, Jocque, needed to be cared for as well as the five apartments in my building. George was perfect for the job—or so I thought.

He drank *all* my liquor and there were repeated complaints from my tenants and friends. Still I gave him the benefit of the doubt. At one point, he was thrown in jail for drug possession. Naturally his version was entirely different than the police, so gullible me gave him another chance. I warned him that if this ever happened again, he was gone.

It did. And he was.

However, I did write a letter to the judge suggesting that George needed rehabilitation, close supervision and encouragement, not a long stay in prison. I also informed the judge that George's daughter would be graduating from college in a few months and needed her father there.

I received a call from George a few weeks later. He thanked me for the letter and had the strange notion that I still wanted him to work for me.

Chapter 11

Miss Iler and The Cafe Atchafalaya simmered in the back of my mind. I still wanted to hear from Iler as to why she had let Bill go. I was also intrigued with Iler herself, and wanted to hear more about her life. So—I picked up the phone and told her that I would like to interview her for a book I was writing. She announced that this was not the first time she had been asked to be interviewed for a book. I inquired as to the name of the book, because I wanted to run out and buy it.

"Redneck Heaven!" she bellowed. "And I said—HELL NO! Mississippi Delta girls are not rednecks and I will absolutely NOT be involved with portraying such. But," she admitted, "after the content and atmosphere of her book was explained—well—I agreed."

She also agreed to mine.

The lunch hour at Cafe Atchafalaya begins at 11:30 a.m. Iler said if I came about ten, she could give me an hour. I needed to buy a tape recorder and, though Radio Shack is just around the corner on Magazine Street, they didn't open until ten. I called Iler, told her I was running late and would be there shortly.

With tape recorder in hand, I arrived at the cafe at 10:20. I walked through the bar and into the dining area where I found Miss Iler—a portable phone pressed to her ear with one hand and a fly swatter in the other. She had a damn good eye because flies were dropping right and left. I was told later that the damn deliveries taking place in the rear of the cafe were an open invitation to every fly residing within the entire state of Louisiana.

After taking another call and disposing of several more flies, Iler settled at a table near the kitchen. She placed the phone close by, but held tight to the swatter. The flies were coming in as fast as she could take them out, and she was determined not to have a restaurant full of them when customers began arriving. Later, as I left the cafe, I saw that *she*—not the flies—had prevailed.

After a marvelous chat, I thanked Miss Iler and rushed back home, eager to get this interview into the computer. I scaled the 23 stairs to the second floor, settled myself at the desk and turned on the recorder.

I was certain that I had not suddenly gone deaf, because I could hear Ruth Brown's *If I Can't Sell It, I'll Keep Sittin' On It* emanating from the CD ROM. But where was my interview? The entire tape was blank.

You dumb shit, I thought. You pushed "play" instead of "record" during the entire interview.

Meekly and with great humility, I picked up the phone and gave Miss Iler the bad news. All she said was, 'now that was really stupid,' and offered herself up for another interview.

Miss Iler Bounds Pope.

I asked about her last name. "You mean Pope, like . . .?"

"Like THE," she informed. "God! That'll probably offend every Catholic alive." Iler laughed and swatted another fly.

Miss Iler's family is from Drew, Mississippi, and her grandparents owned a large plantation in those parts. However, the plantation's next-door neighbor was Parchman Farm, the great prison in the Mississippi Delta, and that fact alone discouraged the building of their plantation home on that particular site. So they built it inside the city limits of Drew. It's the largest home there. And since Iler's mother divorced when Iler was very young, she and her mother spent most of Iler's young life inside this grand plantation-style home.

I found this thing about Parchman Farm very interesting. My cousin, Will Taylor, had written a book about this famed prison called *Down on Parchman Farm*. And being that Will is from Mississippi, I knew Iler would want to meet him. She did.

Iler had abandoned her fly swatter and portable phone for a large bag of green snap beans that she was now snapping into small pieces and throwing into a plastic bowl. And trust me, when she's done cooking those beans, they *will* seduce your pallet. As she snapped, swatted an occasional fly and answered questions about the day's specials, I began my interview.

The first and foremost question still lingering inside my mind was why she had let Bill go. So I asked about the day he had inquired about the waiter's position.

"Well," she said. "He walked through the door and immediately handed me his card. I looked at it and saw his name printed across the front. William Lafayette Holcomb. I immediately recognized the last name and asked if he was from Clarksdale, Mississippi. He said hesitantly, 'Yes, I am.' I then asked if his grandfather had been a dentist. He confirmed that he had. I then informed him that his grandfather had been our family dentist for years. And that's when I decided that Bill Holcomb was family."

"Family?" I said.

"Hell, yes. The guy was from a good Mississippi Delta family and that was good enough for me. I thought."

"Then what was your first clue?"

"He said he didn't need to make much money. That was a hellava clue. The next was when I took him for dinner that night. I noticed that he didn't drink. That was great for me, 'cause I was paying. But I didn't buy the notion that he was a teetotaler. However, I soon learned that Bill knew very little about the inner workings of a restaurant. He may have owned and operated several, but he must have been in a fog while he did it. There was no way I could comfortably turn my restaurant over at any given time to this man. I just couldn't. And I felt bad that I was going to have to renege on my offer. But I had to. And I did suspect that he was an alcoholic. And that's what happened."

I knew Iler had made the right decision. Besides, if Bill had gone to work then, he would not have come to my house that day, and I would not have insisted he go to rehab. I truly felt that the entire scenario had played out as fate would have it.

But Miss Iler was a real character and I was eager to dig around in her life. I had told her how much she reminded me of my Aunt Maggie, but still had not mentioned my aunt's proclivity to stand while peeing.

Of course, I was very interested in the fact that Miss Iler was a lesbian, had been married and had a son whom she absolutely adored. So I began by asking her about her childhood. I suspected that Iler was a very precocious little girl and there were some interesting accounts of those earlier years.

Miss Iler obliged me by recounting the time she and another little girl of equal precociousness had been given their weekly nickels. They immediately left on foot for downtown Drew. As they arrived, they reached inside their pinafores for their nickels. To their gasping horror, their nickels were gone.

About that time, the town banker stopped to ask why they looked so distraught. With trembling chins and down-swept mouths, the girls relayed their dilemma. The kind gentleman gave the girls a soft pat, retrieved two quarters from his pocket, handed them over, and with a smile proceeded on his way.

Since Iler and her friend were not stupid, and a quarter afforded five times the worth of a nickel, they stuffed their newly acquired wealth inside their pinafores, then proceeded to take regular trips to town and look painfully down in the mouth.

One day, Iler's mother happened to open the top drawer of Iler's dresser and saw this wealth of cash. Poor Iler was now faced with her mother wanting to know where in the hell she had gotten all those quarters. So Iler told her.

"Oh my, Jesus," her mother wailed. "You've been panhandling on the streets of Drew." And Iler guessed that, in fact, she had—but more intelligently than most five or six year olds.

"You were only five?" I said, trying to imagine such precociousness at that age.

"I couldn't have been much more than that. I do know that I still wore pinafores when I was in the first grade because I got really bad spanked because Mother was having bridge club, and it had rained and all these worms came out. And I thought, man that is so neat. I'm gonna get some worms in case somebody goes fishing. I had two little puffy pockets—the same pockets I had put my quarters in. Anyway, I filled them up once and I went in to the bridge club. They were all playing, and, you know, I was dressed real cute, because there were people over. Mother said, 'sugar what you got in your pocket?' And I said, 'got some worms,' and put 'em right in the middle of the table.

"Well, of course, they turned the table over and screeched and hollered. And I thought this was Goddamn stupid 'cause I knew Mother fished and stuff. So I figured the other mothers didn't and she had to do it to keep up with them. I, I guess that's what I thought. Good God, that's been a looooong time ago. But, growing up in a little old town—it is kind of funny because see, you gotta have a mother like I had. By the time I learned to drive and all, I'd come in and Mother would say, sumbody saw you turning the corner today. Sumbody saw you over in Cleveland."

"Cleveland?" I said.

"Yeah. It's a little old town about 16 miles away. Anyway, I'd get really mad and I'd try to figure out who was telling on me. I had it narrowed down to three people. And I just purely hated their guts. I mean—I was never even real nice to them. Wasn't real ugly either 'cause I knew I'd get in trouble. Well, as years passed most of them died. I was so ugly to one that—the one who I thought it really was kinda, was the one whose strawberries I'd stomped years back. My punishment did not occur until I was fourteen. He died and my mother made me go to his funeral. 'You stomped his strawberries,' my mother said, 'and now it's payback.' I said, 'Do I really have to?' She said, 'Yip, huh huh.' But I was kinda glad really 'cause I wanted to see if he really was dead 'cause I really did hate him.

"But anyway, years passed and I married. I was home one day and my brother came in. He was about fifteen then. And my mother said, 'Joe, somebody saw you turning the corner really bad.' And Joe said, 'Well, yes ma'am, I won't do that anymore.'

"After Joe left the room I said to Mother, 'Well I know who it is. It's Mr. Brisco. He's the only one living.' Mother said, 'What are you talking about?' I said, 'That sumbody that always told on us? Well, I had it narrowed down to three people and two of um are dead.' Mother said, 'What makes you think it's anybody?' Well—I looked at her dumbfounded. 'You mean to tell me it wasn't anybody?' She said, 'Huh huh.' Then she said, 'If you tell Joe, I'll spank you.' And you know, whether I was grown or not, I thought she might. If she had a mind to do it."

"Sounds like your mother had your devilish humor," I said.

"She did. She was also the prettiest thing in the Delta. After she divorced our father, she had guys coming and going. They were swarming like flies. I loved it. But there was this one guy we loved, so we told him we wanted him to ask our mother to marry him. And he said, 'Well, you know, you'd better ask her.' They'd already talked about it and of course they did.

"So while they were on their honeymoon my brother and I learned THE FINGER. We were so proud of learning the finger. My brother was eight years old and I was eight and a half."

I looked at Iler skeptically. But since I was never very good at math, I let the age thing pass. However, I found out later that Iler had been eleven, not eight and a half.

"And we kept giving it to Grandmother," she said. "And of course my grandmother just laughed. 'Cause she didn't know what it meant either. Had no clue. So we thought that must be really something funny. Kinda like go to hell but in a nice way, ya know, 'cause we didn't know anything else. Well, Mother and Vernon came back from their honeymoon and you know, they brought us all these presents, they were coming in the door with all these presents and we like—da da—shooten the finger. Well, Mother almost had a heart attack. Pulled us upstairs, I remember, and she sat us down and said, 'do you know what that means?'

"We said, 'No.'

"And she said," 'Well I do and if you ever do it again . . .'

'We've been giving it to grandmother and she didn't care.'

"Mom said, 'Has she been giving it to everybody?'

"She was just frantic. She said, 'if my mother has been shooten the bird, I will kill you children.'

"Maybe we really did know that it meant something dirty. I don't know, but I never did shoot it again until I got up in high school. I knew damn well what it meant then.

"Poor Mother. I can just see her now. She was devastated when she walked through that door."

Knowing that I was deathly allergic to cigarette smoke, Iler sprang from the table. "I'm gonna sit over here," she said. "But I'll yell, 'cause I got to have a cigarette. I've been working too hard." Iler sucked in an enormous cloud of smoke, tilted her head and blew it straight up into the air.

"As opposed to a large town," she said. "You know you are loved. Everybody, Paulette. It's not just your mama and daddy and grandma and grandpa and your brothers and sisters—it's everybody. Everybody loved you. I remember so well coming home one weekend. First weekend, I think, when I was in college. And I ran into Archie Manning. (Archie Manning was a very famous quarterback for the New Orleans' Saints in the '70s.) Archie was a little boy; he was about ten years younger than I was. And he said, 'Iler Ann, where have you been? Have you been to college?' And I said, 'Uh huh, I sure have.' He said, 'I'm so glad to see you. Will you stay home?' I said, 'No I, I can't stay home, Archie.' He was just a kid. A little kid.

"One of the greatest things happened in here, just not long ago.

And I still think of them as children although they're all fifty years old. Women ten years younger than I—there were eight of them—were having a little class reunion here at the restaurant. And they came in and made me tell them who they were."

"And?" I said. "How did you do?"

"I—I, did pretty well. I got five out of eight."

"That *is* good. Quite amazing as a matter of fact."

"I was impressed," she admitted boldly. "That sort of thing makes you feel good. And they—they all remembered me."

"How could they not?" The idea of anyone forgetting this woman was ludicrous.

"And lots of them had dated my brother. And later, when I was talking to him about it, 'cause he dated younger girls when he got divorced—his first divorce. Anyway, one of them didn't say she dated him. And I was telling him who all was here and who dated him, and he said, 'Brenda didn't say she dated me?' And I said, 'No.' He said, 'She's the only one I fucked.' And I said, 'Well, that could be it. You just hit it on the nail.' But I said, 'Of course I told that time I caught you in the bed with that Betty Ann Boozeman."

"Who?" I said.

"Betty Ann Boozeman. She was a holier-than-thou child. And ugly—God!"

"You caught him in the bed with her?" I asked.

"Yep. I sure did. And I said that's the ugliest girl. And he said, 'But they all look alike in the dark.'"

I started to crack up, holding my sides with laughter.

"Shit," Iler giggled. "I've got my kitchen going now. They won't be able to work."

But Miss Iler pushed on.

"About everybody in my family is kinda funny. Now my grandmother wasn't very funny . . ."

"Yeah," I said. "But she made you drive her to Memphis when you were twelve."

"Well she was just gutsy. I had a big old fat horse. You could stand on it and everything. For a child, it was the best thing I could of had. And I had been ridin' on her back. Standing up. All over the yard. Well, I came in and announced that I was going to be a trick rider. In the circus. My grandmother didn't bat an eye.

"She said, 'Well, get out there and keep practicing.' She said," 'You know. You can do anything you wanta do. It's your generation.

Your time.'

"You know—I've never backed off of a Goddamn thing."

And I had no doubt of that.

"Now she didn't think that for my mother," Iler said. "She wanted my mother home. Goddamn! There we were, I was seven years old, Mother's dating, and Mother had to be home at midnight. I mean, Goddog. *I* didn't have to be home at midnight when I was eighteen."

"But yo' mama did," I said.

"My mama did. Oh, oh, oh. My grandmother was so strict on my mother. Unbelievable strict on her. And thought I could do no wrong. I came in one night. I was in college. Drunk as a hoot owl. Knew I was drunk, so I got home early. And they were all awake, sitten in the living room. And Mother turned around to grandmother and said, 'MOTHA! Look at her. Drunk as a dog.'

"Grandmother said, 'That child's not drunk, just tired.'

"I thought, if I can just get up these stairs without fallin' down, I'd be a lucky sonabitch. And I didn't fall.

"You know, Mother knew I was drunk one Christmas Eve. I was still in college. And she had bought this huge train set. Enormous. Well, you can't put them together very well drunk. She had my date and me in the floor most of the night—Christmas Eve night putten that thing together. I sobered up before it was over and got it put together with all the diddly dos and stops and everything. But she did stuff like that to me on purpose. So you knew you were going to get in trouble.

"Now my brother got really drunk one night and fell in the john. He was a bad sight when he arrived home and Grandmother was up drinking coffee. Grandmother looked at him. Of course he said he just wanted to die.

"She said, 'My son, now when you dance you have to pay the piper.'

"Mother had to take him to the doctor to get the stitches in his eyes and a Tetanus, after all he'd been in the toilet—with his face. And this real cute little girl he'd been seeing said, 'What—what happened to you?'

"Mother said, 'he fell in the toilet.'

"Well, later he had to go back to school. His car was broken. So he had to go back to school in one of his friend's jeep. An OPEN jeep. With a hangover."

"Another hangover?" I guessed the toilet incident had long since been forgotten.

"Yes," Iler said. "He offered me everything including his allowance for a semester to drive him back. I was married and I said, 'HELL NO. Just like Grandmother said, 'When you dance—' He said, 'I don't even won't to think about it.'

"But they were very lenient with us. I was allowed to drink at the country club."

"What age?" I wanted to know since I knew Bill was allowed to drink in his early teens.

"Fifteen."

"Really? Bill was, too. Home and the country club."

"Well, they knew I was gonna do it. Hell, I drank at home. But Mother told me, when I started datin' and all, in cars, going out—she said, 'Now Iler, I do not want you to go to Andy's Tap Room.' And I said, 'WHY?' And she said, 'Because I just don't want you in there and I mean you better not go in there.' But of course I couldn't wait. And I went all the time and I thought God, Mother is such a fool. This is the nicest place and this is the nicest man. So she's a fool.

"One day we were in Cleveland (that's Mississippi) shopping, my mother and I, and who comes walking down the street but Andy LaGronne. And I thought, Oh. I'm just gonna die. I hope he doesn't speak to me. Well, he spoke to my mother, hugged her and kissed her and said, 'I've been taking a lot of good care of your child.' So, mother and I go on and shop and I said, 'Mother—' She said, 'Iler, I knew if I told you that you *could* go there you know you wouldn't. And it's so nice and clean and good, and Andy's watched after you for three years.'"

I smiled at Iler. "You had a very enlightened and smart mother."

"Oh," she agreed. "I sure did. And you know, she was cute as hell, too. My friends' mothers were fat and life threatening. My mother wore cute clothes. She rode a bike. Oh yeah. We'd go riden, bike riden. And one of my friends said, 'your mother riden around town like that—she otta . . .' I said, 'yeah, your mother would too if she wadden so fat.' My mother rode, played tennis. She swam. She did everything. Oh yeah, she was a cute potato. Her high school room-mate, her roommate from All Saints comes in here occasionally. She lives here."

"All Saints?" I had no idea where that was.

"All Saints. In Vicksburg. They all went there. I went there. But I got thrown out for smoking. And years passed and I have my child, and All Saints in the meantime has become co-ed. I was delighted 'cause I wanted to send my son there. He's really smart and I'm very proud of him. I always say, if you can't do but one thing, do it right. And I did it totally right. But huh, we were out one night, we were with a whole bunch of his little friends and one said, 'Miss Pope, you really went to All Saints?' I said, 'oh yes, but I got kicked out for smoking.'

"My son looked at me and gasped. I said, 'Richard, that's not so bad.' He said, 'Mother, I don't want all my friends to think you smoked pot.' I said, 'Richard. It was a Viceroy cigarette.' He said, 'Cigarette? Well, we can smoke.' I said, 'Do you?' He said, 'Hell no. No.' And he never has. Won't even ride in my car. Rents a car at the airport when he comes in."

"You smoke in your car?" I asked.

"Yep."

"Well, I'd have to rent one, too."

That was enough about smoking. Besides, I wanted to hear about Trent Lott. She had mentioned him earlier. So I said, "Tell me about your wonderful friend, Trent Lott."

Iler did not mince words. "I don't like Trent Lott's fucking ass. That sanctimonious son-of-a-bitch. I've known Trent for a long, long time. My son, Richard, was a Republican and damn near won State Attorney General in Washington State. And his party thought he was going to get 70-80,000 votes and he got 700 thousand plus. But huh, it's kinda funny, I said, 'Richard, you must have kissed every baby in the state of Washington.' He said, 'Not a single one of them under 18, Mother.' But huh, Richard knows I'm gay, and he's very comfortable with it. And Trent made this little statement on national TV that homosexuality is like kleptomania and it could be cured. So Richard gave that a lot of thought. And then he went down and switched parties. Then I wrote Trent a letter. Several page letter. I'd never written a politician in my entire life. My father was a politician, and I think all of um suck. I don't ever write um, but I wrote him, and I told him I was ashamed he was from Mississippi. I was really ashamed of his ignorance. And that I remembered that he wasn't a real nice guy anyway."

Just then the phone rang and Iler picked up the portable. "Hello," she answered. After a short pause, she said, "I'm not going to do anything this time, but I do appreciate you calling. No, I can't. I have grandchildren of my own."

Now I knew this was a lie. Her son Richard was engaged to be married and neither he or his fiancee had any children.

"Okay, bye-bye." Iler hung up the phone. "I hate those calls."

"I do too," I said.

"You know why I hate um? Because this money doesn't all go to these kids. Fifteen per cent of what they collect does. Oh, I don't give anything over the telephone. Not at all. You've gotta see my face. I'm from Mississippi. I wanta see what you look like. I wanta see the cut of your jeans."

"All right," I urged. "So you wrote Trent Lott a letter."

"I sure did. And I never heard a thing from that wimpy bastard. I don't know why either. Because if someone wrote me a letter like that, I would absolutely respond. I mean, you've got to. That's just—"

Iler lifted her fly swatter. "Goddamn!" And she murdered another round of flies. She called back to the kitchen. "All right, ya'll gonna have to come and pick up flies. Son-of-a-bitch. Every time it gets like it's gonna rain—wait a minute, let me go get one I see." And another fly fell to Iler's swatter.

"Miss Iler," I said. "I would love to hear about Richard. How did he handle the divorce and the fact that you had finally admitted your homosexuality?"

Iler smiled and freed her hands of the portable phone and fly swatter. "He wanted to live with his father," she said. "And I understood. Hell, that was a lot for a young man to deal with." Iler narrowed her eyes and gave me a wicked grin.

"And?" I said, eager to know what stirred inside her head.

"It was Thanksgiving, and I called Richard. I said, 'Richard, are you going to be at my house for Thanksgiving?' He said, 'NO.' So, I made plans to go to a friend's house. It was about 40 of us. And Richard calls the day before and said, 'I want to come home.' I called Pat and said that I couldn't come because my son wants to come home. She said, 'I think you otta bring him out here and let him meet all your friends.' Now these were all lesbians, there were no gay men. So I thought about it, and yeah, I should, because I'd already made my plans—and I called him and told him what I had really planned to do and that he could be included. He said, 'Well, I guess I otta meet your friends.'"

"How old was he then?" I asked.

"He was about 17 or 18. And I thought, he probably won't stay. But he stayed to the bitter end and fell in love with everybody. They went out of their way—they were inviting him down town to their law offices to have lunch in the executive dining room—and of course, there's no man living, I don't care if its a lesbian or a straight woman, that doesn't love to be flattered. And he said, 'you know Mom, I really like your gay friends better than I do your straight ones.'—and then he moved in with me and Susan. And we were glad to have him because he could share the chores. He had to mow and edge the yard, take the garbage out and empty the dishwasher, 'cause we hated those things. And everything else was done for him. And he could have a party anytime he wanted to. Which he didn't take advantage of, you know, but he had friends over—and ugh, it was a good thing for all of us. It was a real good thing. And he stayed until the night he didn't come home.

"Well, the first night he didn't come home I forgave him, 'cause it was really funny. His dad had come to the restaurant with a sweet young thing. And ugh, I met her and she was so young and—she was very nice, and very, very young. I mean, she was a young kid. So, about twelve-thirty or one o'clock, Dick, my ex-husband, called and asked if Richard was staying over at my house. I said not that I know of. He said he was spending the weekend with you. And he said that Richard was not in. And I said, well, don't worry about it. And Dick said, but he needs to be in. I said, when did you see him last? He said, well, Holly and I went out for a drink and Richard joined us and since I had this God-awful headache, Richard offered to take her home. And I said, well, there's your answer. And he said, 'What—what are you saying?' And I said, 'What do you think I'm saying? You idiot, he stayed with her. My God, Dick, he's much closer to her age than yours.' And he said, 'Well, you're the most disgusting bitch on earth. You otta go to a shrink.' I said, 'Well, bye. Good-bye.'

Iler shifted her eyes my way and gave me one of her evil grins. "I did the same thing," she admitted.

"The same thing?" I said.

"Yeah. One time this very young woman asked me out. And I thought. God! You are really a baby. But I'm going. Well, Richard was home and I thought, Oh God, I hope he goes out on his date before she comes. Because she's YOUNG and BEAUTIFUL. Well, he didn't. And he met her. I had to introduce him. I mean, I can't be rude. Well, I go out and he goes out and I got home a little before he did, and he came in my room and said, 'Mom, how old was your date?' And I said, I'm not gonna tell you, and he said, 'She's younger than I am.' And I said, that's right. And he said, 'Well, I'll have to hand it to you, she's prettier than my date.'

"But see, he doesn't bat an eye at stuff like that. Once when he was in graduate school, he brought home a billion people for Mardi Gras."

"Oh God!" I said.

"Oh God is right," she lamented. "And I was single at the time. And I decided that I would be—Mamma. I mean, everything short of a frilly apron. Oh, and I cooked and did all this stuff da da da da da, and when Richard got home, I said, now, don't you worry about anything, 'cause I've canceled every plan, I gonna be home. Richard said, 'home for what?' I said, I'm just gonna be Mamma. Richard said, 'Mamma, they know you're gay—shit. You're the only one who seems to have a problem. You know, I was at Uncle Woody's when you took yours and Susan's picture and put it in the desk drawer.' I said, 'Were you?' He said, 'Yeah, didn't you see Uncle Woody take it right back out and put it up?'

"I didn't want that picture out. Susan was sittin in my lap. It was the cutest picture of us. And he got it and framed it."

"Who?" I asked. "Your son?"

"No, Woody, my brother. One of the funniest things my brother ever said as long as I can remember—in my life was one time this really up-tight guy, and I'm gonna let him remain nameless."

"Well, that's all right," I said. "But if you change your mind—"

"This friend of theirs came by Woody's office one day and he said, 'God, I feel so sorry for Brad.' And my brother says 'Why?' The guy says, 'Shelby's coming home for Christmas and he's bringing his LOVER.' Woody said, 'Yeah, and you should feel sorry for me.' And the guy said, 'How come?' Woody said, 'Well, Iler's coming home and she's not bringing her lover and I really like that woman a lot.' The guy said, 'Iler, ain't gay.' Woody said, 'Oh yes she is.' The guy said, 'I dated Iler!' Woody said, 'Probably what made her gay.'

"I did date him. The asshole. You know, my brother doesn't seem to have a problem with it. None of my family does."

"Well, that's the way it should be," I said.

"You know. I had a friend that hadn't told her parents. And we were talking about it. And I asked her. Have they quit asking you when you're gonna get married? And she said, 'Yeah, a long time ago.' I said, 'They know.'

"Now I didn't tell my mother. She guessed it. She said she didn't understand it, but if that's what made me happy, she was all for it.

And my grandmother never knew, didn't need to know. But she always loved all my friends. She just didn't know what they were.

"You know," Iler suddenly announced. "If I didn't already have a date for this swanky-ass party I'm going to, I'd take Bill."

"What kind of a party is it?" I asked.

"It's very formal. It's these two guys I know. They have one of the prettiest houses I've ever seen in my life."

"Where is it?" I wanted to know.

"On Magazine. Just off the corner of Jackson. It's pretty on the outside but not like it is on the inside. It's furnished unbelievably. It would be nice to take Bill. He needs to know there are people like that. They are lovely, gracious and charming."

Bill was well aware of people like that. He simply did not want to be known as "people like that," which was dreadfully frustrating and made no sense at all. Bill had no problem living the life of a drunk, being known as a drunk, openly admit to unemployment, food stamps and such. But heaven forbid he find a healthy, loving and stable relationship with another man. The only relationships he embraced were surreptitious trysts behind doors that housed the pitiful and needy, or the occasional rendezvous with an upper who needed a quick blow job.

None of it made sense. I could no more find reasoning with this than I could turning down a hundred million dollars. But reasoning was one of the crucial elements that, over the years, had slipped slowly and silently into the void.

Chapter 12

What causes someone who has extraordinary intelligence, breeding and wit, to be manipulated by drugs and alcohol? To endure the pain and humiliation of a fringe existence rather than dealing with the pain that could ultimately rescue and put them on a more optimistic track of self worth and success?

For me, the latter seems the easier route.

For Bill, the former.

I had known Bill for close to a year now, so I felt comfortable to begin my probe into the last 47 years of his life. Would I uncover even a morsel of information that could help my friend? Or was help beyond reach or imagination? I didn't care. I was going to plunge headlong and dig as far down as I could.

I had asked Bill about his childhood.

Had he a loving relationship with his father? Did his father tuck him into bed at night; tell him marvelous stories and kiss him goodnight? All the things my own father had done. For me, these acts of love and affection had been commonplace. For Bill, they had not existed. At least not where his father was concerned.

Bill was not the son his father had envisioned. Bill was not a macho little boy. He hated to hunt but did it to please his father. He was extremely intelligent, far ahead of his peers and did not fit in socially. In fact, he finished his schooling at home. However, Bill was blessed with a marvelous personality and a talent for acting. Since he could mesmerize an entire audience with his outrageous stories, Bill Holcomb's young life laid the groundwork for charades of half-truths, lies and imaginary scenarios.

Bill had told me of his adventures as a seventeen year old, how he came to New Orleans and suddenly found himself in the throes of a social order so surreal that even today it would seem like something out of a Salvador Dali painting.

But the alcohol ran fast and furious and Bill found himself back on the Gulf Coast, where chunks of time seemed to have simply dropped from his memory.

One day his father told him to dress and come to his office.

"Did you do it?" I asked.

"Mmm huh," he said. "I, I had had some blackouts. I was showered, dressed, packed and went out to get in my car. But it wasn't there. I had to walk to his office. About two miles. The hottest day in the world. And when I got there, he told me I was going to live in Chicago."

"Chicago?" I said. "Did you know anybody in Chicago?"

"Not a living soul. So, I took the bus from Pass Christian to New Orleans and met Kathy and Edward at St. Charles Tavern. That night they drove me to the airport to catch the night coach to Chicago. I landed in Chicago, found out how to get downtown—I only had fifty dollars."

"Did you know why you had been sent to Chicago?"

"He just wanted me away from him."

"But why Chicago?"

"I don't know. Guess it was the first thing that came to mind. Oh, he had done some business there. I guess he thought his friends there could guide me or whatever. But I didn't want to be anywhere near his fucking friends."

"But why?"

"Because. I knew he had told them I had fucked it all up. Dirty filthy bastard. All he gave me was fifty bucks. And here I was in Chicago at three or three-thirty in the morning. So I took a bus to the Loop. Dawn was coming up. I walked around the Loop for hours. And then I went and checked into the Y. For the next few days I wandered around and tried to acclimate myself.

"One night I went to several nightclubs on Rush Street. I went to see Billy Ekstine at the Scotch Mist. And then I went to a transvestite place across the street, and saw a dancer who looked familiar. After the show was over, I asked the bartender if that girl was from New Orleans. He said that he thought she was. I said that I would love to meet her. So he did and she came out—not still in drag though. We talked for the longest time. She was so flattered that I had recognized her picture and knew her from the My-Oh-My Club. It had been years since I had been there. This chick must have been 80."

I wondered how many years Bill was talking about. At this point, he couldn't have been older than early twenties. This made me wonder how old he had been when he had first seen this performer.

"I mean," Bill said. "I had only been to the My-O-My Club once in my entire life and this guy was great. Anyway, I moved out of the Y and into a very cheap hotel. No job and no money— well, I—I did have a little money left. I had found this job at the *Tribune* newspaper. Calling people asking, you know, telemarketing. Until I blew out the entire electrical system."

"What!"

"Well, I had gone to wash out my headset and mouth set with this S2-37 whatever it is, and sparks ran out all over and closed the *Tribune* for an hour. They asked me not to come back.

"That was the night I went back to the Parkview Hotel, put on shorts, shirt and sandals and headed toward the lake. I don't know if I was going to throw myself in the lake—I probably wouldn't have, it was too cold. But I was really down in the dumps. And this old man— I say old man, he wasn't an old man—he had fallen down and I helped him up. He thanked me very much and I asked him if I could get him a taxi. He said no but I could help him back to his apartment because he had had too much to drink. We walked into his building, got in the elevator and went to his apartment. My God, I couldn't believe the view. It was the most beautiful skyline I'd seen in my entire life.

"He asked me if I'd like to have a drink and I did, of course. And we sat up and we talked almost the whole night long. And he was with a brokerage firm called Whitewell. George, I'd say was my father's age, and I impressed him because even though I didn't know that much about the business world per se, I read a lot and knew enough to have an intelligent conversation.

"Then he asked me if I'd go to bed with him and I said yes and I did. And you know, I don't think we even did anything that night but sleep together. You know—literally. And the next morning—I think the next morning was Saturday and he made me get in a taxi and go back to the hotel to get my things. He said I was going to stay with him."

"Bill," I said. "You could have had a wonderful relationship with him."

"I did. But I did have a great relationship with him. I mean, he did have a hard time keeping it up though."

"But...but even—forget that," I said.

"I—I stayed with him for quite some time But he said, 'now look. I have to take my holiday. I have two weeks off.' Then we started talking about traveling. He said he knew someone in the travel business and that's when he took me to Drake's Travel—the building soon to become the Playboy Club—and George introduced me to Bruno, the owner.

"Now since George was going to Guatemala and I had been there, I planned the entire trip. Bruno said that not even he could have done better and he had been in the travel business for 40 years. So we then went to this very chic bar in the hotel, had several drinks then went back to George's apartment. That night we went to the Barclay Club then went back and talked that night, went to bed, and I guess we did a bunch of stuff.

"But you know, I thought I had been saved."

"Well," I said. "You had."

"Yeah. Well, then he went and bought every newspaper ever printed and read them. That night we went to his friend's house. This guy had open house every night, seven nights a week for cocktails. He was married to the daughter of some big cheese of old Chicago wealth. And this guy had a twin brother that was queer as a three dollar bill. He was a problematic rich kid child and was married.

"And that's when I got launched in Chicago. I mean, I met everybody that was anybody. Started going to black tie affairs, white tie affairs. I called Mamma and told her, you wanted me to come to Chicago, I'm here and I need you to send me all my formal wear and send them now. They arrived almost immediately.

"I then went about to find a job in the travel industry and that's how I ended up at Thomas Cook Travel. We had a very wet lunch so I knew I was going to like the job. Then George comes back from Guatemala and by that time I'm dating this girl from Lake Forest named Susie—like a nut!

"Well, she immediately took to me. She was so in love with me that it was embarrassing."

"Mmm huh," I said. "Just like me and David. I've been there."

Loving a gay man is just about the most torturous thing a woman can go through. I had been there, done that, and *never* wanted to experience it again.

"It was just ridiculous," Bill said. "I mean, it was so bad that I couldn't even get it up. And huh, she then started saying that I should get away from George. She called him Uncle George. She had known him since she was a kid. She said that I should get my own place. Well, I said that I couldn't afford it with what I was making at Thomas Cook. But she said she would find me a room. So she found me an apartment in the chic part of the city. And she paid my first month's rent."

"She wanted you so badly," I said.

"She thought she had me. So we went to all these parties together and all that commotion. And drank swills of scotch every night. I mean, I met wealth, royalty and everything in-between. And I screwed man, woman, separate and together, and holy Christ—I don't know.

"Well, now it was my birthday, and Susie, unbeknownst to me, had gotten tickets to the Black Hawks' game, which in those days were scarcer than hen's teeth. I mean, this hockey team was so popular that you either had to take a cab or a limo. And Susie calls me up and says, 'guess where we're going Monday night.' Well, I knew where *I* was going, I was going to have dinner with Christina, you know, and um, Susie announced all this commotion and I said that I wish she had told me because I had made these plans. And she said, 'how could you have made plans? You don't know anybody here.' And I said, 'gees, well I'm terribly sorry— you know.'

"Well, meanwhile Susie had moved into the same building that George lived in and there was a vacant lot on the corner which gave her visual access to my apartment. But I didn't think anything of it. So that night, I left my apartment, walked across the street to Christina's apartment. When I got there the phone rang. It was for me. So Christina asked who was calling. Susie wouldn't give her name so Christina wouldn't give me the phone. So we dropped that by the way side, had a few drinks and went to the Palmer House. Later we went back to the apartment and carried on and screwed and stuff and had more drinks.

"So then I moved in with Christina. But then her husband came back into town early and you know, I wasn't used to running around with married women and all. Christina made up some wild story about me being there—But God, I was a wreck. And then there we were— the three of us."

"The three of you?"

"Oh yes. He didn't mind me with his wife as long as he was included. But then they had this huge fight and that's when I found out that they weren't really married. I then found out that this guy had worked for Trans Canada, which later became Air Canada, and he was opening their office in London. Well, he had met Christina when she was a dance girl from La De Da, it's called something else now, in London. She was well known in London among cafe society. Anyway she had gone with him to Canada then moved to Chicago. Christina and I lived together, after all of that, for about a year. She ran this very posh retail boutique and we—actually we lived a very mundane kind of life. I mean, we worked, we ate, we drank, we screwed."

"Wait," I said. "Speaking of living with Christina. Haven't you been married before?"

"Yes. I had actually just divorced Anne six months before I moved to Chicago."

"How old were you then? And who was Anne?"

"Twenty-six. And she was Anne Carr Porter from Memphis. The whole la de da. Miss Hutchinson's school, *Les Passés.* You know, the whole Memphis society. She was working at the *Times Picayune* and living in the Quarter. I hadn't seen her in years. We ran into each other at the Press Club. And we sort of had a grand reunion, which ended up, needless to say after *many* gin and tonics, in bed.

"The truth of the matter is, Anne was not found of working, and at that particular time, my Dad was on one of his rolls—you know, full page advertisements in the Sunday paper—you know, he owned half of the Mississippi Gulf Coast. And I suppose I must have looked like a pretty good catch. Poor bitch, because my father never gave me squat that I didn't work for. And that is the gospel truth.

"Anyway, about eight weeks later we got married. And it was a *Delta* wedding in the *grand* tradition. Sometimes I think that Lady Di styled her wedding after ours. Six months later we divorced. She hadn't even finished writing her thank you notes."

"Well, you dumb shit. You shouldn't have gotten married in the first place."

"Screw you. You don't know why I got married. Do you?"

"I have my suspicions."

"There you go into that psychological shit again."

"Then forget it."

"No. The reason that I got married is that my sister, Susan, married John in October and had so much fun with all these grand parties and the liquor flowing, that I decided that I was not going to be outdone by my sister. So bless Pete. When Anne and I announced our engagement, we had so many parties proposed for us, that, if everyone who wanted to entertain us, could have, we would have had to put the marriage off for a year."

"Oh. Well, then I understand," I remarked. "A *damn* good reason for you to get married."

"Well, plus the fact Anne was dead attractive, witty, smart and loved to drink."

"Another good reason. So, now back to Chicago."

"All right. But I got married twice in Chicago."

"What! You've just got to be kidding."

"No. I'm not kidding at all. First there was Christina."

"Good God, Bill. Hadn't you learned your lesson by now?"

"Well, it's really not what you think. It was simply a piece of paper so that Christina could buy a business and stay in the United States."

"Oh. Well, I guess that's okay."

"And then I married her sister for the same reason."

"What a nice guy you are."

"Or a bastard. Don't think I did it just for them."

"Then why?"

"Well, Christina made twice as much money as I did. Had a perfectly beautiful apartment while I was living in a converted telephone booth. Living with Christina was like living a life of pure hedonism. Life started every morning with her sitting in her boudoir putting on her face, sipping a screw driver while I shaved and dressed, and sipped screw drivers with her. Everybody at Thomas Cook said that I was the happiest person they had ever worked with. And the stock of Brach's peppermint candy company split four times in one year."

"What does that have to do with anything?"

"Because, I ate at least two bags of peppermints on my way to work."

"Did you drink during the day and manage to work at Thomas Cook?"

"Mmm huh."

"And you could do that?"

"Mmm huh. Yeah. Hell, my boss did too. Dan was a bigger lush than me. We went out to lunch at least twice a week. We wouldn't leave until about one-thirty or two, and when we left, Laura, the receptionist would very cattily say, see you tomorrow morning, because she knew we wouldn't be back."

"I'm sure she did. So, what about you and Christina?"

"Well, Christina and I stayed together and we talked about getting married. At that time I didn't know how much older she was than I. I mean, she's almost ninety now. You see, when I was twenty-five, twenty-six, she was in her fifties. She was like you. She didn't look a day over thirty. She had this absolutely exquisite looking skin, not one wrinkle, superb body, very statuesque, you know. And could drink like a goat. I mean you and I and an elephant couldn't hold that much even if we had someone to help us. She could walk into a room and everyone knew that Christina was there. And if anyone said anything to her, she'd say, 'oh, fuck you.'"

"She sounds like Pat," I said. "You know, that British sitcom, *Absolutely Fabulous*."

"Very much so," Bill agreed. "One time we went to New York the week before Christmas. That's when her ex beau, Calhoun whatever, that did the Saatchi and Saatchi advertisement, and he took us to lunch at Twenty One and all these fabulous places and the theatre."

"You were making good money by then?" I asked.

"By that time I was. And huh, we had a wonderful time. Good old Northwest was just nine-hundred dollars away."

"Northwest," I reminisced. "I could have been your stewardess. What year was this?"

"Oh, the early seventies."

"Then I wasn't. I quit flying in 1965. But I imagine your father was quite happy with you about now. You were working, making good money. Doing great."

"Oh yes. I was doing fine. Wasn't asking him for a thing. Never did ask him for anything. Anyway, we got back to Chicago and, huh, Christina and I got into a big fight."

"About what?"

"I don't remember. I've forgotten exactly. I think she wanted to move. And I loved our apartment. And she wanted to move to some high rise or something. And I didn't want to move. And I was getting tired of her. And one night we had such a fight that I even called my boss and asked if I could stay with him. He was separated from his wife and had an apartment. He said he would come and get me and we'd figure out what to do. So I packed up everything and I left. And then I moved back to the apartment I had had before.

"Then Thomas Cook gave me the Rotary Club Convention. And

that took me out of commission because I was so busy with the Rotary Club thing. And then I quit. And I didn't know where I was going to go next."

"You quit? Why?"

"Because I was so mad at him making me do Rotary. Then I went to work for Gold Coast Travel for a girl named Sue who was Jewish but claimed she wasn't. And that's how I met Louisa Gillman who was Jewish but didn't look it. She lived on Lake Shore Drive, had this adopted son who was crazy—she had the biggest hair in the whole world, eight fur coats, more memberships in more clubs—she just had more money than God.

"I worked for Susan a year. It was more like playing. I was always on her guest list. She always needed extra men. Talking about working for her—she took me to her apartment and seduced me. HA! What a drag."

"Was it really?"

"Yeah. The maid came in the next morning. It must have been her mother's maid or something, 'cause she went into this big Jewish woman's decline. Oh God, what a fiasco that was."

Chapter 13

The Crain, Holcomb, Dedini (that's Renée's last name) home was running splendidly.

Our routine ticked like a Swiss time piece. Bill had only a week of outpatient treatment left and we were looking forward to having entire days together to collaborate on our book.

Renée had begun working on an elaborate gown for the woman that had recently purchased that sprawling Greek Revival masterpiece at the corner of Third and Coliseum.

Remember way back when—the young girl whose husband, while on their honeymoon, had committed suicide at the Jahrezeiten on Maximillian Strasse? Well, this house was her family home and had recently been purchased by a friend of Buzz Harper's. Buzz was planning all sorts of parties and such for the new owners. And of course, Mr. Harper would be decorating this palatial home with the most exquisite antiques and furnishings known to man. So Renée was anxiously working on one of the many gowns to be worn by the lady of this newly acquired manor. The lady, I might add, is quite beautiful, has a wicked sense of humor and will fit into Garden District society very nicely.

Now Renée, when first arriving in New Orleans, was introduced to a friend of mine who works part time for Buzz Harper. His name is Codie Scott and he's as cute as can be. He's from Plaquemines Parish (we have parishes here, not counties) and at one time worked on the oyster boats out in the Gulf. He is around thirty and has this curious innocence about him that adds to his charm and sex appeal. He also fancies himself a cowboy and designer of country-western wear, which he takes very seriously, and was thrilled to meet Renée.

Renée, not being particularly bored at the sight of this guy, offered her knowledge and years of wisdom in design and a friendship was born. So one day Codie asked Renée if she would mind paying a few of his bills.

No, it's not what you think.

Codie does not have a checking account and he probably never has, so he has to go to the check cashing facilities to pay his electric and phone bills. He also wanted her to pay his cable bill, which was in a different location.

Since Renée was without a car and I had an errand to run, I suggested that we go together. Besides, she wasn't as yet acclimated to our circuitous city and would have probably ended up right back where she started. So we headed up Washington and turned right onto Prytania. That's when Renée's eyes suddenly widened.

Mine did too.

Now I'm pretty used to most of the madness that is ingrained into this city, but I just had to laugh at what I saw rolling up Prytania. Renée was almost bent over with laughter.

In the absolute middle of the left-hand lane was a very nice looking black man in a wheelchair, pushing furiously up Prytania with twelve cars moving at a snail's pace behind him. It occurred to me that not one horn was honking, which is a rarity here in The Big Easy. Renée and I watched in awe and laughter as this procession moved past us. I quickly looked into the rear-view mirror and saw that the man had made a sharp turn onto Washington and was headed toward St. Charles. The procession accelerated and the cars faded out of sight.

Renée looked at me as though this entire scene might have been an aberration. I quickly reminded her that this was the reason she had fallen in love with our city. And like Bill had said to me, this is New Orleans. It's not real.

After my errand was completed, we found ourselves headed down Canal where Cox cable was located. About a block away, we noticed a black man on a bicycle, smack dab in the middle of the street and headed right toward us. Not only was he on the wrong side of the street, he was aimed squarely for the center of my car. Renée let out several blasphemous shrieks and I might have said one or two myself, but Cox cable had appeared and I lurched into their parking lot. Renée slumped into laughter and braced herself against the dashboard. I just shrugged my shoulders and reminded her that she needed to go pay

Codi's cable bill.

About five minutes later, Renée returned and we continued on down Canal. Just as we reached Claiborne, we saw this young and very muscular black guy emerge from around the concrete support that was holding up Interstate 10. He swayed and stumbled, performed a backward jig then propelled himself forward and disappeared around the other side of the concrete support. There was little doubt the poor guy had indulged himself in long hours of hard drink the night before and as Iler's grandmother would say, it was time for him to pay the piper.

So we figured he had collapsed into the bush and would sleep it off. But no sooner than he disappeared, he appeared again. The light turned green, he stumbled into Claiborne, turned his head toward us and without so much as a bent neck, regurgitated last night's consumption into the middle of Claiborne Avenue. This act was over in a flash. He turned his head in the direction he was headed then quickly turned it back and spit. As we passed him, he seemed a bit steadier and had managed the distance across Claiborne.

"Welcome to New Orleans," I said to Renée. "Now where is this check cashing place Codi wants you to go?"

The only check cashing place I was familiar with was on Magazine Street at Jackson where Miss Bonnie always hangs out. I had to go there once when I first moved to New Orleans. I had been so busy with the move and had failed to pay the utility bill. So while I was downstairs talking with one of my tenants, the damn utility company turned off my electricity.

Now there are three ways to get into the penthouse. One is the elevator that opens directly into the apartment (but the utilities were out) and the other two are the back staircases. Since I had just moved there, I had not hidden a key to the back stairs nor did I have one on my key ring. But the key ring would have been of no use anyway, since I had the elevator unlocked and had no need to have my keys. So there I was, both of my Scotty dogs locked in the penthouse and me with no way to get to them. And no amount of yelling and cussing and commotion was getting my electricity turned back on. I even told them I had two babies locked upstairs. But then I admitted they were my dogs and that was that.

So I immediately called Buzz and Les. They knew the bigwigs at Entergy and were on the phone immediately. In the interim, Les called someone to bring over a fifty foot ladder, where he then climbed into my solarium.

Now this was an arresting sight, since Les is drop-dead gorgeous, six-foot-four and had every woman and gay man on that part of St. Charles Avenue in still-pause.

But Les was oblivious to this and climbed inside my solarium and unlocked the stairwell door.

The utilities were activated soon after, but no one told *me*. So I cursed and squealed and made an irate call the next morning. That's when I was told that the utilities had been activated the night before, and that I needed to go down and flip the outside breaker. Anyway, I went to that check cashing place on Magazine the next day and paid the bill.

Codi's check cashing place was in a questionable part of town somewhere around Louisiana and Claiborne. Or maybe Washington and Claiborne. Well, Louisiana becomes Washington or it branches off—never mind. Anyway I found it, waited *forever* for Renée to pay Codi's bills. Finally she came out and got back into the car. She mumbled something about being the only white person in there, then mentioned that she had also been the only white person paying the cable bill. Now Renée doesn't have a prejudiced bone in her body. She's dated black guys and has many black friends. But you must keep in mind, she's from California where the black population is minute compared to the South. I explained that our black population was extensive and not unlike the Mexican and Oriental population she was accustomed to in California.

We then started to pull away from the curb, when I noticed a very large early model car in the middle of the street and precariously close to mine. The driver looked around 90 and seemed to lack even an iota of peripheral vision. He had no idea that I even existed. So Renée and I waited and watched cautiously as this slight of a man maneuvered his enormous car in every direction imaginable. Once I considered tapping my horn but was afraid I would either give the poor guy a heart attack or send him careening into my car. By this time a line was forming, and afraid that the horn blowing was imminent, I decided to take a chance. I waited until the man had made one of his side maneuvers then bolted past him. We made our escape, but our rear view mirror told us that the situation had not changed.

We now had but two more stops before we were safely home. We were headed up St. Charles Avenue when Renée pointed across the street, then positively fell over with laughter. I quickly turned to see what had triggered her outburst. I found myself staring into a large antiques show window filled with an exquisite French parlor suite. There in the corner of the sofa was an old black gentlemen curled up and fast asleep.

Renée, though thoroughly enjoying the antics of her newly acquired city, remarked that she didn't want to push her luck. So after stopping at Harper's Interiors where I picked up a bolt of material, we headed down Magazine toward Felicity. One last stop at the bank and we would head home.

Felicity is one of the last cobblestone streets in New Orleans. Now there's an intersection just before Felicity. And this intersection has three signs. One sign informing that you cannot turn left. Another sign that you cannot turn right and then another sign behind the signs informing again that you cannot turn left.

Renée gazed at those signs as though they had miraculously fallen from outer space. And without a hint of a smile she said, "You just gotta love this city."

Chapter 14

My house was built over one hundred and forty years ago, and with the help of Buzz Harper and Les Wisinger, I have decorated and furnished it as close to that era as possible. And New Orleans' Garden District, being a Mecca for tourists and all, I periodically open my home for tours.

So when Bill lurched into the kitchen one evening, announcing that he had been wicked, and had just invited three young tourists, who were admiring the garden, to a tour of the house, I simply told him to bring them in.

And that he did.

With his on-stage presence and grandiose manner, he took on the part of Master of Crain House. I stayed in the kitchen with my vodka and orange juice, creating an evening meal masterpiece. So I have no idea what manner of fact or fiction was presented to these young tourists.

The tour was completed, and they all ended up in the kitchen, where I was introduced to two adorable girls and one equally adorable guy. They were on a whirl-wind tour of the South and would soon be returning to their homes in Los Angeles. We spent several minutes in joyous conversation about New Orleans and such, with Bill sharing a few of his humorous stories. As Bill flourished inside his dialogue, I noticed that his eyes looked terribly bloodshot. And although I mentioned this briefly, I gave it little thought since his injured eye will periodically become irritated.

After sending our young tourists on their way, Bill went back to the garden to finish the watering. About an hour later, we sat down to dinner, watched a TV program, then decided to go upstairs to my bedroom and watch one of my old movies. Bill cleaned up the kitchen, I let Max out for his nightly constitutional, and went upstairs to get ready for bed and pop "The Spiral Staircase" into the VCR. A few minutes later, Bill and Max appeared. Max settled onto this red pillow and Bill plopped down on my king-size bed. I pushed play on the remote, and we were all in for the night to watch a very old black-and-white scary movie.

I don't think twenty minutes had even passed, when Bill sprang from the bed and announced that he was going downstairs to call his sister, Gussy, who lives in North Carolina. And though it would not have mattered, he assured me that she had an 800 number.

She did not.

I continued watching the movie until I heard Bill yelling that he wanted me to pick up the phone and talk to Gussy. Well, I was thrilled at the thought of talking with one of Bill's sisters and immediately reached for the phone. We had a wonderful conversation, and I assured her that Bill was safe, had finished his out-patient treatment and was working very hard at staying sober. By this time, Bill was back in the bedroom where he resumed his position on the other side of the bed. I said good-bye to Gussy and handed Bill the phone.

And that's when I realized that he was dead drunk.

He had been drinking earlier when I commented on his eyes. But he was now dead drunk, which meant that he had been drinking while he cleaned the kitchen and again when he went downstairs to call his sister.

I could feel the anger rising. That was my first emotion. So when he handed me the phone, I firmly placed it back, sat straight up in the bed and said, "You're drunk!"

Bill's exact words and phrases are a blur. I do remember a lot of babbling and excuses and self pity, and how I didn't understand him. Or how I couldn't know how he felt and all that other pitiful nonsense. Then I remember leaping off the bed several times screeching and hollering at the top of my lungs. I was furious with him and fed up to the gills with his rantings and self-pity. So we carried on for several minutes, me shrieking, him babbling, then momentary bouts of silence. Finally, his babbling became so incoherent that I left the bed, walked to the other side and pulled him to his feet so that I could get him back to his bedroom.

This was not particularly easy. Bill swayed, he stumbled, and he reeled. Several times I thought I would lose my balance and find us both in a heap on the hall floor. But I managed the distance and got him to his bedroom door. I was determined that he would get himself into bed. So I deposited him inside the bedroom and slammed the door.

That night, as I lay in bed, and almost certain that this had been nothing more than a hideous nightmare, I fell asleep inside the rhythm of his snores.

As if the morning was starting out no differently than the last thirty, Bill entered the Red Room with the morning paper, greeted me with his usual *bonjour*, poured his coffee, then headed for the courtyard.

I, on the other hand, sat benumbed inside the leather wing chair, drinking my morning coffee. I stared out through the French doors amazed that he could sit there, as if the previous night had been nothing more than a figment of my imagination. And I think, if only fleetingly, I fancied that it had. Everything looked the same. I was in my usual position, drinking my coffee and watching the *Today Show*. Bill was just outside sitting at the end of the wrought-iron table, and had lit one of his sweet cigars. He was perusing the society section of the paper before tackling his morning crossword puzzle. Max, as always, was stretched out on the flagstones next to his feet. The scene was eerily familiar and seemed in perfect order.

But nothing inside me felt familiar or in any manner of speaking, in perfect order. I felt as though someone had poked me with a large needle, expelling every ounce of energy that I had possessed.

I felt flat.

But there was a residue of anger that lingered, and gave me if but a fraction of determination to get on with my day. From the onset, I had vowed that if Bill took but one drink, he would be out. But this had hit me so unexpectedly, that I was still finding it difficult to perceive. I suppose I didn't want to perceive it.

Everything had been going so smoothly.

Our days had been filled with laughter and humorous conversations. We collaborated on our book and spent hours writing and editing. I felt that Bill was finally releasing years of stored up anger and guilt, and was almost certain the healing had begun. In fact, I was so optimistic that I had felt comfortable enough to leave him to house-sit over the Fourth of July weekend. Buzz and Les have a marvelous apartment on the top floor of the Calhoun Mansion in Charleston, and Daddy and I planned a trip there. Renée had flown back to California for a short visit so that left Bill to watch after the house. When we returned from Charleston, Bill was promptly waiting for us at the airport. Renée had flown in a few days prior and Bill had been equally prompt to meet her. I saw no signs that Bill was anything but on his way to a successful life of sobriety.

However, Renée later informed me that during our absence, Bill had taken the car for hours at a time, giving Renée all sorts of obscure reasons for his long absence. Not wanting to accuse him of something she could not prove, Renée had let it go.

As it turned out, it was over the Fourth of July that Bill refrained from taking his medication. Four days later, the Antabuse had left his system and he was now free to drink. And he had plenty of money to begin another binge of hard drinking.

Still numb and a bit deflated from the previous night's antics, I went about my daily routine. There were several errands I needed to run, so I asked Bill to go with me. We headed out to the post office, the bank, had lunch at a wonderful Chinese restaurant on Oak Street in Riverbend, perused an old nickel and dime store across the street, then head back to the Garden District and the A&P.

In the past, Bill would only pay for a small portion of the groceries. His needs were so few, that twenty dollars was more than enough for a month's toiletries and his sweet cigars. Everything else was furnished for him. But this time, he wanted to pay for the entire purchase. I questioned whether he really needed that much money. Without looking me in the eye, he continued separating the items his food-stamp card would allow and simply mumbled that, yes, he did.

I knew that he did not need sixty or seventy dollars for anything other than his freedom to do as he wished. But by that time, I had decided to simply bow out. What more could I do? Nothing and no one could save Bill from himself—except himself. So we proceeded through the check-out. The bill was over seventy dollars. I used my ATM card, withdrew eighty dollars of which I handed him seventy. We drove home.

After putting away the groceries, we ended up in the Red Room where I confronted him with the previous night.

All right. So I wasn't yet ready to let this go.

We bantered, screeched, squealed and hollered. At one point, I rose from the leather wing-back chair.

"This fiasco would play out famously on Broadway.

"Social Distortion!" I exclaimed, sending my arms flapping about.

This man and his nonsensical ramblings would drive a dead man to hard drink. Yet I prodded, probed, dug and tugged at every emotion I could grasp until he finally threw me a searing glare. "Okay!" he exclaimed "You think you want to hear it, then let's go. I'll tell it." He waived a languid hand toward the staircase.

I said, "You're damn right I wanta hear it." And we headed up the stairs.

It was early afternoon when I turned the tape recorder on and settled in to hear Bill's confession.

"When I came back to New Orleans in 1985," he began. "I—I wanted—I was looking for some place where I was not known as a drunk. All right?"

"Mmm huh," I nodded.

"So I came here to The City That Care Forgot so that I could drink all the time, and no one would know I was an alcoholic, you know. And of course—ha—that lasted about one hour. And then I got a job running a business over at Jackson Brewery, and was making a lot of money. A lot of money. All right? Then I thought, okay, fine, you've got a whole new life, no one knows who you are except your family in New Orleans, which of course I never got in touch with. So, I decided to see *how queer I was.* All right?"

"Mmm huh."

"All right. I knew I was gay. But I—I never wanted to admit it. It—it . . ."

"Okay."

"You know. Stuff like running around with the odd person here in the—all right, so I started going to the baths. Wonderful! I, I was a lot younger. Didn't have a paunch belly or anything. And guys would pick me up and, and use me. That's what I went for. To get my dick blown."

"Right," I said. "That's what people do that go there."

"And then, I—I—I liked it. A lot."

"Of course you did."

"All right? I liked the fact that, you know, they would do—just want to hold you and kiss you and stuff like that—that you know, I thought, huh, huh, good, they like me. They really like me! Hu, hu, and I'm not being Sally Fields—they liked me. Hu, they liked me. All right—of course they *liked me*, you know, 'cause in turn I was kissing them and blowing them and all. There's nothing I haven't done. All right? At all."

"Well, I know that," I said.

"I know you know it! I know you know it. I just don't like to— what the fuck!"

"I know. I know. Now go ahead."

"All right. I—I—"

"You need to be able to say it and be okay with it."

"But I'm not okay with—!"

"But you need to. We'll talk about that later. Go ahead and finish."

"All right. Right."

"All right. Go ahead."

"This—this—went on for years. For years, you know. And I—I, oooooh. And I'm a, I'm a damn good liar as you well know."

"The best."

"All right. You know."

"Kinda," I said. Bill was more transparent than he aspired to be.

"I'd say, you know—the best liar—"

"Kinda," I repeated.

"Kinda," he said. "Except—you know, I—I run into a bitch like you who can read me, and I don't like that atoll."

"I know you don't like that." And I didn't care if he liked it or not.

"And I'm surprised you made it through last night. Ha, ha, ha."

"Do you know," I said. "I didn't even close my door."

"I, I noticed. But, at the same time, you know—you only kill someone you love."

"Thanks a lot, you bastard."

"Ha! Anyway. I fell in love—with a guy—he was so fucking low rent man, ha. I, I don't even know why—"

"Well," I said. "Maybe he made you feel superior. You, you need that. He was low rent."

"Oh God. He was from Alabama. Ha! But he was very presentable and very nice—and also kind of weird. He was a fry cook at Déjà vu restaurant. And—and you know, he loved—he didn't love me. . ."

"He loved the idea of you." I said. "Well, not just the idea, he loved the sex, too."

"You know, I talked different. You know."

"Right."

"You know, I wasn't your typical Quarterite hustler. I tried to be. Ha, but no one would pick me up. I was too old for that. Okay, and I stayed with him for a few nights and Kathy and Edward didn't know where the hell I was. And it drove Kathy mad."

"Oh, I'm sure it did."

"He, he lived in a, huh, talk about squalor. It was like two rooms with no furniture and all, and we'd go home at night, and our provisions for the evening would be two-fifths of vodka. He'd drink one and I'd drink one. And I don't even know what kind of sex we had, we were both so stoned. He could have stuck it up my nose and I wouldn't have known the difference."

"And this was when you were working over at Jack's Brewery and making all that money?"

"Yeah. I was making two-hundred dollars a day."

"And—and you didn't want to get your own place? To have your own...?"

"I, I was having too much of what I thought was—was fu—"

"Fun?" I said.

"Fun."

"And that meant more to you than..."

"Oh yeah."

"Okay."

"And then—then I started going to the—to the queer bars. And you know—happy hour. And then there was always some number that would pick me up. But, but I would turn the tables and tell them that no, you're not picking me up, I'm picking you up. All right? Because, because I was scared to go where they wanted me to go."

"Right. You wanted them to go where you wanted to go."

"Yeah. I didn't..."

"And that was a wise thing to do."

"Well, I didn't wanta get..."

"It really was."

"Yeah. Well, well—huh, it went on for years. And, you know, the whole time—all right, I was, I was—how do you say? Commanding, I was not very docile They would say, you wanna screw me—and I would say, yeah, turn over."

"You would say—oh, they would say, you wanna screw me?"

"Yeah. Oh, I would *never* let anyone screw *me*."

"Yeah. Okay."

"*Never!* Many would certainly try. But *never!* I said, if you value your life. And—and then Kathy found out."

"Mmm huh."

"Well, she didn't really find out. But, but she knew this guy. He'd come in the shop, The Brass Menagerie, and probably the strangest dude I've ever known in my entire life. But she knew him. Like she knew a lot of people in the Garden District. And she knew I was going out to dinner with him. And she said, now Bill, Billy, be careful. You don't know him very well. But, of course, I knew exactly."

"Because you'd been with him?" I said.

"No. I'd not been with him. I just knew him from waiting on him in the shop. And, and you know, I'd become pretty savvy in my association with gay people here in New Orleans. A little innuendo here and there, you know, you can just read people. And Kathy would say, Bill, now be careful. She was the one that said to me, you are weak willed and easily led. She knows me better than you do."

"Well, of course she does." Hell, I had only known Bill for all of maybe a year.

"And I said to Kathy, don't worry about it. I can handle myself."

"Mmm huh."

"And of course, I handled myself right into his bed."

"Well. Of course you did."

"All right. You know—he—he . . ."

"Well, tell me about him though. Was he . . .?"

"You know him."

"Okay. Who was he? Tell me."

"He—I'm not going to tell you his name."

"Yes you can."

"No I'm not. You're just gonna have to guess it."

"Oh. Okay."

"He has an antique shop on Royal Street."

"Oh. You're talking about Henry."

Bill burst out laughing. "Oh God!" he screeched. "I'm not going to say anything anymore."

"Well honey, for God's sake. You tell me I know him, and you tell me he has a shop on Royal Street—of course it's Henry."

"But there are a lot of antique shops on Royal Street."

"But I don't know a whole lot of people on Royal. Anyway it was Henry. I know Henry."

"Oh yeah. It was lovely dinners . . ."

"Sure," I said. "Absolutely."

"And cocktails and the whole lot. Okay. And I thought, well, I guess I'm just as queer as I can be. I liked it."

"Well yeah."

"And all I had to do was lay down. I didn't have to be aggressive. The odd kiss. So what's a kiss. Before dying?"

"Ohhhh. Now that's a movie."

"Yeah. You know—when I came—I died. All right? And that went on for a bit, and then—Edward, who, like Kathy, also has a sixth sense—all right, you know, Henry has a lot of money."

"Mmm. I know it."

"And he does. And he has money. Money *beaucoup*. And Edward had just started this—found this guy outside of Mexico City who did this fabulous iron work."

"I need some iron work for the sides of my house," I said.

"Well let me get it for you. If we're still speaking."

"Even if we're not I'll . . ."

"Ha!"

"I'll search you out somehow."

"Ha! Paulette the Jew."

"Mmm huh!"

"Anyway. I was spending a lot of time with . . ."

"With Henry."

"Huh huh. But not in his house."

"Was he living in that gorgeous house then?"

"I never went to his house."

"So where would you and Henry go?"

"To the Chateau Le Moyne. He had a guy living at home with him."

"Was he with— ? What year was this?"

"I don't know. Late '80s."

"Never mind. So Henry considered you street trash?"

"Yeah."

"Why?"

"Because I never told him exactly who I was. Or anything. You know, I just became the *laybacker*. A new word. But Edward saw us together. We were having coffee one morning at La Madeleine's or the other place that's there on Chartres. And Edward sort of picked up that I knew him. And Henry had said something about something he needed made. And this was right before Carnival.

"And Edward was out of town and he would call me everyday,

bugging me to call Henry to find out how many of this and that he wanted, 'cause if he ordered a larger quantity he could get a better price. But I said, Edward, it's Carnival, people don't—Edward after 23 years don't you know that New Orleans—Edward said, call me, call me back immediately. So I called Henry at the shop and said, look, I've got this job on my hands right now. Edward just called about the iron work you wanted. He wants to know how many you would need, and if you could increase the amount that you need, you'll get a lower price. And Henry said, 'Bill,' he said, 'if you want me to suck your dick, come over right now. But if you want to talk about that iron work, then wait until Carnival is over. I'm in a ball. Tonight. And fuck Edward and his iron work.'"

"That sounds just like Henry," I said.

"And I would have paid for Edward to have heard that. But I called and said, now look. The man is not interested right now. It's Carnival here and you are in Mexico City and having a wonderful time and all. This city is in the throes of Carnival. And Edward, okay, okay?

"So when Edward came back, he said, 'Bill you are sure making the numbers aren't you?' And I said, 'what do you mean, I'm making the number?' And he said, 'well, you know Bill—'

"Now there was this guy who used to work for the paper whom I never had anything to do with, and there was this decorator that came in that I gave a discount to because he was a decorator. And the guy bought like 400 something dollars. And Edward wanted to know if I knew him well. Hell, I didn't know him from Adam's house cat, except he was a decorator and he was far too fake for me anyway. I mean, I like men. I mean, I don't want to be dominated, but I mean, I want a man. I mean, I want someone—it's kinda hard to explain. I mean, I want a man. I don't want a piece of shit. I want someone that can talk with me as a man. If it just so happens that we go to bed together, then we go to bed together."

"Stop!" I shrieked. "Bill, you're rambling. What does all that have to do with what Edward said?"

Bill sighed. "Nothing, I guess. Except, well, I don't know. Edward said that I was obviously not doing very well for him in the type business I pulled in. Which meant he didn't care how much money I was bringing in, he didn't want it from fags."

"I see."

"And I said, 'if you want me to bring business in, then I shall wear a jacket and tie and bring business in. But if you think I'm bringing in business because of my dick, you're out of your mind.' And Edward said, 'Oh! I didn't mean that.' And I thought, the hell you didn't.

"Now, I can get along with people. You know, sort of flirt, wink."

"I can too."

"You sure as hell can. You know how to manipulate. You can! And that's what I did. I manipulated."

"Mmm. All right,"

"Anyway, then, there was this gal, her friend owned this club on Toulouse—a gentleman's club. Right across the street from the Irish Pub. A gay gentleman's club."

"The Irish Pub. I know where that is. Is the club still there."

"Oh yes."

"Would they let me go in there?"

"Ha!"

"Would they?"

"Oh please—"

"Is there a lot of smoking in there?" I asked.

"Oh fuck. Smoking—you can forget that, there's more going on—"

"Yeah, but that doesn't make me sick."

"Ha, ha, ha, ha, ha. Forget it. Anyway, now I had never been to a bath house of this type. And I had always taken my hat off to Bette Midler."

"Wait." I interrupted. "Bette Midler?"

"Yeah. That's where she started off. In the bath houses in New York. That's where she used to sing."

"Did she?"

"Oh yeah. Before she ever did anything, she sang for all the gay people in the bath houses. You know, guys would walk around, with or without—"

"Mmm huh."

"And she'd sing her heart out. Wonderful, wonderful. Great old album of dicks. Ha, ha."

I had to laugh, too. I could just picture Bette in such a place, singing her heart out to a bunch of gay naked bodies. Only the Divine Miss M could have pulled that off.

"So I had some passes to this club. Deluxe passes. All right? So, one Sunday afternoon, I said, Katherine, I'm going to Mass to pray for business."

"So why were you going to Mass?"

"What? Why, I wasn't going to Mass atoll. I was going to the bath house. So, I went, and it had no sign or anything. Just this brass thing. And I rang the bell and the door opened and I walked in. God! I can't explain it."

"Well, work at it," I said.

"You walk in. And there were like three guys on the way out. And they weren't looking at my butt-sprung blue jeans, they were looking at what they hoped would spring out from the front. All right? So, I signed the thing and announced that I had a pass from James. 'Oh yes!' they said, 'you're Bill.' And I said, 'Yes, I am.' And then, there were two rooms up there, TVs, double beds and the whole bit. And a one way window, which I didn't know."

"Where they can look at you but you can't see them," I said.

"Yeah. Now, I'd never been to a place like this. It didn't take me long. At all. And I thought, well, I guess one takes their clothes off—right? I mean, you can't be trotting around in your Bermuda shorts. So I sat down, and naturally, you know me, I had to go take a leak. So when I started back to my room, I felt like the Pied Piper in Hamlet. You know, I had a bunch of rats following me forever. So I went into my room and closed the door."

"By yourself?" I said.

"Mmm huh."

"Okay. And then what?"

"All right. And then. And then Hernandez came in. He was from Mexico City, and—ha—He teaches philosophy at the University of Mexico. And for an hour we had gone to bed and just talked. That was all."

"I bet you enjoyed that, though."

"Oh. It was fun. I thought. This is what a bath house is about?"

"Oh yeah," I said sarcastically.

"Well. Hernandez left and this other guy came in—"

"Just talked and he left?"

"Yeah. And the next guy came in and started doing things I didn't even know were written."

"Like what?"

"No."

"Tell me."

"Like—like sixty nine."

"What do you mean you didn't know that was written? Sixty-nine!"

"Well, I knew what it was. I just hadn't done it."

"Well," I said. "I don't like it. It's like having somebody scratch your back and they expect you to scratch theirs at the same time. But anyway. So— you did sixty-nine."

"Yeah."

"That's the first time you'd ever done that?"

"Yeah. And I thought it was wonderful. All right?"

"A lot of people do."

"Well, I'll let you do it to me."

"Ha!" I laughed.

"Do me. Here I am. Anyway. During the course of the evening, and five hundred partners and whatever, there was always one who wanted to get up my butt."

"And that's when you'd take out your hypodermic needle," I joked."

"Yeah. Noooooooway were they gonna go anywhere up my butt. And anyway. I was just a guy."

"Yes, Bill, just a guy."

"And I went back and I went back and went back and went back. I was going like every night."

"All right. Now let me stop right there. What about catching some sort of venereal disease or AIDS? And this was like the late eighties. And this was when AIDS was running rampant."

"What about precautions? Did they insist . . .?"

"Everywhere. You wear condoms."

"Good. I'm glad to hear that."

"Okay? No, you do."

"Well, yes. If you want to live. You do."

"Right. And there's more— huh, for the way that I read the things, and I also went to the—wanted to have my first AIDS test. And I got really nervous about the whole thing. I thought, oh shit, you know—I'd been with a guy. Regardless of how or where, I mean, I'm dying of AIDS. Now they had big signs and pamphlets and things and you know. And most of the AIDS cases are relative to anal sex. But of course, if you had a cut in your mouth or a sore, well, I didn't suck people off, you know, I did a little head here and there or whatever, but hum, that was just not on my diet. Protein or not."

"So you just mostly preferred that they do you."

"Do me. Yeah."

"Well. That's not very fair."

"There's nothing fair about it."

"Ha."

"Ha, ha. There's *nothing* fair about it. At all. This is why I don't like it. All right. You get these—and I suppose that maybe I fall into that realm often. I mean, those poor people that have no other outlet, so they become the masked invisible people who are strolling the halls of these bath houses looking for what—instant relief? Why don't they stay home and jack off? And dream. Whatever. You know, to me it was just sick. You know, that true sex to me is accompanied by a little bit more than just getting off."

"Well, sure. Yeah."

"Something, something that—and this isn't even Catholic background, it just—it's just part of you and your being. It should be joyous. Not a hurried thing, grabbed in corners and you know, like guys stopping you in the hall and dropping to their knees and start sucking your dick. I mean, you don't even have a hard on. At all. I mean. It's pathetic."

"But there are a lot of pathetic people, Bill."

"And this is why I don't like to be—"

"But a gay relationship doesn't have to be that way."

"I know it, but . . ."

"You do know that?"

"Well yes. I do. I know that."

"All right."

"I know that."

"Any kind of relationship. Gay, heterosexual, whatever. It can go either way."

"But there—there—I'm not—but after I'd been going there for some time, and kinda knew the people behind the counter and all this kind of stuff, there was this old guy. *Old.* Older than me now. Ha, ha, ha, really old guy."

"You mean like 70 or 80 years old?"

"Oh yeah."

"And just needed whatever he needed."

"Right. And he'd come in. And I'd already come twice anyway. But all he wanted to do was just lie there and touch."

"That was before Viagra," I said. "And they just needed the closeness. Whatever."

"Right. I guess I probably pacified more old men that way than an old man's home. So, I did it and did it and did it."

Bill and I talked several minutes longer about other relationships that had passed through his life. However, the one thing that presently and urgently haunted him was the intense love he had formed for his heterosexual friend Brian. He couldn't seem to let that go. And I knew it was Brian that kept Bill returning to that forlorn Rendezvous Tavern.

"I gotta have a smoke," Bill insisted. He turned from the office and headed downstairs for the courtyard.

Chapter 15

"Bill," I said. "You are in an impossible situation. Brian is heterosexual and other than your friendship and food stamp card, he has zero interest in you. I know what I'm talking about."

"I don't care," he said. "I love Brian. I will always love Brian. I just don't care."

"And those were my exact words when David finally admitted to me that he was gay. I loved him so much that his admission had no meaning. The only meaning in my life was David. I couldn't think beyond that. My own child had taken a back seat to David. I loved him, I wanted him and I couldn't let him go.

"And when he was in New York for those three long months to try and find himself, I decided that I was going to find out what this homosexuality was all about. I was all of twenty-four, had been a stewardess for two airlines, had a one-year-old child, and thought I was damn worldly.

"I wasn't the least bit worldly. I was naïve. And I certainly knew nothing about homosexuality. And you know, I ended up having an affair with a woman for six months. I was so distraught over David that I wanted to lose myself inside his own world. I guess I must have felt closer to him for it. Hell, I don't know. But then David came back, and we were suppose to get married. It didn't take long for us to realize that our life together was hopelessly impossible. I couldn't compete with other men. Other women, yes. But other men? Bill, I had to let go. It almost killed me. But I had no other choice. I had to let go."

"I can't," he said. The tears were now streaming down his face. "I love him. I love him. I will always love him."

"I know you love him. But neither you nor I can do anything about that. Only time and the will to move on with your life can diminish that feeling." I caressed his arm. "I will do everything I can to help you. I just can't do it for you. You have to find the courage and determination somewhere inside *you*. If you don't, then you will only seep further into your own misery. And you still won't have Brian. Bill, you've got to find the strength to pull yourself out of this morbid malaise. Then you can be someone Brian can look up to. Not someone Brian uses and discards. But a role model for Brian. God knows he could use one.

"Doesn't the idea of that stimulate you at all? You, Bill Holcomb, a role model for all those lost souls out there. Think what you could accomplish, the people you could help. My God, Bill, you've experienced the grandiose and the dregs. You've crawled inside the filth and decay of deprivation. You've done it and seen it all. You are a product of it. Jesus! With your intelligence and wit, it's limitless to what you could accomplish. Why, Bill? Why do you chose to wallow in self pity?"

Bill raised his head slightly, then lifted his blood-shot eyes. They were filled with tears. He looked inside the space between us. "Tell me about you," he said.

"Me! Tell you about me? I've told you *everything* there is to know about me. I've already laid out my sordid life to you. What do you want to know that I've not already told you?"

"Why are you always so up?" he said grudgingly.

"I'm *not* always up."

"Oh, yes you are."

"I certainly am not. However, I choose not to spend my time down in the mouth and moping about like some pitiful creature."

"But you're always—so hopeful."

"Well, yeah," I said. "I'd sure as hell rather live with hope than the pitiful life you've chosen. I'll be damned if I'm going to live like you. I'm not a quitter. And I'm stubborn."

"I'm stubborn, too," he said. "That's why I'm where I am today."

"And that's bullshit," I barked. "You're not stubborn, you're lazy and full of self pity. Damn you, Bill Holcomb. You aren't the only child who had a difficult life. Your life has been a piece of cake compared to most. And you son-of-a-bitch, I had problems and inhibitions and embarrassments just like you did.

"You talk about how you didn't fit in when you were a child. How you were only interested in academics. How you were ostracized, weren't popular. But you turned it all around didn't you? You became the on-stage personality, weaving fabulous stories. You could have done amazing things with that talent. But no, you threw it away and opted for self pity instead.

"But self-pity bores the hell out of me. You see, Bill, I was your exact opposite. Academics was as foreign to me as reading a Chinese novel. Hell, the first six years of elementary school was nothing more than a blur. I can't begin to tell you how many times I was crushed with embarrassment. The only way I got to junior high was through my ability to memorize. And junior high and high school weren't much better. But I knew I had three things going for me. I was extremely athletic, I had an out-going personality and I was attractive. So—I took what I had and did the very best I could with it. I wasn't considered smart or intelligent or any of the things I wished I could be. But I was popular, a damn good athlete, a cheerleader, a homecoming queen and all that other insignificant nonsense.

"And then I decided to go to college. Now that was a joke. I only did it because I was too young to fly. I wanted to be a glamorous stewardess. And believe me, they were considered glamorous in the early sixties. So I went to college one year, rarely made anything above a D, and broke my engagement to Johnny, my high school boyfriend. He deserved better than me, anyway. Then I fell madly in love with one of the most popular guys on campus and lost him within six months because I went out with one of his fraternity brothers.

"I don't know why I'm telling you this," I said. "I've already told you the worst of it."

"Tell me anyway." Bill said passing his gaze across my face.

I guess I thought that a more in-depth history of my life might trigger an undiscovered emotion inside this man. Whatever I thought, I laid out my own life in as much detail as I could.

"Talk about a life spiraling out of control," I said. "After that insignificant year at The University of Tennessee at Martin, I was hired by Southern Airways and moved to Atlanta, Georgia. I thought I was hot stuff. This was 1962 and in 1963 I left Southern and was hired by Northwest. My old stewardess buddies and I still refer to ourselves as the Sky Sluts. And I guess that's exactly what we were. It was the '60s and nothing mattered but pure unadulterated pleasure.

"I was living in Minneapolis, Minnesota, flying for Northwest, and indulging in mad partying at the Essex Square Apartments where the Minnesota Vikings lived during season. That's when I met this most incredible man. We fell for each other almost immediately. I tried to play the innocent young girl and refused to go to bed with him. That didn't go over so well, so I finally came around to his way of thinking. And then I got pregnant. I came around to his way of thinking for a second time.

"You know Bill," I said. "Some would consider me sinful, perverted, and a murderer. At least you're not a murderer. You're only sinful and perverted. So I guess I'm one up on you."

Bill only looked at me with dazed eyes and chuckled.

At that point, I probably should have just given up. But I still had a shred of hope that I could get through to him. So I kept on talking.

"Nothing I could say or do would change the fact that the man that I had fallen in love with was not ready to get married, least of all have a family. So I found myself in his home town, staying with a friend of the family, and lying on a bed while a nurse inserted a tube inside my uterus. That night I went into labor, rushed to the bathroom and watched as this tiny fetus left my body. The one thing I recall as it hung there from the umbilical cord, was that it would have been tall like his father. It seemed to have a very long back. And then it was gone. I had flushed it down the toilet."

I looked at Bill, but his eyes were distant. He wasn't listening. His thoughts were too consumed with Brian. But I kept right on.

"Football season had ended, so I now had a long distance relationship. I would fly through Atlanta on my way to Miami where we would meet for a little more than ten to fifteen minutes. It was difficult, but we were managing. I was so in love. But as the months progressed, I found that I was also very lonely. So what would it hurt if I went out from time to time?

"Here is a profound example of the hurt that it caused.

"I don't recall how I met this guy. I do remember that he and another stewardess friend of mine had dated. She became pregnant and refused to marry the guy. She now lived in another state with her child. The guy would carry pictures of his baby with him and I truly thought he was a nice guy. So I agreed to have lunch with him one day. After lunch, he said that he was in-between apartments and was staying at a local motel."

This caught Bill's attention. He looked at me as if to say, you've got to be kidding. But I was dead serious. I was only twenty-one at the time and hadn't enough sense to come in out of the rain. So I actually thought nothing of going to this guy's motel room. God, was I naïve.

"I not only ended up in his hotel room, I ended up on his bed with him all over me. And this is the first time I've ever admitted this to a living soul. I was so naive and so turned on by the eroticism of the moment, that this guy proceeded to rape me while I proceeded to enjoy every last minute of it. As I pushed and pleaded and begged and made all manner of commotion, he threatened to snap my neck if I didn't let him do what he wanted. I became terribly caught up in this drama. And not once did I experience fear, anger or anything the least bit connected with rape. Rape did not enter my mind. But clearly, and without doubt, that was exactly what was happening. However, after it was over, they guy got down on his knees and begged forgiveness. This only added to the illusion that I had not been raped.

"My first emotion after this incident, was the fear of being pregnant. But little did I know that pregnancy would be the least of my fears.

"About a week or so after a glorious trip to Panama City with my boyfriend, I received a call. I'll never forget his words. 'You've given me the Clap.' Now I had no earthly idea what the Clap was. The first thing out of my mouth was, 'I'm so sorry.' I had no idea what I was sorry about, but by the tone of his voice, I knew I needed to be sorry. However, when I admitted I didn't know what the Clap was, he quickly informed me that it was gonorrhea.

"I was horrified. And I immediately denied it. There was no way I could have given that to him. He must have gotten it from someone else. But he swore that he had not been with anyone but me.

"I not only found out that I had this embarrassing disease, I also learned that this other guy I had spent but a few minutes with was known to have had it. I was devastated to say the least. I had not only been unfaithful to the man that I loved, but I had given him this horrible thing.

"So—what was I going to do? I guess I could have continued to claim my innocence, insisting that I was the victim not him. But I didn't. I told him that I had been raped. And that I had not wanted him to know. And I stayed with that story until now.

"After it was all said and done, nothing I could say or do would take away the pain that this man felt. He simply could not handle that I had been with another man let alone had given him this disease. And I don't think he truly ever believed my rape story. And why should he.

It was distorted at best.

"When he left me that day to drive back to Atlanta, I felt as though I was suffocating. I cried, fell to his feet and begged him to forgive me. But his pain was too great, and his pride too strong. He pushed me away and walked out the door.

"I lived in a fog for the next several months, relied on diet pills to get me through each day and continued feeding my sexual desires when I felt like it. And this led to my second abortion. Then one night the phone rang. And it was HIM. He was with another pro football team, was living outside of Buffalo New York, and was drinking Black Russians. He wanted me to fly up to Buffalo and spend a week with him.

"The joy and exhilaration that I felt at that moment was indescribable. I must have danced around my apartment for hours before collapsing into bed. He was giving me another chance, and I was going to do everything in my power to win back his love and respect. But I soon learned that his reason for having me there was nothing more than for his own enjoyment. He had already become interested in someone else. Talked with her on the phone my entire visit. He did admit that he still loved me, but there was no way he could ever trust me again. So when I got on the airplane to fly back to Minneapolis, I knew that I would never see him again.

"All I wanted to do was curl up into a ball, hide somewhere far, far away and hopefully die within a short period of time. But I didn't. I continued flying and going through the motions of getting on with my life. Until a few weeks later when I realized that I was pregnant again.

"Hope! I had not felt hope like that in a long time. I was pregnant. Why I thought this would change anything, I don't know. Of course it didn't. He was even less interested after receiving this bombshell. But you know, I still clung to that hope that I could some day, some how, win back his love. "So, I told him that I needed three-hundred dollars for an abortion. I had the money within three days. I called my chiropractor.

"This would be hysterical if it weren't so pathetic.

"Two months prior to this, my roommate had needed an abortion. I think every living soul must have had at least one abortion in the sixties. It had become an epidemic. And my chiropractor had connections with a doctor who was performing abortions for $600. So another friend and I took my roommate to the chiropractor's office. My roommate was told that the doctor needed to remain anonymous, and she would have to wear a blindfold. The blindfold was positioned, the cervical tube was inserted and within three days she miscarried. And that was that.

"But it didn't take me long to figure out that the only doctor present that night was my chiropractor. He was the one doing the abortions and pocketing six hundred dollars a procedure. He was making a fortune.

"So I called him and told him that I knew. And that I had no money but needed help. He agreed. The next night I drove to his apartment rather than his office, and on top of his kitchen table, he inserted the tube. The procedure was like something out of a horror movie. I don't know why he had so much trouble with it, but it took him forever. I felt like a raw piece of meat. But I put it out of my mind and drove back to my apartment. The next day, I walked into Northwest personnel, told them I wanted to get back to the south and resigned.

"The south had nothing to do with it. I wanted to be as close to *him* as possible and Delta Air Lines' headquarters was in Atlanta and that was my goal.

"I then took the three-hundred dollars that was to go for the abortion and paid off my bills. Football season had ended and one of the players from Alabama was driving back in his car. I rented a U-Haul, loaded it with my furniture, and hooked it to the back of his car. I also had a car, so I followed him all the way home to Jackson, Tennessee. He then continued on to Alabama.

"My parents, who are the most wonderful parents a child could ever hope for, had no idea that I was pregnant. Let alone that I had this tube inside me and was waiting to miscarry, which should have happened long before now. So there I was, the other end of this tube taped to my stomach and still no miscarriage. After days of this, I finally called my chiropractor. He told me to take the tube out immediately. But it was no use. No matter how hard I tried, it would not come out. I was by now bleeding through the tube and was starting to panic.

"I had no other choice. I had to tell my mother. And I had to tell her everything. So I did. The next day we were headed to Memphis to see a doctor. Memphis was far enough away from Jackson that no one in Jackson would ever know. And I suppose no one ever did, until now.

"The doctor removed the tube, informed my mother and me that we couldn't imagine how many of these botched abortions he had seen. He also gave us hope that my baby would live. So Mother and I, on our way back to Jackson, stopped at a jewelry story, purchased a gold wedding band, and collaborated on our story. It went something like this: My husband was furious when I became pregnant and since I wouldn't have an abortion, he abandoned me.

"Well, the scenario wasn't too far from the truth and worked to my advantage. Six and a half months later, I gave birth to a three pound, eleven ounce baby boy. When the nurse came into my hospital room to gather information for my baby's birth certificate, naturally she assumed that I was married. I had taken the father's last name the minute I purchased that gold wedding band. So for the last six or so months, I had been using his name. The nurse asked me all the pertinent questions for the birth certificate, and I answered every question with honesty. Not once did she ask if I was married.

"Three and a half years of more immorality and heartache, I met a man that not even I have the words to describe. Other than to say that he was the only man on this planet that I could have ever married and lived with for the next thirty years. There was nothing about my past that I needed left unsaid. He accepted me unconditionally. From the abortions to my gay love affair and everything in-between. One year after we met, we were married. Two months later, he adopted my son Steve. A year later, we had a little girl. We named her Ashley.

"Eleven years later when Steve was fifteen, I felt that I needed to tell him the truth about what had happened between his father and me. Why his father refused to see him. And the real reason he had been born premature. If Steve had not been the precocious child that he was, and if we had not had the most phenomenal relationship, I might not have told him so early on. But somehow, both of my children are mentally and spiritually light-years ahead of their mother.

"And Bill, you know what Steve said when I told him the truth?"

"Mmm uh."

"He said, 'You know, Mom. I really was meant to be here—wasn't I?'

"He said that, Bill. I told my fifteen year old son that his father didn't want him and that his mother tried to get rid of him. And that was his response! And look at you, sitting there wallowing in all that self pity."

Bill gave little response to what I had just told him. He was too wrapped up in his own pain and misery to even care. He was too wrapped up in Brian.

"I need to tell Brian exactly how I feel," he said. "I'm going to tell him that I'm gay and that I love him. Not just as a friend. But that I'm in love with him."

"Are you sure you want to do that?"

"I have to," he said. "Because—he'll probably tell me to get lost and then I'll be forced to get out of his life. It's the only way."

"Probably," I agreed. "But what if he doesn't. What if he admits that he loves you, too?"

"Ha! I'll probably run."

"Probably. But either way, you will have removed yourself from the temptation. You'll never get over Brian as long as you're with him."

"I know," he said. "I know."

"All right. Then go. Take the car and go."

Chapter 16

Three hours had passed and Bill was still at The Rendezvous.

Of course he was still at The Rendezvous. Did I honestly think he would go there, say his piece and obediently return? How gullible could I be? Very, I suppose. But three hours was pushing it and besides, he had my car. So I picked up the phone and called The Rendezvous. The barmaid answered and I asked for Brian. He was on the phone within seconds. He said that Bill was not drinking, so I asked to speak to him. When he came to the phone, I asked him to come home immediately. He assured me that he was on his way. An hour later, I called again. This time I asked for Murphy. Murphy informed me that Bill was drunk and that he would drive him home.

As they drove into the driveway, I saw this look of glee on Bill's face as he fumbled with the car door. After several awkward maneuvers, he managed his exit from the car and began his assent up the three stairs to the back door. He then pointed to Murphy who was standing just behind the car. I quickly opened the door to hear Bill announce, "Look who I've brought."

I thanked Murphy for getting my car and Bill safely home and ordered Bill into the house.

The level of vibrato inside the Red Room that night was unparalleled. If my house were not constructed of several feet of brick and concrete, I'm sure the Garden District Patrol would have been summoned. After a good hour of reproach, criticism, castigation, scolding and vile tongue lashing, I picked up the phone and called Dr. Harry Johnson. He was at my back door within thirty minutes.

Actually, the three of us had a most enjoyable evening. I indulged in several vodkas and orange juice, Harry preferred a martini and Bill was too drunk to care. We talked, we laughed and from time to time, Bill would prance about the Red Room performing various soliloquies from Shakespeare to Neil Simon. Nothing we could have said to Bill that night would have altered his thinking. His way of thinking had not found alteration for the past 50 some-odd years. So the gloves were off and a fun evening was had by all.

Bill slept late the next morning, so I went about my daily routine of writing, exercising, attending to various complaints at the apartment building and preparing for my friend, Alice, to arrive from Atlanta. Bill finally emerged from his bedroom and found his way to the kitchen. I knew it was too soon to encourage him to resume his Antabuse, but I did insist that he take his Prozac.

Talk about denial. I was consumed with it. Did I really think this man was going to come around to my way of thinking? Still, I went about my day as though I did and said nothing about the previous evening.

Four o'clock was approaching and it was time to drive to the airport to pick up Alice. So I walked out into the courtyard where Bill was working his crossword puzzle. I handed him this letter and left for the airport:

Dear Bill,

Writing my thoughts rather than speaking them has always been easier and more effective. So that's what I'm doing now.

My feelings for you should be clear. I've relayed them to you often enough. But I think I should make our situation crystal clear, so I am taking this opportunity to do just that. You need to understand that I am serious, sincere and will absolutely follow through with my convictions. The rest, I leave up to you.

If you want to continue living with me then these are the parameters, rules or whatever you choose to call them. I will not and can not have you here if you drink. As for taking the Antabuse, that's entirely up to you. As for the Prozac, I am of the opinion that the benefits outweigh the side effects. However, there are other drugs that have little side effects. That, too, is entirely up to you.

I know that you have pain, sorrow and all sorts of

haunting emotions. But Bill, there is no living soul that doesn't. And I can assure you that your pain is minute compared to some. I will also say that some of that pain is brought on by you and no one else. But all of it is under your will to either do something about it or simply let it take over. So far, you have chosen the latter.

Laziness, selfishness, moaning and groaning run thin with me. You've had years to wallow in self pity and laziness and such. I don't want to hear it any longer, other than within a constructive environment. I am always here to listen and help you work through it. BUT, do not postulate self pity and hopelessness. Your problem is far from hopeless and I sure as hell don't pity you.

I think often of Robert, Chuck's partner, and the degradation and abuse he suffered as a child. I can't even conceive of what that must have been like. But you don't see him wallowing in self pity. He was determined to make something of himself. And his reservoir of knowledge is limited. Can you imagine how it compares to yours? The difference here, is that Robert wanted something out of life and went after it. Can you imagine how far you could go with only a fraction of that sort of determination and ambition?

And then there's my girlfriend who lost, within seconds, her husband and three children to a drunk driver. She was left with one child. She found her reason to live after simply wanting to die.

As I said, your life and the way you choose to live it is entirely up to you. You just need to know that if you choose to drink again, I will immediately and without thought, show you the door. I don't care what time of day or night it is. You will go.

I hope against hope that this won't happen. But with your track record, even I am clinging to but a shred of that hope. The ball is in your court. See what you can do with it.

I love you, Pet

I had now been away from the house for approximately an hour. Not knowing what to expect when Alice and I arrived, I tried to fill her in on the situation. She had never met Bill, and I hated the idea that their first meeting might find him in a drunken stupor.

It did.

After I introduced Alice to Bill, it was obvious that he had been hitting the bottle during my absence. He was *on*. Showering Alice with copious compliments and witty remarks. During a short interlude, Bill assured me that he understood my letter fully and thanked me for it.

As I puttered in the kitchen preparing the evening meal, Alice and Bill sat in the Red Room. Alice was a product of an alcoholic father and had little sympathy where Bill was concerned. Their conversation would grow intense, then level off to a quiet lull, only to escalate again. Alice had great words of wisdom to offer Bill, and though I felt minutely hopeful, I knew her words were falling on deaf ears.

The next morning Bill was still not up when Alice and I left the house. That was around 11:30, and though I was concerned, I guessed that he simply needed to sleep it off. But I stopped by The Brass Menagerie and informed Kathy and Edward of Bill's condition. Since Kathy had lived with this for over thirty years, she advised me to let Bill sleep. She warned me not to even wake him to eat. He would need at least twenty-four hours of sleep if he was going to emerge well and sober.

Again I felt hopeful. Bill had read my letter and was going to find his way back to sobriety. So I would let him sleep, and when he awoke, we would start anew. But starting anew was not in his scheme of things. When Alice and I returned home, Bill was nowhere to be found. And frankly, after Bill had told me the previous night that his confession to Brian had not gone well, I wasn't so sure that he had returned to The Rendezvous. But he had, and around six p.m., he appeared at my back door.

Not intending for Bill to find his way back into my house, I had locked the back door. The front gate is always locked as is the gate to the courtyard. But I had forgotten the spare key inside the small storeroom. As I turned from the Red Room to enter the kitchen, I saw him. He had managed to retrieve the spare key, but was having great difficulty inserting it into the lock. As I approached the backdoor, he looked up. With eyes at half-mast, he waived the key in front of me, then lowered his gaze and angled it toward the key hole for another try.

I pulled open the door and lifted the key from between his fingers. I closed the door, locked it and walked back into the Red Room, proceeded down the hall, up the stairs and—I don't know. I guess I went to find Alice.

It was over. I had told Bill that I would put him out if he continued drinking. And I had. With nothing but the clothes on his back. An hour or so later, Renée, Alice and I were in the kitchen. Not wanting Bill to show up at my backdoor, I decided to close and lock the outside double louvered doors. As I reached out to pull them shut, I saw Bill sitting on the brick ledge at the front of my driveway. I suppose he had been sitting there for the last hour. The sight of him startled me at first, but I quickly pulled the doors shut, locked them and closed the back door. I turned to Renée and Alice.

"My God," I said. "He's sitting out there on the ledge. In this wretched heat."

"Don't you even think of letting him back in here," Alice said.

"You can't," Renée agreed. "You gave him an ultimatum, more chances than he deserved, and you have to stick to it."

I knew they were right. And as I peered through the drapes, watching him, his arms flapping about as though he were talking to an imaginary person, I knew I couldn't give in. But I suppose I needed further assistance with this dilemma. So I picked up the phone and called Harry Johnson. This was his response:

"Take Bill a blanket and a can of beans. And tell him to be careful not to let you hit him with your car when you drive in your driveway."

Now Harry was dead serious about this. But Renée and Alice were telling me not to react to Bill in any way, shape, form or fashion. And frankly, I didn't want to have to approach him. Not then, not in his drunken stupor, and maybe not ever. But Harry finally talked me into it. So I hung up the phone ready to retrieve a blanket and a can of beans. But when I looked out onto my driveway, Bill was wandering off. I let out a sigh of relief, and tried to put him out of my mind. Of course I didn't. We talked about him over several vodkas and orange juice, and a dinner of flaming hot pasta.

The next day, I gathered all his clothes and toiletries, put them in shopping bags, and stored them in the upstairs closet. As I was cleaning out the chest of drawers, I found an empty pint of very cheap vodka. Three days later Kathy said that she had run into Brian at the A&P. Brian told her that Bill was at the bar drinking ice water. Kathy informed me that I would be hearing from him soon.

She knew him well. The next day I received a call. Bill said he would like to stop by and pick up his things. That afternoon he appeared, gathered several bags of clothes and announced he would return shortly for the remainder. Before he left, he apologized for what he had put me through, then proceeded to give me the news that Critter had been found murdered the night before. I remembered hearing about a man that had been found shot in the St. Thomas Projects, but his name had not been revealed. He was slumped over his steering wheel. I wondered if he had been in the Jeep Cherokee that he had helped himself to a few years back. I also wondered how soon it would be before I received the same tragic news about Bill. But that was out of my hands now.

When Bill returned, my cousin, Will Taylor and his wife had arrived and were in the kitchen. Bill greeted them and proceeded to gather the remainder of his clothes. I left Bill to his task and went up stairs. When I returned, Will motioned to a box of clothes. He informed me that Bill had requested that I throw it out.

I opened the box to see what I had packed inside. The sight could not have been more prophetic. Bill needed no words for this. No grandiose posturing or dialogue. His message was profound, absolute, and perfectly clear. Bill Holcomb was receding back into the dark abyss where he could escape his pain and indulge his pity. He would have no use for sport coats, suits—certainly not a tux.

Into the face of society's demands, he had thrown his last possessions.

Chapter 17

GRAND AND SECRET ORDER OF THE OBITUARY COCKTAIL

Buvez toujours et ne mourez jamais
(Drink always and never die)

Dorian Bennett, one of New Orleans' top realtors, founded this prestigious club. Most of the real estate signs from the French Quarter to the Garden District and beyond bear either his name or that of my friend and neighbor, Martha Ann Samuels who is the realtor for Buzz Harper and Anne Rice. Dorian is my realtor for the simple fact that he represented the apartment building that Daddy and I purchased back in 1996.

Uncle Buzz assured me that this building was one of the best buys around, and since I had the unbearable urge to move to New Orleans, Dorian and I schemed, connived and collaborated daily over the phone. Daddy finally flew to New Orleans, looked at the building and made an offer. Within a matter of days, we were proud owners of the stately apartment building on St. Charles Avenue. I had never laid eyes on the thing, but if Uncle Buzz says it's beautiful and a great buy, that's all I need to know. And of course, if it hadn't been the buy of the millennium, Daddy Des would not have made the purchase.

Not wanting to keep most of the furnishings we had acquired over the years, I held an estate sale and came away with several thousand dollars. I immediately put that money into the hands of my Uncle Buzz and told him to do his magic. I packed the remainder of our possessions, called the moving company and sent them on their way. I also called my daughter's mother-in-law, Joyce, and told her I wasn't about to put my Scotties in the belly of an airplane and for her to be ready to head for New Orleans. The next day I put Jocque and Max in my Corvette convertible, bid my good-byes to Los Gatos, California, and drove to Apple Valley. I picked up Joyce and we were off to The Big Easy, where I met Dorian for the first time.

And Dorian and I have been fast friends ever since.

Dorian was a good friend of the playwright, Tennessee Williams. Back in the sixties, Tennessee fancied a young Dorian, but no amount of pursuing or persuasion could bring young Dorian around. So Tennessee was forced to accept his loss and settle for Dorian's friendship—not a love affair.

Two weeks or so after I had thrown Bill out of the house, The Obituary Cocktail Society, which meets every Friday at a different bar, was meeting at Broussard's, one of my favorites. My friend, David Armstrong (now he's another story) plays the piano at Broussard's as well as the Bombay Club across the street.

I did not want to miss this particular Friday night gathering of the Obituary Cocktail Society, but I was faced with my usual problem.

With the debt that I have amassed over the years, I do not have the luxury of mad drinking and fine dining. Only when Daddy is in town or Uncle Buzz or Les or Ray are kind enough to include me, am I fortunate enough to indulge myself. But I was set on going that night, and I wanted to take Renée with me. We both needed a night out on the town, and if Daddy had been there, the three of us would have done just that. So thinking that Daddy would probably be up at 6:00 a.m., California time, preparing to go to the health club, I called—and woke him out of a sound asleep. Still, I stated my case and asked if he would pay for a night out at Broussard's.

An overwhelming silence ensued. It lasted so long that I began to lose hope and wished that I had called much later in the day. So I told him to just forget it. It didn't matter and never mind. I worked at sounding pitiful—wanted him to feel like a heel. It must have worked 'cause he finally said yes. So that night, I pulled out the credit card called United Cab. Renée and I headed for the French Quarter.

Knowing that my good friend, Dorian, had known Tennessee Williams, I was curious to dig around a bit inside the playwright's tumultuous life. It had occurred to me that Tennessee Williams and William Lafayette Holcomb had much in common.

The cocktail hour went splendidly. The author of *The Obituary Cocktail* coffee table book, Kerri McCaffety, had joined us, and as everyone proceeded to get pleasantly wasted, they passed around books for her to sign. This impressive book cost me 43 dollars at the Garden District Book Shop, and is probably one of my better purchases. It is a marvelous history of New Orleans' crumbling taverns and opulent saloons.

As Kerri McCaffety so eloquently penned:

> "New Orleans, with over 3,000 gin joints—more per capita than anywhere else in the United States—uncorked its drinking tradition with the first shipload of weary Frenchmen needing a place to sit, brag and languish in the heat. It has never abandoned its European/Caribbean, opulence-in-exile heritage even during Reconstruction and Prohibition, and clings to it still. Where else can you get a "go cup," bar hop at four in the morning, or sit out a tropical storm drinking Hurricane Punch in the same crumbling cottage where pirates plotted military matters two centuries ago?"

The City That Time and Care Forgot embraces us still with its diversity, immorality and exotic pulchritude. A crumbling edifice, its venerable soul lures, seduces and claims another victim.

Dorian and I, honored and proud that we also had succumbed to this inexplicable city, were now three sheets to the wind as we left the bar and entered the dining area. Finally after much ado, our table was filled with Dorian's wife Kel to his left, me to his right, Renée across from us and seven others placed throughout. Renée decided that she would forego another drink, Dorian and I both should have simply gone home, but we ordered one glass of wine instead. We then proceeded to order dinner and savor our meal.

If there is one particular thing that I am notorious for, it's drinking, eating, then heading straight for the bed. I absolutely do not drink after I've eaten, and if you ever come to my house for dinner, you will notice that I silently disappear. This is by no means a Southern tradition.

It is my tradition.

However, it works quite well when Daddy is around. He is the life of the party, will tell the most outrageous jokes, and can drink an elephant under the table into the wee hours of the morning. When morning arrives, I never know in what part of the house I might find him.

So, if you do happen to end up at my dinner table, fear not, Daddy will not leave you stranded as I am wont to do.

So that night at Broussard's, I had eaten and was ready to head home. I handed my credit card to Dorian who had as much business figuring food costs as an inebriated snail. I made an appointment for the next week to discuss his friendship with Tennessee Williams and would retrieve my credit card at that time.

The next week Dorian picked me up. As we headed to Cannon's for lunch, he informed me that the man sitting at the head of our table at Broussard's had graciously indulged himself by ordering several bottles of very expensive wine. Dorian, when splitting up the bill for that night, simply divided it by ten and charged our credit cards. This meant that my and Renée's bill was in excess of two-hundred dollars and that did not include the drinks we had at the bar.

If my parsimonious husband had been present that night, inebriation would *not* have played even a minute part in the bill figuring. He would have had the thing down to the exact cent of what we had spent. Those infamous bottles of wine enjoyed by who knows who would not have been taken into consideration.

But Dorian promised to speak with this man at our next Obituary Cocktail affair, which would be held at the Bombay Club that night. And knowing that I couldn't spend my money on mad drinking and such, he insisted that Renée and I come along at his treat.

I accepted. So did Renée.

The son-of-a-bitch that had ordered the expensive wine did not show. Dorian, ever the Southern gentleman, paid for our drinks, and Renée and I were forced to spring for our dinner.

Now we're broke again. No more mad drinking and succulent dining without Daddy. However, I have since met this enigmatic man and have fallen madly in love with him. Especially after he treated me to a marvelous dinner at my neighborhood café, Commander's Palace, and a $700 bottle of *Récolte* 1982 Grand Vin de Léoville du Marquis de Las Cases *Saint-Julien*. His name is Dale Rathke and he's my new best friend.

So Dorian and I settled into our luncheon booth at Cannon's, ordered two scrumptious salads and dove into zealous conversation about his friendship with Tennessee Williams.

Foregoing any hope of a sexual liaison, Tennessee came to admire young Dorian, who was a talented artist as well as a trained concert pianist. For over a decade their friendship had grown into one of deep respect and genuine admiration.

As Dorian said, "Tennessee may get looped, which of course he usually did, but he never made direct advances toward me. I always knew he was interested in me, but you know, for me—you know, the biggest thrill was to be with this unbelievable individual who had created my favorite all-time plays of life. Just the idea that this human being, you know, is there and has accomplished so much, you know, in bringing out the inner madness of dysfunctional families and all these other things that are just so inherent in the South. I mean, he's just amazing to know. And he was absolutely just the most attentive fan. And that's what I'd say."

"He was your fan and you were his," I said.

"Exactly. He—was—a—fan—of—me."

"What kind of paintings had you done?"

"I had some realistic paintings and other artwork and drawings and stuff like that that I had on the walls in this apartment that I had at 819 Bourbon Street, which is a whole 'nother story. That building is just— was a killer building. It was the Elmo Avet building. Elmo was very famous for his antique store."

"What was the name of his antique store?" I asked.

"The Elmo Avet Antique Store—and it was on Chartres Street, I believe. And he was known for the most outrageous things in the world. Like—he would have Marie Antoinette's bed, stuff like that. I mean, he would go for the truly over-the-top-stuff. I mean fabulous stuff like he had Mae West's bed for sale. You know. And he had this phenomenal building on Bourbon that was his old home and had been made into apartments."

"Properly?" I asked.

"Properly. I mean it was just gorgeous. Basically, it's one of the finest buildings in the French Quarter."

"How the hell could you afford that? How old were you then?"

"Well—because, because the landlady was related to Elmo, and she had inherited the property. She had the rents incredibly reasonable, because this building was in the wildest part of the French Quarter. I mean, it was a magnificent building. But you've got Pete's, The Bourbon Pub and Lafitte's over at the other end. So they're all right there. So I learned real quick that I couldn't wait out in front of the building for friends when they were coming to pick me up."

"Yeah," I said. "Because you'd get picked up before your friends got there."

"I learned—exactly. I learned that I couldn't dawdle around at the mailbox and stuff like that."

"Now what year—are we talking about the '60s?"

"Huh, no. The '70s. Like '76 maybe '77 through '80."

"Okay—then how exactly did you meet Tennessee?"

"Well—I had wanted to take this apartment that Tennessee had for rent. He had this apartment building in the ten-hundred block of Dumaine Street. So, I knew Tennessee was there. I knew he existed, but I'd never met him. He was just always this person I knew was there but had never met and was a fan of. But my mother wouldn't let me take it. She was absolutely sure that Tennessee Williams would be all over me like bread on butter. Okay? And that was her deal. She made a huge fit about it. I couldn't even go there. So I turned the apartment on to a friend of mine, and he took it."

And I said, "So Dorian took the apartment on Bourbon Street."

"Yeah. My mother met the landlady and everything was fine 'cause the landlady was 70-something years old. And the most wonderful human being I ever met. I mean, she took me for one hour—interviewed the shit out of me. I mean, she kept asking me one pointed question after another. And finally her little five-foot-two wonderful self from Donaldsonville, Louisiana, placed her little—her little staunch finger—right on my chest."

'Dawlin,' she said. 'If you want this apartment, it's yours.'

"What was the woman's name?"

"Dorothy," he said. "Dorothy Casso. She was wonderful. She'd do things like once when I was in the hospital, she'd come with a box of jelly candies, she'd defrost my icebox, she'd bring me my week's mail. She was wonderful and the apartment was wonderful."

"How much rent were you paying?"

"Three hundred dollars a month. And it was the most glorious apartment you can imagine. Glorious architectural details, fourteen foot ceilings, great chandeliers, I had a beautiful little entrance and dining room. I had a huge living room that I put so much furniture in that literally, when I moved from the apartment and into the house that I bought, it was full. I mean I had great storage in the apartment, a second floor bedroom with a balcony overlooking Bourbon Street."

"Okay. So how did you meet Tennessee?"

"All right. Tennessee knew my friend Barry from Arkansas. The nicest man on the face of the planet. But Barry died. It's a long story.

He was just a great guy. Very entertaining and all."

"Barry was gay," I said.

"Oh yeah. I don't pay any attention to that kind of stuff. I have gay friends, straight friends and everything else."

"As do I. It just doesn't matter."

"Absolutely not. And I love 'um all. And huh, Tennessee was spending some time with Barry. I don't think they were sleeping together or anything. They were just great friends. He had a job as a psychiatric nurse. So that tells you a little bit. He was a very fascinating kind of guy. And that kept Tennessee I'm sure, busy. 'Cause Barry, he could keep you entertained beyond belief. And he was hysterically funny and just a great guy. So—Tennessee was in town."

"Wait," I said. "Now where—Tennessee had an apartment? He kept an apartment—"

"Tennessee owned this building in the ten-hundred block of Dumaine Street and his apartment was on the second floor with a balcony."

"Okay. Where did he really actually live? In Los Angeles? New York?"

"Oh God no. No, no. Tennessee spent as much time at the apartments here, Key West and New York. And whatever, you know, little diversities he might take, et cetera. But he was here a lot. I mean—a lot. And our friendship started over this one encounter. This one meeting."

"All right. What meeting?"

"Well. Barry had told me that Tennessee really liked this one particular type of drug. And it was illegal as hell. It was called a Black Molly. Now I had never heard of a Black Molly and I had never done a Black Molly. But—Tennessee liked Black Mollys and I wanted to meet Tennessee, so I said, why don't I get you some Black Mollys? And Barry said, oh, if you could do that, that would make Tennessee really happy. And you know, yada yada yada, and there was this wonderful doctor that I knew. He was Renée's lover—"

"Who the hell is Renée?"

"Renée was this artist that I knew. Because I painted. You know, I painted and played piano and stuff and I know a lot of people. Okay?"

"Well, sure."

"So—here we go. I tell Barry. I can get the Black Mollys. Barry said, why don't you come over. But I said. Oh no. I said, if I get the Black Mollys and Tennessee wants the Black Mollys, then Tennessee comes here to get the Black Mollys.

"To your place." I confirmed.

"Right. To my place. That's how that plays out."

"I don't blame you."

"And they said fine. When can we come? So I scheduled an appointment for late one afternoon. I think it was around fall, the weather was really nice. I was standing out on the balcony, the breeze was good, and here they come walking around the corner. I looked down there—"

"Your stomach must have leapt into your heart."

"Exactly. I thought, I don't believe that. I really believed that Barry was pulling my leg. I mean, this man was so incredibly famous. Anyway, they came over. I was, you know, maybe twenty-two, twenty-three, cute and all this stuff. Twenty-eight inch waist, thirty inch waist. Whatever."

"Kind of the way you look now," I commented. "Since you've been working out."

"Exactly. But huh. He came up. And we sat around, and we talked and I showed him some of my paintings and we talked some more, and he was very entertaining. Then he saw the piano. He asked me if I played and I said yes. So he asked if I would please play something for him. And I said, 'are you sure?' It's really just a hobby, sure I had classical training at one point in time but I could be rough.

"But here sat this fabulous piano that I'd had for about three years. It was Ignace Jan Paderewski's piano. He was one of the finest classical performers over the past couple of hundred years. He was twice Prime Minister of Poland. And his entire story is a whole 'nother story, and the piano is a whole 'nother story. Anyway, here sits this piano. It's been fully restored and I play that piano. I sit and play Liszt's *Liberstraum*. The first movement of it. I took him through the whole first movement of it. And he loved it. And—he asked me to play again."

"Was he having a drink while you were doing this?"

"Of course. We were all having cocktails. It was probably white wine, or scotch or bourbon or gin or vodka or whatever."

"Or any kind of alcohol."

"Yeah, and we were all just sitting there, and I hadn't relinquished his Black Mollys that he wanted so—"

"Had he asked for them yet?"

"No. No he hadn't. He was being very polite and very hospitable. But he knew that I had them."

"Mmm huh."

"And he knew that I had requested that he come there. And what else was said, I don't know. And that's okay. Nothing was ever said. But, okay, I played again. He was enthralled, really enjoyed what I did and asked me to play again. Now, we might have all been really drunk and I might have been playing really good, or maybe I was really playing great and we weren't so drunk. Who knows? Okay. So I played it again. And he loved it. And—because—because when you really stop and listen to Liszt's *Liberstraum*, and when you hear that first—that whole first movement, that is an incredible experience.

"I mean, it's not like—I mean, it's not Chopin, it's not Bach, it's, it's not Mozart, it's not Beethoven—it's absolutely the most seductive, the most beautiful music you can possibly envision. I mean, it's Liszt's *Liberstraum*. It's a love song. As passionate as it gets. I mean, if you don't feel something after listening to that, you should not listen to music. You should find some other avenue. So, when Tennessee asked me to play, I played that piece. And I don't know exactly why I played it. Except that I knew I played it well. And I knew that I wanted him to hear me play well. As well as I could. And it was a complex, convoluted piece that would appeal to someone like Tennessee Williams.

"So now I've played it for a third time. Here I am, a little trained monkey. But I thought, that's okay, I'm twenty-three years old, but I'm sitting here playing for Tennessee Williams."

"How old was Tennessee?"

"Oh, I don't know. Hell, then anybody over forty was ancient. Now I'm forty-seven and anybody over eighty is ancient. It's all a matter of perspective. But, I don't know. He was over forty, he could have been sixty or maybe even fifty. But it didn't matter. He was very in tune. He was very engaging. And he was incredibly articulate and phenomenally entertaining and so wonderful to be around. I mean, he was just so flattering and so effusive. And, you know, maybe he had another agenda, but it felt, you know, and it sounded great, I mean it sounded great. I'm much more comfortable now with flattery I receive or compliments now, but then, you know, it made me feel so self conscious. But, but anyway, it was great so I played it for the fourth time. He asked me to play it again, so I did. But I told him that before I played it—'Before I play this for you, I'm going to insist on something.' And he said 'what?' And I said, 'anything that I have in here that has your name on it, be it books, playbills, whatever—you've got to sign them. And that's all there is to it.' 'Oh,' he said, 'but of course. No problem.'

"Now he knew that I was just this little puppy fan of his. I was just a peripheral of this wide fan club of the earth that loved this man's work. So I play the piece for the fourth time and then run to go find this stuff for him to autograph. And I don't have a clue where anything is and I don't have much time because I needed to be out there entertaining. So I'm tearing through my apartment, scrambling around to find if only one book. And I did. I found one book, and it was his memoirs. I brought it over to him, actually the book didn't even belong to me. But I've never returned the book. I couldn't. And, it was an old girlfriend's, and she never asked for it back and if she had I'd have just bought her another one. She wasn't getten that one. I hadn't even read this book, but I'd seen so much of his work and everything else, and this was the first thing I'd put my hands on. He writes a beautiful, beautiful passage. Just basically, you know, a little love script in a way, or a fan script about how much he enjoyed meeting me and that he had a great love for my art and my music, you know, something like that. It wasn't gross or over done. It was just nice. And then the next day—"

"But did you give him the Black Mollys?"

"Oh. Of course. I gave them to Barry and he gave them to Tennessee. I mean, there was no direct exchange. I mean, I didn't hand him the pills and say, 'here, you drug addict. These are for you.' 'Cause you know. I'm from Hammond, Louisiana. I'm so out on the outside. You know, in the '50s when everybody was being a hippie, I was just trying to read, write, think, play the piano. You know, I was a nerd. Basically—I was a nerd. I was a major nerd. I was absolutely a nerd. A nerd. A nerd. Major nerd. Straight A's. Major nerd. But you know."

"Yeah. But unlike Bill Holcomb, you didn't end up an alcoholic and all that."

"Oh no, no, no. I—I really don't drink other than my drinking club. I don't drink. Never drink. Don't drink wine, don't drink anything. Huh, it's very, very rare. And—with this drinking club—two drinks, and if I'm really tempted, maybe three—on a Friday."

"I know. We had three at Broussard's and we were snockered."

"Yeah. But anyway—here we go. The next morning there's a buzz at my door, and it's a Saturday. I'm almost sure. A Saturday or Sunday 'cause I wasn't doing anything. And I'm a workaholic. So Monday through Friday you know where I am."

"Now wait. How were you making your living then?"

"In the real estate business. I started real estate one year out of college. And when I got into the business, within one year I made myself full-time. And, I made myself successful. So basically, my first six months I was part time and—"

"Who were you working for then? Martha Ann Samuels?"

"No, no, no. Back then I was with Robert F. Hudson. A wonderful guy. He had a class-act firm over on Rampart Street. For a guy like me, the esthetics were appealing, the place looked great, and so, that's where I worked."

"Okay. So the buzzer rang."

"Yeah. The buzzer rang. And it was someone who had been sent to bring me a photograph of Tennessee that he had autographed for me. And there was a lovely message attached to the autograph. And the inscription said—it was in French—and English translates to 'There was a time.' And I think he was simply saying that he enjoyed meeting me, listening to me play the piano and I think he thought that sending the photograph would definitely touch my heart. And it did. I was very, very touched. And he gave me his numbers and I put them down in my book. Now how many times do you get to put someone like Tennessee Williams' numbers in your book?

"And so, he asked, when he was in town, you know, if I minded getting together for drinks. And I said, Great. I'd love to. So, so then, we'd join up. At least one night when he was in town, we'd get together and have drinks at Lafitte's piano bar."

"The gay bar?"

"No, no. The other one."

"Oh, Lafitte's Blacksmith Shop? That's Daddy's all time favorite."

"Yeah. The, Who Knew What Anybody Was, place." You know—that's most of the problem with people today. You know?"

"Yeah. I most certainly do know."

"Anyway. We sat and he said he'd love to hear me sing."

"What!" I said. "My God. Is there anything you can't do?"

"Yeah."

"What?"

"Tax returns. And mechanical stuff. I can't build bird houses. I mean, there's a lot of stuff I can't do. A lot of stuff."

"So," I said. "Has Tennessee yet to approach you?"

"No. No. And really, the approaches that were made—they were..."

"Subtle?"

"They were subtle enough. They were clear and if I was interested, I could have taken it to the next level, but I wasn't."

"And he never made you feel uncomfortable?"

"Never made me feel uncomfortable. There was only one time when he basically spilled this whole thing of red wine on this nice new jacket that I had—and stuff—and thinking that maybe it was an accident and maybe it wasn't, but it certainly was a lot of wine just to be an accident, and he wanted—for me to basically take my shirt off. And—and I didn't. And—and so, that was the end of that. And it went nowhere.

"But it was just really nice knowing him. I would just help him with projects and things, with his house and stuff. Not for money. I was never paid. But as a friend. I was his friend. And so, I would go there and oversee some of the work he was having done. God knows where he was getting these workers from. He would get the cheapest workers on the face of the planet. They wouldn't even have shoes."

"God! He sounds dangerously like Daddy."

"Right. Ha, ha. I mean he must have gotten them off a Honduras milk truck or something. I have no idea what. But they didn't speak English either, so I'd go over there, and—and I'd tell Tennessee, I don't know what you've got working back there, but they are working, and, you know, I'm not sure what caliber or anything, but all I know is that they're there.

"And, we'd just always get together. And he'd travel, and he'd call me from New York, call me from Key West, and just to chat. There was never anything crude, rude, suggestive, huh, malicious or unkind."

"Do you think he was lonely?"

"He liked the friendship. He just liked me. As a person."

"I understand."

"Now, I would never go out with him and his other friends. I, I knew some of them. I knew who they were, but I was never invited to that or any of the parties he might throw. Pool side and stuff like that. That's just not where he would invite me. You know. He basically kept me separate. He kept me separate from his friends."

"What about alcohol and drugs?" I asked. "How much of that influenced his life?"

"Well, I can tell you this. Totally drunk and drugged out of his mind, he had a brain ten times more fabulous than anybody who is totally sober."

"That's more or less the way it is with Bill. How their minds can function at that level is beyond reason. But Bill Holcomb can remember stuff sloppy drunk that I can't stone sober."

"Right. And I saw Tennessee with Eric Paulsom. When Eric Paulsom did that interview—that's the first time I had seen Tennessee when I knew him. I was sitting at the Theatre of Performing Arts. And I saw him sitting there, the whole house full of people to hear Tennessee in a repartee with Eric Paulsom. And I believe that interview was recorded. And he was phenomenal."

"But he was always drunk or drugged out, yet was clear as a bell?"

"No. I wouldn't say he was always drunk and drugged out. He really wasn't. And when we would got out or something, he was never drunk or drugged out. Never drunk. Never drugged out. And sure, we'd end up drunk. You know. I wasn't doing any drugs. You don't drink and do drugs at the same time. But he—he was at a different level. Anyway, he was not always drunk and drugged out. And that's exactly what I told the people that were checking his sanity when he died. And I had to deal with that court battle that was going on."

"Tell me about that."

"Well—they wanted some character references, because that school who had received all his money was being sued by Tennessee's brother. Anyway, the last time I saw him, I had this little dinner party—"

"Was this in the early '80s, just before he died?"

"Before he died. Right before he left for New York. It was then, in New York, that he died. I went out and bought 30-40 antheridiums, and Beverly and I threw this little dinner party for four. It was Beverly and me and Tennessee and a guy he brought named—Sky—Blue Sky, Red Sky, whatever. Or Moonglow—something. But a nice guy, you know. Tennessee was in a state of depression like I'd never seen. I'd never seen him like that."

"But he still came to your dinner party."

"Oh yeah. But he was very clear—very clear that he was unhappy. And what had happened was—I believe it was right when *Moise and The World of Reason*, or something with some other play or book to do about the way the critics were handling it."

"So you think he was depressed over a bad review?"

"I think that was the only thing that could touch him at that point. I think that was the only thing that could touch him or really hurt him.

Bad reviews or if someone maliciously, you know, attacked his work. He loved his work. He was an artist. A pure artist. You know, he lived frugally. He was very modest about the way he lived. And he had a ton of money. And I understand where he came from."

"Where *did* he come from?"

"He came from the Depression, you know. As far as the money thing. He was a poor man's son with this great talent."

"Where was he from?"

"Well, originally from Memphis or some place around there. And then he was living with his grandfather who was a preacher down in some part of Mississippi for a while. But he was from St. Louis. That's where he spent his formative years."

"Okay. So he's over at your house for the party, and you could tell that he was really depressed."

"Oh God, yes. And he hadn't visited me in my new home and I wanted him to come by."

"Where was your new home?"

"In the 800 block of Frenchman Street. It was a beautiful old Creole cottage that I had renovated—just a special thing. That was in the early '80s when there was all this Vietnamese boat people going on. My best way of dealing with feeling sorry about things and being depressed and such, is to always take myself outside of who I am, where I am, and look at how bad things *could* be. And so, that's what I did with Tennessee 'cause I saw what was going on there. And I said to him, 'Tennessee, you are depressed. You are very depressed. I mean, I've never seen this in you. You know, and all I've got to say is that you've got the world by the tail. You are inconceivable—your talent—what you have given to the world. I mean, think about the Vietnamese boat people, where they, you know, got like 60-some odd people in a boat that can't fit ten. You know, and they're out there fighting off the sharks and everything else just trying to find some place to go.'"

"Absolutely," I said. "That's precisely the kind of stuff I think about when I start feeling sorry for myself. I allow it for about ten to twenty minutes at the most. I can't let it last much longer."

"No. No, you can't. I mean, that's the most nonproductive stuff. It's terrible. I mean, if you want to feel sorry for yourself, go to some leper colony or something. I mean, you know—give me a break. I don't care for it at all."

"So what did Tennessee say? What was his reaction?"

"He heard me. And we talked. And then we went on to other

things. I was about to get him into the Tennessee that I knew. But this was no longer the Tennessee that I knew. I mean. I still loved him. I loved him. He was great."

"But," I said, "depression can be a chemical thing inside the brain."

"Yeah. And it also could have been drug-related. Because—I know that, that as up as you get, the drug will take you just as far down. I mean, it's not—no one can ride those things. No matter how good they think they are. The drug world will take you down. So, Tennessee is up in New York, and we've chatted a couple of times. He's planning on coming back to New Orleans, yada yada. And so I'm busy about doing what I do."

"Did he seem better when you were talking with him?"

"Yeah. He was fine. I mean, basically they were just conversations that we had. We didn't have what you'd call in-depth personal friendship conversations over the phone. Those were more like when we'd be together talking and sharing thoughts and getting beyond the surface.

"So one day, I was going down the street, doing what I do, showing buildings, walking the dog, going home, just having a great life, when I saw all these flowers decorating Tennessee Williams' gate. Well, I thought, Tennessee's in town and someone has sent him a great big bouquet of calla lilies. I didn't think anything about the calla lilies at all. I didn't see the significance of the death wreath.

"And the odd thing was that there was this great big security guy back in the back. I kept trying to get this guy's attention to find out if Tennessee was back in town, you know, yada yada. But obviously he was told to answer nothing. To anyone. And so, basically I believed that Tennessee must be in town, and I was going to buzz his door and say hello.

"Then one of his tenants comes out of the building. So I ask the tenant 'cause the dumb old security guard won't tell me a bloody thing. So I ask him if Tennessee's in town. And the guy says, haven't you heard? And I said, no. Heard what? What are you talking about?"

"You still don't have a clue?" I said.

"No! And the guy says, 'Tennessee is dead. Tennessee is dead. Tennessee—is dead.'

"And I'm telling you. I thought—that is really—I couldn't believe it. I just couldn't believe it. So . . ."

"And how did he die?"

"Only Tennessee could fully tell you. But, he died of asphyxiation with one of those plastic aerosol things from a can. Now, you know, there's speculation that I've heard that he was snorting, you know, nasally injecting these chemicals, and—it could have easily been that—you know, prying it loose for some reason and it got inside his mouth and he gagged on it."

"But he was doing drugs."

"I don't—I don't know. I never heard. If I heard, I've forgotten. You know, if any chemical substance was found in him. But the odds are there probably was. Certainly alcohol. But then I basically had to deal with the fact that—he was dead."

"Then you got a call?"

"I got a call from some attorney from the school."

"What's with this school? What school?"

"It was some school in Florida. I don't remember the exact details. If the school wasn't in Florida, the attorneys were. Anyway, he had left all of his money to this school. These attorneys were calling me to basically ask me about Tennessee's state of mind. They said that they knew that I had a friendship with him. So they wanted to know about his state of mind when he made that will—whether he had possibly made a mistake. The allegations were that he was not in his right mind when he willed all that money, his estate, to the college. So I told them that the years that I had known Tennessee, the man was incredibly in charge of his business, totally sane, as sane as anybody you'd ever want to meet, and totally capably of handling his affairs, totally aware of everything going on in the world.

"And the funny—well it wasn't funny, but once when I had introduced Tennessee to a friend of mine as we were walking down Bourbon Street to go to the piano bar, and I said to this friend of mine—I want you to meet, you know, Tennessee Williams. Donald, this is Tennessee, Tennessee this is Donald Melina. And Donald Melina says, 'That's not Tennessee Williams, Tennessee Williams is dead.'

"Now he said that right there to Tennessee's face. And I'm sure that that's not the first Tennessee ever heard that. You know, when you're that famous and you've got that much art out there, some people just don't know. And this guy just didn't know, obviously. Which was a real surprise to me, because I found out later that Donald had an acting background. So of all people that should know, he should have. And I said to him, 'All I'm going to tell you right now, buddy, is that when you figure out the truth, you're gonna be mighty embarrassed. That's all I'm gonna tell you, buddy. So, have a good day, good-bye, and come on, Tennessee.'

"You know, Tennessee was this short little old man. But vibrant and you know, he loved everything. The stars, the moon, the sky, that old bag woman, he loved that sick old dog over there. I mean—he just loved it all. Everything there was about life. I mean, he was totally out there, to take it in. That was what his whole thing was."

"Then why did he have to abuse alcohol and take drugs all the time?"

"To deal with—a lot of things. I think he's a classic example of a Southern dysfunctional family."

"And also his homosexuality," I speculated. "I mean, the era in which he was born. It's almost like Oscar Wilde."

"Right. But his fame, so far—you know, superceded all of that. I mean, I can't imagine it being—everybody knew— who he was, what he was about. And I was raised by an Italian Catholic mother. It really wasn't a secret what he was."

And Bill Holcomb's homosexuality was never really a secret either. It seemed, that through the years, Bill had more of a problem with it than any of his family. Certainly his friends had no problem with it. So—did he truly hate his identity as he had professed to me? Was this what had torn him apart through the years, leaving him a beaten and pitiful excuse for a human being? Or did he simply use this as a ruse to gain pity for his own laziness and self-depravation?

Chapter 18

Spring fades into summer and Bill Holcomb's presence still lingers. His ashtray, ostensibly comprised of a rare and expensive metal, sits on the patio table filled with stale ashes and cigar butts. The newspapers arrive daily, unread and looking pitifully forlorn. His jar of ice coffee remains in the back corner of my refrigerator, as if awaiting his return. And the box of sport coats, suits and tux, are stored safely in the Red Room closet.

Discarding those last articles of clothing was beyond my ability. Those clothes represented the Bill Holcomb I wanted and needed him to be. I couldn't possibly bring myself to carelessly throw them out, as he had instructed, or give them back to the thrift stores where they had previously been purchased.

But reality had finally seeped into my thick skull. What I wanted wasn't the issue. Wasn't the cure. Bill held the power to make his own decisions, to choose his own path in life. And the path had been chosen long before he had met me. His family's infinite outpouring of love and money to save him had long since been gobbled up. Bill Holcomb's message rang loud and clear.

Leave me alone to live my life as I chose.

Those insistent words still played inside my head. I remember the pitch of his voice, the tone of his pain and the look of absolute defeat. And still, I was unwilling to accept it. I had to give it one last shot. God! I just hate failure.

A week or so had passed since Bill's return to The Rendezvous. A letter addressed to him had been mailed to my house. I had had the letter for several days, so I decided to stop by The Rendezvous and hand it over. It was around 4:00 p.m. The "Open" sign was hanging on the front door of the tavern, so I parked the car and proceeded across Magazine. As I entered this mouth of darkness, the first person I saw was Bill. Without hesitation, I walked toward him, held out my hand and presented him with the letter. He thanked me, I said he was welcome, then turned and walked out. Naturally, he was drinking.

My second visit to deliver his mail, I found him sitting at the end of the bar. He quickly rose from the barstool, smiled, took his mail, then asked how I was. I smiled slightly, acknowledged that I was fine and asked about him. He informed me that he was pretty good. I responded with a polite gesture and walked out.

About a week later. Ray, Codie, Renée and I decided to have dinner at one of our favorite local restaurants. So we piled into the car and headed to Joey K's at Seventh and Magazine, which is only two blocks from my house.

Now the four of us have spent many an evening drinking and dining at Joey K's. And there have been some evenings that I'm sure Clay, the owner, and probably most of his staff, had felt an unbearable urge to toss us out on our ears. The martinis run smooth there, so mad drinking has been known to happen accompanied by raised voices and hysterical laughter. This particular evening was tame by comparison, because I only had one martini, Ray was nursing his health (he has diabetes and absolutely should not drink—ever) and Renée and Codi were simply abstaining. So after a wonderful meal of Joey K's lamb shanks, we headed home. As we approached The Rendezvous, I blurted out the ridiculous suggestion that we stop and see our friend Bill. Renée and Codi said, 'Yes, let's do.' Ray wheeled his car into a nearby parking space, mumbling slight obscenities under his breath.

I, of course, led the way. Ray was adamantly mouthing words of abstract horror that he was about to enter such a place, but I pushed open the door and made our entrance. The first person I saw was Murphy, sitting nearest the door. Brian was behind the bar dumping ice into the cooler because Murphy was too cheap to buy refrigeration, and Bill stood about midway into the room. I walked up to the barmaid and ordered a Budweiser. By this time Bill was looking pleasantly stunned, while my entourage had begun to settle into the moment. I gave Bill a generous hug, then he introduced us to Tillie, the barmaid. I walked to the jukebox, picked out a few tunes, then proceeded to tell Bill what was on my mind.

"I have let go of my ambitions for you," I said. "But that doesn't mean I've stopped loving you. You never begged for any of it. I want you to know that I accept you, your lifestyle, whatever. I may not like it or agree with it, but it's the life you have chosen. My love and friendship does not hinge on conditions."

Bill and I talked and philosophized until my Budweiser began screaming at me to go. I announced to my friends that it was time to depart.

The next morning, Bill showed up at my back door fortified with several beers. I had asked him the night before if he would come by and give me one more interview for the book. There were still some unanswered questions and time gaps that I needed to reconcile. He was ten minutes late and apologized profusely. This was entirely unnecessary, but the ingratiating apologies were coming from the alcohol, not Bill.

We climbed the stairs to my office.

"All right," I said. "Let's go back to when you took that drunken binge/whirlwind tour around the world. What year was that?"

"I think it was about 1972."

"Okay. And you had spent how much?"

"I think it was about $12,000 on my American Express card."

"Good God!" I said. "That was an enormous amount of money in the seventies. What prompted you to do such a thing?"

"The reason I did it was because I didn't think I was going to live very much longer. Because I was throwing down booze all the time. You know, 24-hours a day, every waking minute."

"Why? Do you know why?"

"Well, the only thing that comes to mind right now, is that I wasn't making very much money any longer and I was running with the elite, elite of Chicago."

"You mean, that was making you want to drink?"

"Well, yeah, when you can't reciprocate, and you're an alcoholic, unfortunately you just *take*."

"All right. So you had been living in London and working for American Express Travel."

"Right."

"What happened when this disastrous tour came to an end?"

"I was flat broke, so my only choice was to go back home to Clarksdale. My parents had moved back to Clarksdale after living on the Gulf Coast for several years. And when I arrived, they saw the condition I was in and sent me to the Baptist Hospital Chemical Dependence Center in Jackson, Mississippi. I went through the 28-day program then went back home to Clarksdale. And that's when my father bought me this bookstore. He knew that I loved to read and he thought this bookstore would be ideal. So he bought the Volume One Bookstore for me for $6,000.00. And I ran it, and I loved it. It was fun."

"Well, you love to read."

"Yeah. But then I found out that you don't have much time to read in your own store. You're doing all this other shit."

"Yeah. That's right. There's tons of shit to do."

"And then this couple came by and wanted to buy it. And since I had already repaid my father the money he'd put up for it, I sold it to them for twelve grand.

"Oh—now I'm digressing, but—my father bought the business, not the building. He owned the building. But that Christmas, I was so impressed by the fact that my father had bought me this business, I put an envelope on the Christmas tree addressed to him with a check for $6,000. And that's the first time I'd ever seen my father cry in my entire life. And he said, 'Son, I can't believe this.' And I said, 'but look what you did for me.' And—and then came along the restaurant."

"He bought the restaurant for you?"

"He—you see, he owned the whole block. Delta Sunflower Square. He bought it. Piece, by piece, by piece, by piece. 'Cause it was going into like slums. He did and redid and had an artist from Austin, Texas, named Brad Beasley who came and did all the designs. Where there was an alley it became an outside mall. Huh, Paul Harvey even came and brought a plane full of people in. It was one of the most important urban renewal things that had ever been done. And Brad Beasley, being the artist that he was, went around collecting all these wonderful things for the warehouse restaurant. It was two stories tall, wide plank floors and all that stuff. And Jack Houston from Oxford came and ran it for him for the first year. It was like the only restaurant in Clarksdale except for the Holiday Inn."

"And this was in the '60s?"

"Yeah. And next to it was the River Road Bar. And my brother-in-law owned it. My sister Gussy's husband. And at that time he was working for my Uncle Pat's law firm, which is the largest law firm in the State of Mississippi. Uncle Pat was my father's brother. It was Holcomb and Curtis for years then it became Holcomb, Dunbar and you know, about twelve other names. Then they were in Oxford, Jackson, Clarksdale and all over. So David, who had married my sister Gussy when they were at Ole Miss—we were living on the coast then, and David had come down to ask my father for Gussy's hand in marriage.

"My father said, 'No' 'cause Gussy was just a sophomore at Ole Miss and David was in his first year in law school. And my father said, 'can't you just wait a little longer?' Now, unbeknownst to us then, David wanted into the Holcomb law firm."

"Mmm huh."

"Right. And so. Much against my parent's wishes, Gussy and David became engaged anyway. And Gussy put on her own wedding in Clarksdale. She did."

"I like her."

"Absolutely. And she did."

"Well, did your mother and father attend?"

"They did. My parents did. Yes. But, I mean, you're young, you're determined and you're gonna do it. So Gussy and David did. I mean, it's better than running off to Batesville, you know. So—I'm digressing somewhat, but anyway, Gussy and David were married for two years, and she became pregnant. She was delivered of this very healthy baby boy. And then something went wrong. The second day of the child's life, it was necessary to rush the infant to St. Jude's in Memphis. And Gussy, you know, is still laid up in the bed. So my mother rode in the ambulance with the baby, and by the time they got to Tunica, the child was about as blue as your jeans. And mother made the ambulance stop, got out on the side of the road and got water out of the ditch and baptized the baby."

"Your mother baptized the baby?" I said.

"You can do that. You know, my mother is more Catholic than I am. So she baptized the baby and it died, you know, before they even got to Memphis. So I think, probably, that had a lot to do with the disintegration of the marriage."

"Well, sometimes it does."

"Yeah. I—I think—not that they hated each other—"

"With me, it would bring me closer to my husband. But it does tear some people apart."

"Well, in this case, I think it did. About a year later, I mean, of course—now there's no child or anything, and David's making *beaucoup* money working for Uncle Pat's firm."

"So he did get a job with the firm?"

"Oh—oh yeeeaaah. You know dat. Ha. And they had a beautiful home. I mean, kids that age. I mean, it was as if they lived in THIS house. Okay? At age 25. All right? So then—David, who owned the bar, the corner grocery, worked for Uncle Pat—I mean, he was a wheeler dealer, but he was also sort of a grease ball. I'm sorry. Nice looking, clean cut, but you felt that sort of unctuous thing when you were around him. So he and Gussy went to Palm Beach on holiday with friends they knew from school. And while they were there, David's eye was taken with one of the girls from Atlanta."

"Oh my God!," I exclaimed. "I thought you meant that David had lost his eye."

"HA! Well, his eye *was* lost. This young lady, who was also married. And for almost six months, one week even two weeks a month David went to Atlanta on business. At a cocktail party one night, my sister, I think after having a couple of martinis, went up to Uncle Pat and said, 'Uncle Pat, why do you keep sending David to Atlanta?' Where as, Uncle Pat said, 'We don't have any business in Atlanta.' WELL, then the nickel dropped. She called me the next day. She said, 'Bubba, would you like to have lunch?' Now you know me. Take me to lunch and I'll go. So, we went to the club."

"This is in Clarksdale?"

"Yeah. And we went to the club for lunch and she said, 'what would you think If I told you I wanted to live on an island?' And I said, 'Gussy, I'd love to live on an island.' And she said, 'what if I told you it was Manhattan?' I said, 'Manhattan? You and David moving to Manhattan?' And then she said, 'Let me tell you—' Then she, she broke down crying. And my heart went into a hundred pieces. I mean, because she's my really favorite sister. Well, it doesn't matter whether she's my favorite or not, but still, it tore me apart 'cause I—I just didn't think things like that were suppose to take place."

"What! That affairs don't take place? Good God, Bill. You know better than that."

"Well, I know, I know. But you don't think about your sister and her husband. And the fact that they just lost a kid. You know—all this shit and all. It—it just didn't seem fair."

"Nothing's fair, Bill."

"No. Nothing is. We know that."

"Yeah."

"So. I said, 'My God. Gussy, have you told Mom and Dad?' And she said, 'No, I'm going to tell them tonight. Will you come with me?' And I said, 'You've got it.' You know—my mother's so fucking Catholic. Boy, is that an oxymoron."

"It is."

"My mother's so fucking Catholic and my father's a convert which is worse—all right?"

"What was your father?"

"A Methodist. So, we go to the house, ostensibly for dinner. Just the two of us. And Gussy said, 'Bill and I have something we need to talk to you about.' So we're sitting there. No one will start the conversation. I mean, my parents are definitely suspect, 'cause why on earth would Gussy and I, because she's got a husband at home and Gussy and I are looking at each other, and you know—the ham."

"You did it."

"Yep, 'cause you know, I couldn't stand it. Hell, we'd be there for eleven years if we don't do something about this. So I said, 'Huh, Gussy, can I take the floor?' And she immediately started crying. So I said, 'Mom, Dad—I said, there's something I need to tell you all.' I said, 'I feel as Gussy's brother that she's too upset to talk about it right now,' and I said, 'David's having an affair and Gussy wants a divorce.'

"My mother said, 'David's running around with another woman?' And I said, 'Yes ma'am. He sure is.' And she said, 'Divorce him.' Which just sliced me."

"You couldn't believe it," I said.

"I couldn't. I really couldn't. She said, 'Divorce him. Divorce him. Get him out of your life.'"

"I like your mother."

"Yeah. You'd like her. 'Get him out of your life,' she said. 'You don't need that. You just don't need that.' So, she divorced him. And that's when she moved to New York and met Elliott who she's married to now, very happily.

"Anyway, David had this bar called The River Road that I took over. And those were the most fun days I can remember. I owned the bar, I bought it myself."

"You bought it from David."

"Yeap. And I paid my father rent, 'cause I told you, he owned the whole block. And it was a rent that was based on a minimum and a maximum of the percentage that you take in. And I paid him the maximum every single month. I didn't cheat him. You know, sometimes when families are in business, you think, well, I'll hold back. But no. I never did. Never did. And, to be very honest with you—and I'm not lying. I already knew that I was an alcoholic—all right—I definitely was—I drank less and lived better when I owned that damn bar."

"Then why don't you have it anymore. Why?"

"I sold it. I sold it because I got so tired of hiding from the people—I mean, I drank. You know, but everyone in a small town looks at you. They know exactly what you're doing. All right? I mean, once I had a luncheon at the restaurant next door, and I ran out of white wine. It was a ladies' luncheon, and I had to run to Compassi's Liquor Store to get a jug of cheap-ass wine. Before I even got back, they called my mother and told her I had a bottle of wine in my hand. I mean, you can't fart in a small town. You know that."

"Yes. I do know that."

"I just got tired of all the incriminations and all that kind of stuff. And that's when I thought I'd come back here to New Orleans where no one would know. And here we are. Full circle. Now, before I got back here—I didn't have any place to go. I didn't have anything."

"Now wait. You sold the bar. You want to come back here. Why don't you have any money?"

"Because I sent it to my son."

I knew that Bill had a son because he had mentioned him that day in the counselor's office at DePaul's Hospital.

"Your son," I said casually. "You sent everything to your son. Does he know what your name is?"

Silence.

"Well, tell me. We won't mention his name. If we don't mention his name it won't hurt him."

"Right. Right. He has no idea who I am."

"Have you ever seen him?"

"Four times."

"When was the last time?"

"When I was in London."

"And that was when?"

"Eighty-three."

"And how old was he then? What were the circumstances?"

"I went to see him because I knew where he was going to school."

"Okay."

"He's thirty-one now."

"Very close to my son's age," I said.

"Anyway, I sent the money to him 'cause—"

"Through his mom? How did you get it to him?"

"Through a trust fund."

"So you knew he got it."

"Oh yeah. He got it. A lot of ill will in that marriage."

"But there wasn't a marriage."

"No. No, but there was a lot of ill will."

"How long were you with her?"

"Long enough to have a son. What does that tell you?"

"Well—did you just know each other over night. What?"

"We, we met at a party. I—I, I was very impressed. She was a good friend of Christina's."

"Well, I figured that."

"Yeah. And she was also Lord and Ladies and all this commotion."

"Were you living with Christina then?"

"Yeah."

"Okay. Did Christina know that you had gone to bed with her?"

"Yes."

"Yes?

"Yeah."

"Did all of you go to bed together?"

"Yeah."

"Yeah? And was Christina's boyfriend there?"

"No."

"Just the two women and you?"

"Yeah."

"And she got pregnant."

"You've got a way of pulling stuff out of—I swear to Christ!"

"Never mind. So, she got pregnant."

"Right."

"And how did you know she got pregnant?"

"She informed me."

"How?"

"By telex. All right?"

"How did she tell you this? What did she want? If she was all this Lord and Lady type person, why would she do this?"

"She just wanted me to know that we were having a child."

"Okay. All right. You deserve to know."

"Right. And she asked if I wanted to get married."

"Okay."

"And I said, do you want to get married?"

"Mmm huh."

"My, my first feeling was that, all right, if I'm going to have a baby, he's going to need a dad. Right?"

"Right."

"So I said, when do you want to get married? She said, 'I'd rather not.' And—and I felt somewhat half let off the hook and half not."

"Yeah. I understand that. And she said she'd rather not and you said okay. So why are we all mad at each other? Why was there ill will?"

Silence.

"Come on, Bill. Now tell me. You can."

"Because. Because, the first time I contacted her again. My— my—my—"

"Your son?"

"My—my son was already born. Like two going on three years old. And—"

"Wait. How did you learn about his life in the interim? Did you— were you in contact with her at all?"

"Through Christina."

"Christina. All right."

"I know. And it gets more convoluted by the moment."

"Should I be surprised?"

Bill ignored that comment. "I was in London. And I went to this— a kind of fancy party. And I had a really knock-out date. I mean knock-out. I mean, even an old fag like me got turned on. I mean she was really something."

"Was she from England?"

"Yeah. And what's-her-name—who's name I just can't say."

"Who? The mother—?"

"My—my ex unwife."

"Yeah. You don't need to say her name."

"All right, I won't. She was at the same party."

"Just happened to be?" I asked.

"Yeah. Just happened to be. We moved in rarefied circles, my dear."

"I know, I know. But now, this was before you had come back to New Orleans and started working for American Express. You were still in Chicago."

"Right. All right. She came up to me at this party. And everyone is drinking champagne and carrying on like there was no tomorrow. I—I honestly didn't recognize her at first."

"You're kidding."

"I really didn't. She had dyed her hair and gotten all gussied up—whatever. And she came over and she said—in her best British accent, 'Well, fancy seeing you here.' It sounded like the oldest and worst cliché in the world. But that's exactly what she said. And I said, 'How are you?' And she said, 'I'm fine.' Then I said, 'May I present—' and she slapped the shit out of me—and my date. Whack, whack. Just like that."

"This is the truth!" I said.

"She stormed out of the room. And that was the whole rift."

"Wait a minute. This woman gets pregnant because she's having *a ménage a trois*. And then she tells you she'd rather not get married. Why is she so angry, for crying out loud?"

"I have no idea. But—I'll tell you one thing, and I—I don't have the clipping, but if you want to call London, it was on the front page of *The Daily Mirror*. H. H. Munro, who writes under the name of Saki did the piece. He's the Liz Smith of London."

"Really?"

"Really. My only claim to fame. My God."

"How did someone happen to take a picture at just that moment?"

"Oh. This was the type of party that the paparazzi was just everywhere. There were a lot of movie stars there, you know, and stuff. Hell, half of um I didn't know from Adam's house cat. This made cover, because at the time this happened, my ex-unwife was divorcing this highly placed man in the House of Parliament. I mean, this was a scandalous divorce."

"Bill," I asked. "Why in the world would she make such a scene? You honestly don't know why she hauled off and slapped you and your date?"

"I don't. I don't know. Except she probably had a gazoogal amount of champagne in her when she did it. I don't know. Because, she's—she's still well known in London."

"Okay. Then that's why we're not going to mention her name."

"Oh. I don't mind mentioning *her* name."

"I thought you said you didn't want to."

"Well, I don't. But I'll tell you. Just don't put it in print."

"I won't know her, will I?"

"Maybe not."

"I probably wouldn't know her."

"Her name doesn't matter anyway."

"So now. What did you do then?"

"Okay. So now I have sent my son all of my money. I have no money to get to New Orleans. So I call this guy—now this is kind of an interesting part of it, too. I call this guy, a guy named George Morgan. He lived in Columbia, Mississippi."

"So how did you know George Morgan?"

"He was in the hospital with me in Jackson. The 28-day program I had been in. And I thought he was a really nice guy. He had come to Clarksdale with his wife, Carlene, to visit and we went to dinner together. They were a little country, but they were nice. Nice people. I'd helped him get oil leases through my Uncle Pat's firm. And he had always said, if you need anything in the world, just call me. So I was desperate, I called him. He sent a friend of his who's a Baptist minister. Drove all the way up from Columbia. You know, Columbia is not far from New Orleans. Just on the other side of Bogalusa. So he called this minister friend of his to come to Clarksdale to pick me up. And I'm sitten with a bag about the size of your purse."

"Then you had nothing."

"I didn't take anything else with me at all. That's when I left everything in Clarksdale. To this day I've not seen any of it."

"You've never been back to Clarksdale since then?"

"No."

"And this is what year?"

"Eighty-four."

"And had your father just about had enough of you?"

"He was pretty pissed off."

"Then he had just had it."

"Yeah. So this—this young minister comes and picks me up. My God it was like four in the morning when we got back to Columbia, Mississippi to the Morgan's. And I—well, this is sort of again one of those digressions. But I never shall forget when I got out of the car. It was one of those strange things. I looked up at the sky. It's when one of those crescent moons has a star in the center. And I thought, well, well this is a good sign. All right? And I stayed with them for a couple of weeks. And then George started asking me to call some of my friends to do oil lease things. I said, 'George, you know, first of all, I'm sort of on the QT. All right? And I don't really know much of anybody else who has a lot of money to speculate. And, so then I became kidnapped."

"George kidnapped you?"

"They, they wouldn't let me leave."

"Why?"

"Well, they kept making me call this person, that person, this person. So, anyway, three weeks and God, I was just stuck. And here we go again."

"All right," I said. "Here we go."

"There was a small hurricane that was coming through New Orleans. Not a big major or anything. And it blew through Columbia. And I had been waiting for my utility deposit check from Clarksdale— I called the utility company in Clarksdale and gave them George's— actually it wasn't Columbia, Mississippi. It was Kokomo, Mississippi. This teeny little town just north of Columbia—to have that utility check sent to me"

"The utility check from the bar and restaurant?"

"Yeah. The deposit that I had put up."

"Did you live with your mother and dad during this time?"

"No. I had my apartment which was also on top of the, you know, the whole block. So, anyway—it was rain, hail, everything. Typical hurricane weather. And I asked George if I could use the truck to go and check the mail. And sure enough, there was my check. So, even though George had been to rehab and all that kind of stuff, he still drank. On the sly and everything—all right? And we had driven into Hattiesburg a couple of times during my stay there, you know. And we'd stop. Now Carlene was not really a drinker, but she loved Margaritas. So I went to the bank and got the check cashed, and then bought all the makings for Margaritas. And the weather is hell, blowing like a son-of-a-bitch. Back at the house, we all have several drinks. And Carlene can only hold one drink and she folded. Completely."

"And," I said. "You and George made love. Didn't you?"

"Yes."

"Did that shock you?"

"Shocked the shit out of me."

"Did it? 'Cause you had no clue."

"None. None."

"How did it come about? Do you remember how it transpired?"

"Yeah. I do. He asked me if—if I'd go in the back. They, they had a kind of big shed in the back. And he, George never made really anything in his life very much. He lived on land his parents had given him. But he was always one of these people who was in the oil speculation business. Well—he had gotten into Amway. Right?"

"Oh yeah."

"When it, you know, first started. So he said, I want you to come see these Amway things that I have in the back."

"And this hurricane is raging," I said.

"Oh yeah. And the Tequila also. So we went in the back. And he said, 'I want you to suck my dick.'"

"He just said it, boom, like that?"

"Yeah."

"Now did he—or maybe you don't know this. Did he always know that you were gay? Or did he suspect it or did you ever talk about it?"

"Never!"

"Never mentioned?"

"Never. He and Carlene and I had been to dinner together numerous times. He's got four kids, which doesn't mean—"

"That means nothing."

"And—and I was so stunned that—I said, I said, 'you're crazy. Look, I'm not queer.'"

"I do hate that word, Bill," I said.

"Well, I don't like it either, but anyway. I said, NO. And he said, 'Yes, you will.' And then, I said 'Okay, you suck mine, I'll suck yours. All right?' And that's what we did. Then I left that afternoon and I hitchhiked here to New Orleans."

"And you did have money now."

"I hitchhiked because there in Columbia or whatever, I would have had to wait a year for a train or a bus or anything."

"Did you stay at his house that night?"

"Noooo. I left right after that. I put my dick back in my britches and left. And got to New Orleans late at night. It was well after midnight, and, hum, I went to the bathhouses."

"Wait. So when you very first came here, you knew about the bathhouses?"

"Yeah."

"So you lied to me before when you said you didn't know about them."

"Yeah. But I told you I'd stop lying to you. And I have."

"Okay. So you know about the bathhouses, so you knew where you could go."

"Yeah. But I went mostly for a cheap place to stay."

"All right."

"But of course once there, you're up for grabs."

"So you can get into those places any time day or night?"

"Twenty-four hours a day."

"Now wait. Do you have money?"

"Oh yeah. Remember, I cashed the utility deposit check."

"That's right. Well, then you're lucky that George didn't take your money."

"Yeah. But you see. What he took from me, was in essence a bit of dignity."

"I know. You had a long-time friendship with this guy and his wife."

"Right. And you know. If he had just said to me, 'Bill, I'm gay, would you go to bed with me.' You don't just say, 'suck my dick.'"

"Yeah. And then you say no, and he says, oh yes you will."

"That's the thing I don't like about a lot of homosexuals."

"Honey, heterosexual people do the very same thing. And I wouldn't like it either. But they do the same thing. It's degrading, whether it's a homosexual or heterosexual situation. So it doesn't matter."

"Yeah. Just like the barmaid said last night, 'Do you know why they call me head nurse?' And I said, 'No.' And she said, 'My knees are always dirty.' Ha, ha, ha. All right? She's a trip."

"Is she?"

"Guess who she's sleeping with?"

"Who? Murphy?"

"No."

"Brian?"

"And me."

"Both of you?"

"Yeap."

"I'd say you're pretty hard up."

"Well—screw you, Manou."

"So you and Brian are having a good old time. Whatever."

"Yeah," Bill laughed. "We are—this is really, really kinda funny, because she, she got—she lost her apartment last week, and she knocks on—she's really a—she's an okay gal. She's really okay. You know. She ain't never going to be on the cover of *Town and Country*. She's not going to be queen of Comus or anything like that. But she's fun. She's a Duke from North Carolina. All right? She's an RN. She is, really. And she's plenty smart, too. And she also has these terrific pair of bosoms."

"Oh yes," I said. "I remember them from last night."

"So, she had no place to stay, so she knocked on Brian's blanket. 'Do you mind if I come in?' So I told her she could have my bed, which is a chair. All right? So she came in and Brian got up and went to lay on the roof and she laid down for a bit. And Brian came back a little while later and we had a couple of beers, and then Brian said, 'I have to go to the A&P.' I was grateful because I can lay down on the bed now, 'cause I hadn't laid down on a prone surface since I left your house. I mean, it had almost gotten to the point that I was almost concave from sitting in that chair. So I laid down and she laid down next to me. You know, and one thing led to the other."

"What time was this?" I wanted to know.

"Early afternoon."

"Well, it's a good thing I didn't come to search you out for some reason."

"Oh. You would have loved it."

"I would have absolutely loved it. I would have opened that blanket, thought I was hallucinating and turned around and walked *away*."

"Believe me, you really would have thought you were hallucinating."

"Oh, this is too funny. So it's during the day, Brian has gone to the A&P, and there you are with Tillie?"

"Yes. And the next thing I know, it's happening. I mean, it was fine and everything. No great passion, but it was fine. So, it's over, and I go sit in my chair and she goes to the bathroom and Brian comes back, and—really this is funny."

"Now does Brian have a clue of what's happening here?"

"Oh, no, no."

"So he has no clue."

"Oh no. No clue. All right. So after Brian comes back, about an hour later, Marcus comes by and says, 'Bill, you wanna run to the store for me?' I should work for the postal department. I'm on the road more than anybody else. I'm the oldest person who lives there, and I'm the one they always send running."

"Right. And Marcus lives there."

"Yeah. You know, the painter, the great big guy."

"Oh yeah. I know who you're talking about."

"So Marcus says, 'Bill, I'll buy if you fly.'"

"Well, that's what I always say, too. I'll buy if you'll fly. I never want to go out."

"And that always means like an extra pack of cigarettes for me, you know, or an extra beer. So I said, sure. So I go."

"It's a good thing our A&P is close."

"Oh yeah. Or we'd all die of starvation. So I go and when I come back, Marcus is sitting on the roof. I said, okay, here's your beer, bud, here's your change. See you in a little while. And he says, I don't think you wanna go in the room right now."

"What! She's going at it again—with Brian?"

"With Brian. Right. And I say, 'Oh but do I ever.' So when I get to his blanket, he's just finishing. He turns and looks at me and not a word was said. And you know, it's true, it's not the first time that bar-maids have sought harbor, and they know that Brian and I will protect them. Take care of them."

Brian and Bill protecting anyone or anything was ludicrous. And I decided that Bill's entire tale of carnal pleasures was just another one of his many lies or alcohol-induced hallucinations.

Bill threw up his arms. "Now—Toes..."

"Toes? Who's Toes?" I wasn't sure I wanted to know anyone by the name of Toes.

"He's the one that came up and talked to you last night."

"The cemetery guy?"

"Yes."

"Oh, God. He called me today."

"He didn't."

"He did. But I'll tell you about that later."

"Jesus. You know, that son-of-a-bitch's mother pays his rent just to keep him out of her house? But anyway. Toes comes in and says something to the effect that—isn't it my turn to go with Tillie? And Brian and I both said, 'What are you talking about? Tillie is our good friend.' And he said, 'Well, oh well, I just took it for granted that ya'll were banging her.' And I said, 'Toes, you're so, so, obscene. Get the fuck out of the room.' I'm mean, I actually pushed him out of the room. I really did. I'm not much of a fighter. But he just irritates me so much. And after I pushed him out, I looked toward Brian and he looked at me, and I said, 'Brian I—' and he said, 'Bill I—I fucked her.' And I said, 'so did I.'"

"But we're not going to tell anybody."

The next night, with cocktail supplies in hand (one can of frozen orange juice and one large glass) I turned on Eighth Street and parked the car. I was going to spend the cocktail hour with my friend Bill and his raffish renters. As I walked around the corner onto Magazine, Bill was waiting impatiently by the front door. He wore a black sleeveless tee shirt that Tillie had given him, cut offs and loafers. His beard was bushy and his eyes weak from an undetermined amount of beer.

Knowing my aversion to cigarette smoke, he escorted me inside, and strategically placed me at the end of the bar closest to the door. Brian and Murphy were half way down the bar. Brian was smoking cigarettes and drinking beer. Murphy was just drinking beer. A guy I'd never met was at the far end of the bar sucking down a tall one. Some other guy was playing a game of one-sided pool. A very attractive bar-maid named Michelle promptly greeted me with a smile. Bill handed her my frozen orange juice, while I proceeded to dictate the appropriate amount of water she should add to the blender. I then instructed that my glass be filled to the brim with ice and a double helping of vodka. The expediency and proficiency of this ritual left me in awe. I certainly could not have done a better job.

With drink in hand I turned to Bill, who by now had ordered himself another beer, and asked him about Garland who, only days before, had been plucked from The Rendezvous and escorted to central lockup because of old warrants. His bail was set at $10,000 which insured that Garland was going nowhere. Twelve percent of $10,0000 is $1,200 and if Garland had that kind of money, he would not reside at The Rendezvous. But it seemed that he was able to lower the bail and only a hundred dollars would spring him. So with the money he had made on his last roofing job, Garland was now available to walk back through The Rendezvous' door from which he had recently departed. And that's precisely what he did, not five minutes after I arrived.

Now Garland is probably no taller than five-six or seven. He's as cute as a button underneath his rough appearance, and has the most beautiful smile albeit missing one large front tooth. I would love to take him into my care and transform him into the gent I know is hiding beneath his filmed surface. But my lesson of unrequested transformation has been learned, so Garland will remain intact.

Before arriving at The Rendezvous, I stopped by Radio Shack and picked up another supply of tapes for my recorder. I popped one in and was ready for whatever conversations might ensue during the cocktail hour. And I can assure you, there were many. Not ten minutes had elapsed when Marcus, who has the frame of a giant and the face of an angel, joined us. Marcus and I had met previously when he stopped by to give me an estimate on painting my house. So, as he and Bill and I plunged into liquor induced conversation, Tillie emerged through the darkness and joined our group. Now I did not inform Tillie that I had been privy to a conversation regarding her recent sexual encounters with Brian and Bill, but I dabbled around the edges just to let her know that I was not totally in the dark. With the tape recorder spinning, Tillie began spouting obscene one-liner jokes. I suddenly wished that Daddy could be present, but then I quickly rethought my wishes and decided that Tillie and Daddy had no business together inside The Rendezvous Tavern.

My tape recorder was getting an earful of distorted lives, poignant excuses, self-depravation and professed dreams and ambitions that couldn't possibly be accomplished without a serious attitude adjustment. As I listened to Bill and Tillie's repartee, I became so utterly confused that I began questioning my own sanity. Tillie, once an RN, was giving her reason for abandoning this respected career. It had something to do with a back injury whereas she promptly turned around and displayed a scar that covered most of her spine. She then proceeded to explain that she no longer took the pain medicine and had simply learned to live with constant, chronic pain.

I could see, however, that all she had done was replace the pain medicine with alcohol and illegal drugs. And rather than take her education and put it to use in another field, she had chosen a life of ultimate destruction. And after hearing about the day she and Bill set out to a friend's house to smoke hash and drink alcohol, only to wake up the next morning with no clue as to where this friend's house was because they didn't exactly remember getting there, I was having trouble conceiving their professed hopes and dreams. Although, I must say that Bill admits to having very little ambition and doesn't really project his mind much further than the moment. But Tillie talked of her poems, her love for writing and her love for painting. I wondered in what condition she would find herself when finally deciding to make good those dreams. I also wondered about her two children who were obviously not living with her.

As my tape recorder filled with her raw confessions of a life in chaos, I held my tongue and never once asked why. My understanding of why did not matter. And I saw and heard little to give hope that Tillie would ever care.

Bill and I talked and joked and danced and talked some more. And before I knew it, I had gone way past my drinking limit. I was dangerously close to drunk. So I pushed my glass across the bar, asked Michelle to put it under her care and bade farewell. Since Bill looked no different than when I first arrived, I asked him to drive me home. Besides, he's in a different drinking league than I, and I knew damn well that I had no business behind the wheel of a car. Well, Bill probably didn't either, but since my house is in spitting distance of The Rendezvous, I felt relatively certain that driving at a snail's pace up Eighth to Chestnut and to safety could be accomplished.

We arrived home where I promptly dished out a plate of pinto beans covered with cheese, hot salsa, sour cream and black olives. Renée joined us and I proceeded to sober up then I drove Bill back to The Rendezvous.

The next morning I pushed play on the tape recorder to recount the blurred events of the previous evening.

The damn thing was blank. I had failed to push the record button. Again!

Another round at The Rendezvous Tavern was imminent.

Chapter 19

During the cocktail hour at The Rendezvous, I had mentioned my interview with Dorian. Bill looked at me rather strangely, and said, "Tennessee? You mean Tom?"

"Tom?" I said. "Who's Tom?"

"Thomas Lanier Williams. Tennessee."

"Bill," I said. "You expect me to believe that you knew him?"

"Why the fuck not? I'm, I'm not lying to you. The only thing that pisses me off is the fact that Tom's brother, Dakin, tries to take all the glory from his deceased brother. Dakin was never worth shit. He never did anything. He never did anything. Okay? He sold used cars in West Memphis, Arkansas. He was named after his and Tennessee's granddad, Walter Edwin Dakin who was my granddad's roommate at Vanderbuilt. All right?

"Dr. Dakin, you know, he was an Episcopal priest at St. George's in Clarksdale. And the most beloved. Even Monsignor McKenna, who was our Catholic patriarch, forever got together with Father Dakin to try and have racial harmony. Of course it didn't work. But—it really did work, because they both went into—well, we really didn't have slums, but they went into troublesome areas to keep the peace, because at that time in the '60s, there was racial unrest. They went in to try and placate the mood of the whole thing. One Sunday two black couples and their children came to St. George's for the eleven o'clock service. Half the congregation walked out and within ten days St. Marks started."

"What do you mean, St. Marks started?"

"I mean, the congregation left St. George's, formed their own church and called it St. Mark's Episcopal, because, as W. O. Dismuke believed, those niggers had no business praying to HIS God. And besides, the parishioners considered Monsignor McKenna and Dr. Dakin nigger lovers."

"You know Bill, how about let's not spend any time and energy on that subject. I was born and raised with that shit. I didn't understand it then, and I sure as hell don't understand it now. Do you know that my grandmother actually told me that it was in the Bible that the black man was put on this earth to serve the white man? Can you believe that?"

"Hey, back then the Southerner could make the Bible say pretty much anything to suit their prejudices. God, could they twist stuff around. Still can."

"Yeah. Anyway, tell me more about Tennessee (Tom). I can't believe you knew him. I had no idea. I must tell Dorian."

"Of course I knew him. He lived in Clarksdale for eleven years. And—now, the Cutrers were one of the founding fathers of Clarksdale. In a couple of Tennessee Williams' plays, he mentions the Cutrers and the Moonlake Casino which is like 20 miles north of Clarksdale. He mentions them by name, in his works. The Cutrers were a family with tons and tons and tons of money. And this was in the days when cotton was selling for a dollar a pound. You got dollar cotton man, and you got forty acres—you got it. And old man John Cutrer cornered the cotton market.

"They had these lavish parties. I mean lavish. My God, their house was probably the first house in the Mississippi Delta with French windows, French doors and servants and champagne and the whole thing. My grandparents went to Mr. Cutrer's parties. They haven't gotten over it yet. And they're both dead. I'm not kidding you. As a matter of fact, right now, I mean, as we speak, the Cutrer's house came up for sale, and the Catholic church owned it. I went to grammar school in Clarksdale was at St. Elizabeth which was in the old Cutrer's house. And just about seven months ago it came up for sale. And—you'll never guess who bought it."

"Your father."

"Right. $750 thousand."

"That's all?"

"That's all."

"Did Stella tell you this?" I asked. Stella is an old friend who keeps Bill updated on the happenings in Clarksdale. She had sent her last two letters to my address.

"Yeah, yeah. So my father bought the house and deeded it to Delta State University. He just didn't want it to be torn down. It's a beautiful house. You know, neo-Italianate, and I can remember being in the second grade inside this room with all the French doors and windows, and Sister—I used to call her Sister Accelerator, because she pushed her foot down so much I thought she was driving a car. She was trying to drive us to make us learn. I can also remember that I won this spelling bee."

"You would."

"Yeah, all right, to the sixth grade. That was in the days that all the nuns were wearing flying whites and all this kind of shit. Oh God! They wouldn't like me saying shit. But anyway, that's just the way it was. And the lay of the land at that time was that behind the house was this great slope down to a lower plateau of land where St. Elizabeth's is now. Old man Cutrer left it in trust to one of his daughters no one ever saw, at least I never did, I'm sure some did, but she was like dishonored or unhonored or to be thought of not again."

"Really? But he left her this land?"

"Yeah. Left her all this land. She was living in Vienna."

"Oh, Vienna. God, I thought you said Indiana.'

"HA! That would have been a fuck up."

"I know."

"Poor soul would come right out of her grave. Beaten me first and you second. Because she was not an Indiana person. At all. She was a Viennese. I never saw her, I never met her—I've seen pictures. And she was gorgeous."

"And you don't know why she was considered the black sheep of the family?"

"No. I don't know. I'm sure there's a story in there somewhere. But I don't know what it is. Anyway, she left her legacy of the Cutrer's to St. Elizabeth's. And then they built the new church down below, and she's like, she's like—I wish I could think of the word I'm trying to use. Goddamnit! I talk too fucking quick. She was like our saint. There were two St. Theresa's."

"One is at The Rendezvous," I said.

"NO, no, no, no, no. Oh God, Pet. You could have gone years without saying that. No. Now, St. Theresa Avila, the Spanish St.

Theresa in the Catholic church. And St. Theresa of Hungry was the one who was helping the poor all the time. And she had become like a closet convert. And her husband, the king, was horrified that she would dare to take care of these poor people. One night she went out and she had in the fold of her gown, she had 20 loaves of bread that she was going to give to these poor people. I mean, it was in the middle of January or February. Freezing cold. And the king followed her and said, all right, I know what you're doing, whereas she opened her cloak and white roses fell out."

"I love that story," I said.

"I—I do too. It's one of my really favorites."

"What did the old fart do then—faint?"

"Grabbed his butt and went home, I hope. But—but as much bullshit as the nuns and the priests gave me—still that story has always stayed in my mind. And who knows, it may be true."

"It may be."

"But, back to Tom or Tennessee—when he first lived in Clarksdale, I was so young that I wasn't aware of his talent. I wouldn't have known a playwright from a preacher. And I actually think that this was—probably before *Streetcar*, 'cause I think *Streetcar* was around 1947 or so. And that was his projectile into fame. Anyway, Clarksdale had a small, and I'm talking small, eclectic group of artistically-minded people. And here is this guy with all this talent, his Panama hat and cigar, which he pulled off with great panache, not to mention the bourbon.

"My aunt Dot who was my dad's sister, a well-known artist, I mean she had her "Dot's Tuesdays." That's when her house was open, like for the other artists or whosoever in town, who was interesting, 'cause remember, we are starved for any diversity to take our minds off the paucity of our lives. And Tennessee was like—along came Jones—he kinda changed everything. People who didn't understand, you know, the artist-type person thought that maybe Tennessee was simply out in the field gazing at the cotton in a moment of artistic silence. Whereas in reality, he was on his way to Hirschberg's in Friars' Point where the soda jerk was easily jerked. His name was Myron, he was a little slow, and he was a student at Friars' Point Elementary School. He only got to the seventh grade, but the poor guy's only claim to fame was, when suiting out for gym, all the other guys practically passed out, because Myron had a twelve-inch dick. And that was soft. So I think you might be able to understand why Tennessee was hiking up to Hirschberg's.

"Now, you know, I mean, the dudes that were making fun of Myron's dick were probably envious, but never in their rural mindedness, ever dreamed or imagined or even thought that Myron's dick would end up in Tennessee's mouth. Where it lingered for about six months. And believe me, Tennessee would love my reminiscence. And he would. Tennessee pulled no bones about his sexuality, his alcoholism or his drugs. He just didn't give a fuck. But I have to intersperse this: He was the kindest man I ever knew in my life and the most talented. Very few people knew that Tom could play the piano. He could sit down and go through a Chopin Polonaise to shame Ignace Paderewski. He also had a great love of animals. And the Clarksdale SPCA was about as big as a crushed beer can. He owned a cat called Pyewaket, which was probably the only Maltese cat in Mississippi. And some of the rednecks, used to their alley cats and hound dogs, viewed this as a formidable stigma."

"Did you ever go to his home in Key West?"

"Heaven's yes. All the time. The first time was with my grandfather, and I honestly didn't know that Tennessee was living in Key West. So PaPa and I left Clarksdale, 'cause he wanted to go to Key West and fish. I drove all night down the Tamarind Trail. We get to the Keys and we stop in Key Largo and PaPa says we don't have too much further to go—now PaPa and I didn't mind what we said to each other, in fact, he would encourage me in a way, because I was so totally different from my Dad. I'm sure that my father never said fuck in front of his father in his life. And the only reason I would say it in front of my granddad is because he would die laughing and say, let's have another bourbon. He would, Pet. You would just love this guy. And that's probably some of the most truthful words I've ever said."

"He sounds very much like my Aunt Maggie."

"Exactly. So, on I drive in a straight-stick Mercury, and I've never driven a straight-stick in my life, and we arrive in Key West. I ask PaPa, where are we going to stay?"

"Wait a minute. You mean you're driving down to Key West and you don't know you're going to see Tennessee?"

"No. Because PaPa wanted to fish. That's all I knew. So, we get to Key West and PaPa says, go find a phone book."

"Your PaPa doesn't know Tennessee's number?"

"Nope. They hadn't seen each other in years."

"And he had a listed number?"

"Yeap. Under the name of Tom Williams. So, I get the phone

book, dial the number and he answers. I said, this is William Lafayette and Pascal David Holcomb, and we have come to see you. He said, get your butt right over here. I said, I would love to, but where the fuck are you? He said, I'll come get you. Which he did in some kind of a piece of car, I don't know.

"So we, anyway, we were ensconced inside his house. PaPa had two bourbons (he may have had three or four). I, with my eyes as big as saucers, because I'm sitting there talking to this guy who's the greatest playwright in the world, and here I am feeling like a sharecropper from Mississippi, and I'm having rum and coke. I got PaPa up and put him to bed 'cause you gotta remember, PaPa is in his late '70s and just gotten over a stroke. And when I put PaPa to bed, he turned and looked me in the eye and said, 'Be careful, son.' Now that just blew my balls off. Here is this man in his very late '70s, who I never dreamed knew what an aberration was, winking at me and telling me to be careful. So, of course, what do you think I did?"

"Well, actually, I'm not exactly sure what you were thinking, let alone what you did."

"The first thought that came to my mind, after leaving PaPa all covered up in his bourbon haze, was, I want another rum."

"To fortify your courage?"

"Sure. But what happened though, was totally different from what I expected."

"What exactly were you expecting?"

"I thought I was going to go to bed with him. You know, hop in the hay. And I would have been proud to do it. Instead, we sat and talked for like five hours."

"About how old was Tennessee then? How old were you?"

"I think I was 16 or 17, going on 80. Tennessee was, I guess, around late 50s. And the beauty of our conversation was, that we reminisced about Clarksdale, St. George's, the whole lot. To this day, I'm sorry that I didn't go to bed with him."

"Well, he probably had more respect for your PaPa than to approach you."

"Yeah. But two people can have—you know, it's such an intangible thing that you only feel in your soul. You don't feel it sexually or even mentally, it's like some psychic aura. It is."

"I know. I know exactly what you mean."

"And we stayed one week, and I've been in some of the finest homes and entertained by some of the most gracious people, but I've never seen such hospitality in my life. His home was not lavish or grand, but extremely comfortable. I think that probably him reading me and realizing that I was closeted, he invited some guys over. Now they were not nelly. Not nelly at all."

"Well, who cares if they were?"

"Oh shut up. I think they were friends of his from New York and they were all just like him. They were just guys."

"Oh shit! Of course they were guys. Why do you always have to try and be so un-gay?"

"Because, I told you, I don't want people poking their fingers at me and saying, 'look at that queer.'"

"No one does. No one wants any kind of prejudicial slur thrown at them. So let's not beat that to death again."

"No, let's not. Anyway, remember you telling me about when Tennessee and Dorian were walking down Bourbon Street, shortly before Tennessee died, and they ran into this guy, Donald Milano?"

"Yeah. The guy didn't believe it was Tennessee. Said Tennessee was dead."

"Wrong."

"Wrong? What's that suppose to mean?"

"Because. Donald and Tennessee were lovers. Not long-time lovers like Tennessee and Frank Merlo, but lovers. And by this time they had split, well, they really hadn't split."

"Then why did Donald pretend not to know him. Why did Tennessee pretend not to know Donald?"

"I think Tennessee perceived what Donald was trying to do. You know, by this time, Tennessee was very much into his bourbon, his drugs and surrounded by his sycophantical fans."

"Bill, what exactly does that mean?"

"Basically, it's a cock sucker."

"Is that one word or two words?"

"I don't know. I don't do that often."

"Bill, that has nothing to do with how to spell the thing. Never mind."

"Anyway, if you want my expertise at this point, let me just read to you—and I knew how to spell it too."

"No, you didn't. You had to search for it."

"What do you mean, I didn't? I knew it didn't start with a P. You were trying to put some psychoanalytical shit on me."

"Forget it. Read me Webster's meaning of the word."

"Okay, but I'm going to shorten it. It says, a person who seeks favor by flattering people of wealth or influence—parasite or toady. Someone who sucks blood. That's a sycophant.

"And most people who liked Tom took advantage of his fame, because obviously their lives were dull and mundane. So, Donald was probably scorned. You know, Tennessee was like Baskin Robins, every night he went out, whatever flavor he found, he liked. And my own personal feeling is that when he wrote *One Arm and Other Stories*, which included *Desire and The Black Masseuse*, about a guy named Antonio who lived on Toulouse in the French Quarter, he rather let his easy tricks and also his friends know that he was gonna matriculate the way he chose. He didn't care, he didn't have to."

"Did you ever see Tennessee again after your trip to Key West?"

"Yeah. I saw him in New York. Ran into him on Third Avenue. Christina and I were going to Sign of the Dove for lunch. He had a play coming out called *Small Craft Warnings*. And he appeared to be very happy and doing well. Oh, he was a little crocked, but so were we. And the play opened that night and the critics slammed it to death. And that was the last time Tennessee Williams has been on Broadway other than revivals of his brilliant plays. He was going downhill. He had just lost it.

"You know, you can't do bourbon, Tuinal, all prescription drugs. My God, he died of—he had been through three days of rehab at a black church in Harlem, and on the way home he stopped and got like a pint—and he had been on Lithium medication, and took the pint and drank every drop. He still had four tablets of Lithium, so he made it back to the Chelsea Hotel, went to his room and was going to take the Lithium. His hands must have been shaking so violently that he used his mouth to loosen the cap. The cap lodged inside his esophagus and he was asphyxiated. The maid found him the next morning."

"Oh Bill," I said. "Such a waste."

Chapter 20

Oscar Wilde's *Picture of Dorian Gray* has always intrigued me. Mr. Wilde's poignant novel of wicked indulgence and immortality which views the decay of Dorian Gray's soul through his portrait, seems so tragically similar to Bill's life. One passage, when paraphrased, seems to describe Bill's life so appropriately: William Lafayette Holcomb set himself only in life to the serious study of the aristocratic art of doing absolutely nothing. He lived only for pleasure, and his greatest pleasure was observing the pleasures of others while experiencing none of his own.

Bill spends his empty hours passed out in Brian's chair or staggering up Magazine Street to Walgreen's and the A&P for cigarettes and beer. He will call from time to time, but he rarely stops by anymore. Days of sobriety are few, but occasionally I will answer the phone and hear that bright familiar voice.

"Hi Pet, it's Bill." His mind is clear, his humor quick and his spirits elevated.

I received just such a call one day, then the very next I was summoned downstairs by an insistent doorbell. It was around 8 a.m. and I couldn't imagine who would be laying on my doorbell at that hour. As I reached down to turn the key, I could see through the louvers a pair of brown loafers on familiar sockless feet. My first thought was that Bill had come by for coffee and the morning paper. But when I pushed the doors back, I could tell there was nothing social about his presence.

He lurched into my kitchen then headed straight into the Red Room and slouched down on the leather sofa. I situated myself next to him in the leather wing chair. I couldn't imagine what he was about to say.

"Pet. Pet, it's Brian. He's dying."

"What! What do you mean, he's dying? What happened?"

"His body. It's, it's just shut down. His liver is the size of Maine and the rest of his organs have stopped working. Pet, Brian's going to die. He's going to die."

Yes, I thought. Brian is going to die. He has systematically poisoned his entire body, and it's time to pay the piper. My anger started to boil. Here sat Bill across from me in his anguish and sorrow, helpless to save the person he loved, because that person had long ago resigned himself to his own destruction.

I looked at Bill with steel eyes. "And you're next," I said. "You're next to die and I'm next to grieve. So there you have it. You can't resist the power of evil and the devil wins."

I jerked him up from the sofa and wrapped my arms around him. Nothing I could say would comfort him, so I just held him.

Dr. Johnson called me the next day and informed me that Brian had little chance of survival. His liver was virtually beyond repair. So—Bill and everyone else at The Rendezvous had yet another excuse to drown their sorrows in drugs and alcohol. I was the only sober friend left to sit by Brian's bedside. The nurses in ICU had called security on this inebriated lot and guarded Brian with utmost care.

The last time I saw Brian, I had been by his bed for several hours, rubbing his arm, stroking his head and mouthing words of comfort of which he could not hear. Every tube imaginable had been inserted into his body, and the care I saw the doctors and nurses at Touro give to this derelict man was an astounding display of humanity. I sat there and marveled at the tenacity they displayed to keep him alive. To them, Brian was no less important than the wealthiest or most prominent of their patients. Brian was a human being, and his life was in jeopardy.

Four days after Brian's admittance to Touro emergency, I received a phone call from a woman who identified herself as Kathy, Brian's sister from Phoenix, Arizona. Bill had rummaged through Brian's belongings and had found several names and phone numbers. He and Tillie had placed the calls, left messages and were hopefully awaiting a return call. It was Kathy's phone call that gave me the news that Brian had passed away at 3 a.m. the previous morning. Although I knew his death was inevitable, the finality of it saddened me terribly. I also felt a dark foreboding that Bill's death wasn't far behind. I went immediately to Dr. Johnson's office, had a good cry and begged him to help me find a way to rescue my friend before it was too late.

My and Bill's doctor is very wise, and unusually caring. He said to me, "Paulette, think of Bill as your pet. Your injured puppy. You've done all that you can do. So give him a place to sleep when he's in need and a square meal from time to time. He knows that you love him."

We had a memorial cocktail party for Brian at The Rendezvous a few days later. Brian left behind an ex-wife, a son, two grandchildren and a sister. He was originally from Hermosa Beach, California, an avid surfer and sailor. He loved the Sacramento Delta and the Pacific Ocean. Bill and I are giving Brian's ashes to my husband so that he can cast them from the Golden Gate Bridge, across the bay and out to sea. We know that Brian would wish this.

Murphy has now offered Renée a part time job as bartender. And much to my amazement, she has accepted. Renée is now bringing in a gallimaufry of people from all walks of life. Murphy has never seen his raffish bar infused with such class, and he is reveling in it. Renée has quite suddenly become the Queen of The Rendezvous. Her tips are generous, and every night she comes home, dumps her brown paper sack onto the bed and counts her take for the night. The job is convenient and, for now, serves her well.

The night of Brian's memorial gathering, Bill and I went upstairs to their room, retrieved the box of ashes and silently walked back to my house. We made another drink, sat out on the patio under an angry sky streaked with bolts of lightening and claps of thunder. We laughed, we cried, we drank.

I then dished up two bowls of navy beans, and we sat in the Red Room eating and listening to music. After dinner we went upstairs with Brian's ashes in tow, where I tucked Bill in bed, held him, cried with him, and kissed him goodnight.

Bill, however, did not fall into quite slumber. Unbeknownst to me, he left his room, descended the stairs and proceeded to drink himself into a stupor. When Renée arrived home from The Rendezvous, Bill was staggering into the kitchen from the dining room declaring that he needed to eat.

Two days later, Tillie called around 11 a.m., announced that she needed to get the hell out of that hot hole of a room and wanted me to come and get her. So I hopped in the car and drove to The Rendezvous. Bill was inside his doorless digs passed out, half on half off of Brian's filthy mattress. I gently touched his leg and called his name. He awoke with a jolt, and with my help lifted himself to his wobbly feet. I informed him that I was taking him and Tillie to the cool confines of my house.

Upon arriving home, I ordered Bill upstairs to take a shower. Renée grabbed Tillie and proceeded to wash and style her hair. All of this was preceded by Bill and Tillie grabbing a drink of vodka for support. After Bill's shower, I styled his beautiful silver hair, dowsed him with my husband's Escada cologne, then led him into my office where we went over several editorial points of our book. After that, Renée and I stuffed them into the car and drove them back to The Rendezvous.

The next morning I received another call from Tillie announcing that she had hurt her back and she and Bill were calling from a pay phone at PJ's Coffee House on Magazine. There was little doubt that Tillie was stinking drunk, which meant that Bill was in no better condition. As Renée and I drove down Magazine toward PJ's, we spotted these two wretched creatures huddled around a patio table. I honked the horn which threw Bill into a spasm. Tillie was fumbling inside her purse while Bill was gingerly working his way around the table to help his crippled friend from her chair and down the stone stairway toward my car.

Renée and I were doubled over with laughter, because it was just about the funniest sight we'd ever seen. These poor derelicts, we found out later, had been out all night drinking, partaking in various assortments of drugs and had yet to find rest. In fact, they had somehow ended up at the A&P without Tillie's purse, so Tillie told Bill to walk back to The Rendezvous and get it for her. He obediently proceeded down Magazine to retrieve the purse. However, on the way back to the A&P a policeman stopped him and asked him where he had gotten the purse. The policeman was certain that Bill had lifted the thing from some poor unfortunate soul. Bill announced with an indignant tone that the purse he was carrying was HIS. The policeman must have found this to be credible, because he accepted Bill's explanation and allowed him to go on his merry way.

Now that Renée has injected The Rendezvous with a dose of class, I periodically spend my cocktail hour in my very own no smoking section at the front of the bar. I have furnished two aromatherapy candles that flicker brightly, and a glass of dry roasted peanuts for *hors d'oeuvre*. My special glass and frozen orange juice, which I have also furnished awaits my arrival. Murphy, of course, furnishes the vodka. And he charges me FULL price.

Bill and I dance the cocktail hour away to his favorite song, *Private Dancer*, as well as an assortment of country picks and Tony Bennett.

Yesterday, Bill dropped off a letter that he had written Brian's sister. It read:

September 17, 2000

Dear Kathy,

Forgive me for being so remiss in sending you the enclosed. I feel that getting this off to you is the final chapter in Brian's life that I selfishly do not want to relinquish.

Desmond Crain, Paulette's husband, is taking Brian's ashes to San Francisco Sunday and placing him in the Pacific he so loved.

A great regret was his self-imposed alienation from his family. You were all spoken of often and kindly. Actually, I never heard Brian say an unkind word about anyone.

To say he was my friend would bespeak an injustice to our relationship. Indeed, he was my brother and I loved him as one. He was loved by all who knew him. Jim Murphy, for whom he worked has felt the loss deeply, and it seems that not a day passes by that a guy doesn't come in to find Brian is no longer with us. Kathy, most of these guys are pretty macho types, and I've watched more than one go to the back of the bar to cry privately.

You asked me if he was homeless and if he had any friends. Well, his home wasn't exactly what you'd find in Beverly Hills, but the warmth and hospitality it exuded beat the hell out of any mansion. He took me in when I was having a bad time. We would all congregate in "Brian's Room" whether to watch his Rams play or just shoot the breeze. What a wonderful, kind, warm man he was. The turnout for his memorial that Murphy held was outstanding.

While our loss is incomprehensible, I know he would have preferred not to live in an altered state, and we all know that he is in a better place hanging ten and waiting for the "Big One."

Kathy, please keep in touch. I would consider it a privilege to someday meet you and Shane. I can be reached at:

[ed. Note: actual contact information listed on the letter is not reprinted here due to security concerns.]

Again, my deepest felt condolences to all of Brian's family. Know he was loved and pray for him as we do.

With love,

William L. Holcomb

I have resigned myself to the reality that I cannot change Bill. So I love him and care for him as Dr. Johnson suggested. And as I finalize this book, Bill is sleeping soundly in my guest room with Brian's ashes on the bedside table next to him. My refrigerator is stocked with his favorite Busch beer. That's my only hope of getting him out of that filthy dive and away from hard liquor and the sundry drugs that filter in and out of his life. But yesterday, when I rescued him from the upstairs porch of The Rendezvous, he said something that gave me a glimmer of optimism.

"Pet," he said with a horrid sort of laughter. "You'll never guess how I was awakened this morning."

He was right. Not in my wildest dreams would I attempt to guess this. So I simply said, "How?"

"Well," he said. "Around eight this morning, an anxious hand on my leg awakened me. I looked up to see this dreadful looking woman looming over me. She said, 'I'm looking for John.' I said, 'I'm sorry, but I'm Bill.' She said, 'Well, I've got eight dollars of pussy to sell.'

"I swear, Pet, if the mattress had not already been on the floor, I would have slid off the thing. Horrid images of my dick falling off swirled through my mind. Can you imagine the diseases you could get for eight fucking dollars? I swear, Pet, I've got to get out of there. You know, I've just got to get out."

As Bill sleeps off another day's boozing, I sit here at my computer finalizing our book and nurturing my last bit of hope, that someday he will find the will and the courage to lift himself from death's gaping door.

I wait patiently, hopefully and with love.

Epilogue

The sun rises, the sun sets—the moon illuminates the darkness. Another day fades into the past.

As I reflect on the last 50 some-odd-years of my life, I find but little regret. My sins and mistakes are like sinuous fibers, and remain tightly woven inside my being. Without them I would not have come to be the person that I am. Spiritually I am at peace, mentally I am strong, and physically I am fortunate. I have weathered all the storms, remain blissfully optimistic and have never lost my ability to hope. I have been blessed with loving parents, a soul mate for a sister, a devoted husband, a thirty-year marriage and two exceptional children. So far my life has been filled with a combination of ingredients. I could not have learned without the sorrow, without the heartache. And I could not have understood without the experiences. Not a single moment of my life would I change. It is impossible to gain wisdom without tasting what life offers. And it is capable of offering a diverse assortment of choices, indiscretions and alternatives.

Bill's life was no different. He too had all the ingredients. Yet he chose a twisted, more destructive path.

Like the Harper's blurb says of our exotic city—New Orleans—I never could find out exactly who Bill Holcomb was. I looked for him without much enlightenment. He is dropped down there somewhere in the marshes of society and aristocracy, the common folk and the depraved. He is below one and tangled up among the others. Or he might some day fade into oblivion and disappear. How he got there I never could discover. When he first came into view, he was headed North; on Magazine, he abruptly turned his life and made a bold push to the South in order to avoid confrontation, turned momentarily East, then back South again toward Canal Street, into the French Quarter and went no one knows where.

Bill's life has forever headed South. The detours along the way were only peripheral and meaningless—painful interruptions he had no intention of dealing with. Who he is beneath all of this wasteland, we'll probably never know. I'm not sure that he even knows. Whoever he is was lost long ago. And possibly he was right when he told me how much he intensely disliked himself. Maybe the self he referred to was his true self, not the person he had become. I once thought I wanted to get inside his mind, fight his demons, conquer his fears. I'm no longer enticed or determined to peer inside. I'm too afraid of what I might find, afraid that the evil that haunts him is far too dangerous.

I, too, have joined that vast group who realizes that no one can save this man from himself. He simply is not interested in salvation. Yet I will always hold dear the memories of our late-night dinners, our talks in the Red Room, a movie, an occasional cocktail hour at The Rendezvous, and our walks through the Garden District. Most of all, I will forever see him in animated glory, prancing about, his arms and 'hands aloft, the tilt of his head, the wicked gleam in his eye and that undeniable erudite mannerism and speech. He will always be on stage in my memory, like a work of art, performing his masterful stories.

Author's Note

As I stand here in the Red Room, looking out across my beautiful garden filled with blossoming snapdragons and begonias, I reflect on how, in just a short time, life alters its course.

My precious little Max is now gone, lying atop his red-fringed pillow beneath the flowering snapdragons. It seems that after twenty-eight years of a thirty-one year marriage, I have fallen in love with my husband. Strange, I did not realize that I wasn't in love. Curious how one can shut down a part of his or herself without awareness. And even more curious how I came to realize this. Since we can no longer be apart, we have leased the house, furniture and all. I will be moving back to California until Daddy's corporate climb has run its course.

Leaving New Orleans and my beautiful home is sadly difficult. There are so many memories lingering throughout the crumbling sidewalks of the Garden District and caught between these heavy walls. I can feel them, almost see them as I leave the Red Room, walk down the long hall and enter the front parlor. As I look toward the second parlor where my and Daddy's portraits hang, I can hear and feel the laughter of many a cocktail party. I see Uncle Buzz's portrait on the opposite wall, seated regally with his gold-handled walking stick. I can hear Bill inside one of his many soliloquies as he prances about. My dear friend, David Armstrong, plays his sultry New Orleans' jazz on my piano beneath the staircase.

It's almost impossible for me to leave my beloved New Orleans, yet impossible to be away from my husband. I feel happiness, sadness and excitement. So much has taken place here in such a short period of time. Lives so drastically changed. It seems an entire lifetime really that has swept through this historic old place.

One life, though, remains rooted deep inside its torment. A life that knows no change. No hope. A life that desires nothing more than pity and to be left alone inside the squalor of The Rendezvous.

As my plane wings its way westward, Bill's words still linger distantly.

'Pet, this is New Orleans. It's not real.'

April 26, 2001

Printed in the United States
21215LVS00001B/7-30